THE TAROT & ASTROLOGY HANDBOOK

THE TAROT & ASTROLOGY HANDBOOK

The Quintessential Guide for Harnessing the Wisdom of the Stars to Better Interpret the Cards

ARGUS KALDEA

Tarot Reader, Astrologer and creator of @MoonPriest

PAGE STREET PUBLISHING CO.

PAGE STREET
PUBLISHING CO.

First published in 2023 by
Page Street Publishing Co.
27 Congress Street, Suite 1511
Salem, MA 01970
www.pagestreetpublishing.com

Distributed by Macmillan, sales in Canada by The Canadian Manda Group.

27 26 25 24 23 1 2 3 4 5

ISBN-13: 978-1-64567-974-5
ISBN-10: 1-64567-974-8

Library of Congress Control Number: 2022947212

Cover and book design by Katie Beasley for Page Street Publishing Co.

Printed and bound in the United States

DEDICATION

For the watchers of the wheel.

For the questions you cannot seem to answer in life: Address the cards and address the stars.

Everything far will become near, and everything near will become far, for you will remember the truth of who you really are.

CONTENTS

INTRODUCTION

Congratulations on finding this book, my love. Just by virtue of being interested in learning more about the sacred tools of tarot and astrology, you are committing to knowing yourself in this life. What a gift to give yourself in a world where so many of us roam, feeling unnecessarily lost. Not because we don't know what's coming, but because we don't know ourselves.

The 78 cards of the tarot illustrate a path of self-discovery and eventual self-realization. They are the 78 steps on a path of coming home to yourself, and the beauty of it is that it doesn't matter which step you begin on. All roads lead home. You're coming home, my love, and you cannot fathom how much joy it brings me to be able to help awaken this inner compass of yours.

Yes, there are methods to the madness we call life, and the tarot is one of them. By depicting a host of universal human experiences, the tarot opens you up to the fact that your struggles are not as unique as you may think. Indeed, if there is one thing you will learn from me along this journey together through the 78 cards of the tarot, it is that you are never truly alone. These steps have been walked and will be walked by everyone around you, for we are all turning, growing and evolving on the wheel of life. And to have overcome these steps, to have walked through these psychological and spiritual doors, is to have attained profound wisdom not only for your life, but for the lives of everyone around you.

The tarot connects you to the universal web of human experience because it speaks the language of your subconscious, and your subconscious holds the mythos of man that we all share and are called by. When you can connect and relate to others with these mythic symbols, a profound compassion will stir within your soul, and you will begin to notice the beautiful unfolding of both your own journey here and that of those around you.

If you are ready for me to take you on this journey, my love, I ask that you let me lead you from your heart. The heart always knows home. No matter where it finds itself in the trials, tribulations and chaos of this physical experience . . . it knows, it knows, it knows. As we walk through this journey—these 78 doors to the truth of who you are—you will find yourself stopping along the way and saying, "Here, here I am!" And you will witness how perfect the unfolding of your life really is and always has been. You will find yourself on this wheel, you will accept the cycles of your life and know what is currently being asked of you in order to evolve into the most authentic and liberated version of who you really are.

Along our journey through the four elemental suits of the tarot, you will encounter cards both from the "major arcana" and the "minor arcana." As I introduce you to these images, you will come to understand the major arcana as cards that represent archetypal consciousness. Archetypes are what connect us to universal spiritual experiences and cosmic laws. The minor arcana, as you will see, visually connects us more with our physical human experiences in life as we work to evolve our personality. Contained within the minor arcana are also court cards and these take the form of a page, knight, queen and king for each of the four suits. The court cards give us a direct way to connect with a personified image of a certain consciousness that is operating within us or being reflected to us by the people in our lives. Yes, you will meet some interesting characters along this journey.

THE PATH IS THE GOAL

Before we begin, I want to share with you a phrase that was said to me by someone I met along my own journey of writing this guide for you: *Der Weg ist das Ziel*. It is a German expression that roughly translates to "The path is the goal." The woman who said this to me was just casually expressing how she felt exploring the city of Athens, enjoying walking the streets and not going anywhere in particular. Unknowingly, she had perfectly captured the essence of the tarot in these few words.

There is no destination for our journey together, my love. My only hope is that by learning this path and knowing where you are on this path, you will have the wisdom to be able to respond a little differently to your present. To stop reacting so much from the patterns of where you have been and to start responding in ways that lift you higher into greater personal fulfillment and into a more sovereign expression of who you are.

So, come with me now. I will take good care of you along this journey, and there is no pressure to complete it in a specific way or in a specific time. Remember, *Der Weg ist das Ziel*. I will do my best to share with you everything I have learned so that you, too, may be able to show the way to someone at a crossroads, to be a star on the path of a lost traveler, to be the whisper in a gentle breeze that says, "All paths eventually lead home."

THE MAJOR AND MINOR ARCANA

Some of you may already know that the 78 cards of the tarot are divided into the major arcana (or trump cards) and the minor arcana (or "pips," numbered one through ten). I have deliberately chosen not to fully separate them from one another in this guide, as the major arcana represent the overseeing cosmic laws that are influencing the human journey (that is represented in the minor arcana).

In reality, the experiences represented by the major and minor arcana are not separate; they are many times not even sequential. They are interweaved throughout the course of your journey in inconceivably perfect ways, specific to the journey of your soul. That is why I will be guiding you through the human journey of the minor arcana, whereupon we will inevitably stumble across the cosmic laws of the major arcana at differing points along the way. It may help you, my love, to think of the minor arcana cards as describing the physical course of your life and the major arcana cards as describing the spiritual course of the soul.

It is the interweaving of these two journeys into one that will bring wholeness, completion and the physical actualization of your spirit in this life. It is the melding of these two paths that will bring your personal heaven to earth for all to enjoy. To be committed to the journey that we are about to embark on is to always remain on a path pointed toward realizing your limitless potential in this life.

In the way that it has been constructed, this guide can be both read as a story and as a reference. For some points in life call for the resonance of the heart and others call for practical wisdom, this guide contains both. It is for you to use in the way that you find serves your Highest Good. On some days, you may only require a few words from here, on others several more. Years may pass and something here may strike you again in a completely new way.

This guide has been written to evolve with your journey. The words have been selected to speak the one truth in a myriad of ways. So that you can always land somewhere along this journey. So that you can find and nestle into wherever your heart currently is along the road. We are all on many different journeys, my love, but we all belong to the same wheel of time. You are never alone, you are always coming home and, in the rushing rivers of life, there are certain wisdoms that will always serve as your stepping stones.

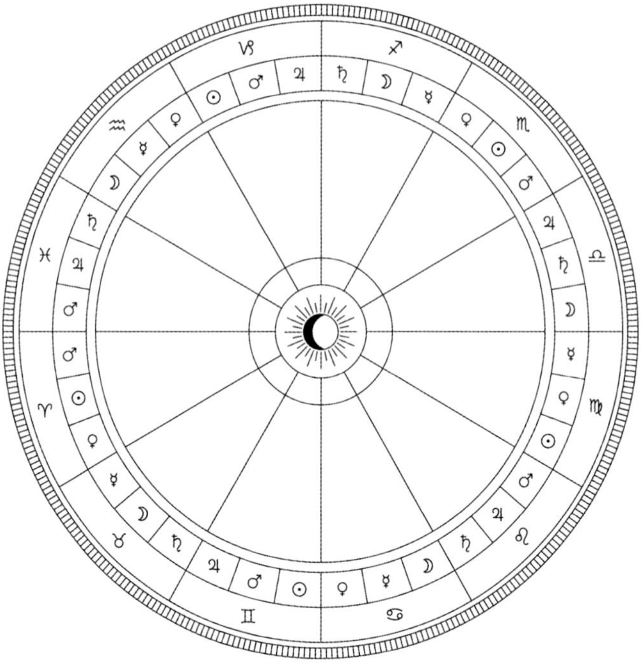

THE ASTROLOGICAL CORRESPONDENCES OF THE TAROT

Across our journey together, you will uncover the profound meanings of each and every card in the tarot through an astrological lens. You will learn about the astrological correlations that are connected to all 78 cards. This connection between the tools of tarot and astrology will teach the tarot reader astrology and the astrologer the tarot. And for the soul exploring life, it will teach them a little more about themselves. And so, where do the astrological correspondences of the tarot arise from? To put it simply, it comes down to two key concepts: the Chaldean Order and the astrological decans.

THE CHALDEAN ORDER

The Chaldean Order is a planetary sequence that arranges the seven celestial bodies (excluding the newer discoveries of Uranus, Neptune and Pluto) based on their apparent velocity from the perspective of Earth. The order is from the slowest- to the fastest-moving celestial body as a result of their orbit: Saturn, Jupiter, Mars, sun, Venus, Mercury, moon. You will notice this sequence as you move through the astrological correspondences of the minor arcana! So, how does this apply specifically to the tarot? This is where the decans become important.

THE DECANS

According to classical astrology, the 12 signs of the zodiac are each divided into three decans. This creates 36 decans that each take up ten degrees of the full astrological wheel. Each decan is also ruled by one of the seven planets mentioned in the Chaldean Order. The first decan begins with Mars in Aries and the sequence of the Chaldean Order continues from there. It is this sequence that combines the Chaldean Order with the astrological decans that became the basis for the astrological correspondence of the 78 cards of the tarot. In any case, you need not get too caught up in the technicalities, my love. The history of alchemy and hermetic science is a little beyond the scope of this particular guide and we really must be on our way, for a long journey lies ahead of us.

A NOTE ON RETROGRADES AND REVERSALS

Oh, and I almost forgot! I could have sworn Mercury ended its retrograde a couple of weeks ago . . . so where will I ascribe my forgetfulness to now? Take accountability for my own actions, you say? Not a chance. Sometimes, my love, the only way to go forward in your journey is to first go back. Retrograde in astrology refers to when a planet appears to move backward through the sky due to our perspective from Earth. When a planet is retrograding, its themes are brought into greater focus and there is an emphasis on resolving the past. This can also represent a time of introspection, delay, reevaluation, consolidation, the discovery of deeper information and a new approach that will better assist you moving forward in your journey.

I have applied the knowledge of retrogrades in astrology directly to the concept of reversals in the practice of reading tarot. Reversals refer to tarot cards that appear upside-down in a reading. In my practice, reversed tarot cards are treated with the same themes of retrograde planets in astrology. You will find more information on this at the end of each card's description in this guide. Keep in mind: Many who practice reading tarot do not make use of reversed cards. Give yourself the freedom to discern what works and does not work for your practice.

And so, are you ready to begin now? The truth is that you have already begun. And you will never be done. And how could a great manifester of realities ever be done, my love? There is too much for you here to joyfully create and too many creations ahead of you to enjoy. Let us "begin" anyway then. Somewhere, anywhere . . . into the unknown . . .

A NOTE ON GENDERED LANGUAGE

Before we go further, I would also like to emphasize that the depictions in the tarot are heteronormative and binary in their expressions of gender, sexuality, race and culture. The depictions themselves are far from a perfect representation of the world we live in today. Though this does not justify the lack of representation in these cards, I would like to assert that all 78 cards are metaphorical archetypes that exist within all of us.

The binaries of empress and emperor, and kings and queens, refer to forms of energy that are not exclusive to those that identify with that particular gender or sexual orientation. All of us have a responsibility to individually integrate the forces represented by both the Emperor and Empress and so on.

Someone who identifies as male can embody the force that is their inner Empress, just as much as someone who identifies as female or nonbinary can embody the force that is their inner emperor. These are forces, not people. Unfortunately, we are still very limited in our language for many of the themes that this guide covers. To counteract this, I have attempted to use differing pronouns for many of the cards; however, many still suffer from their inherently gender-conforming and racial depictions.

It is my hope that you will be able to look past these physical depictions at times and locate the source of the force that exists within you, not in the world of appearances. I want to affirm that the tarot is for every soul that opens itself to it. You are seen and valued in your gender identity and gender expression, sexual orientation, race and culture. And, if anything, correct use of the tarot will allow you to go beyond the world of binaries and discern where you do not conform to certain societal norms. After all, the tarot is here to help guide you to the truth of who you really are. And to those who do not conform, it is the most rewarding.

#0 ◆ THE FOOL

MAJOR ARCANA

Astrological Correlation: Air and Uranus

You must be quite the Fool to begin this journey, my love. I don't mean to insult you, but it is precisely this ignorance to both your past and future that allows you to have the courage to step into a new beginning in your present. Look here, how the Fool walks with their chest open and proud. They are led by the heart. Are you foolish enough to be led by your heart? Are you ignorant enough to trust a feeling? To follow the vague and uncharted territory of who you really are?

Those that have had the courage to do so are often dismissed as fools by the predictable and socially conventional. Predictability and logic are the enemy of the Fool and, consequently, the enemy of new beginnings. So ripe with potential is this card that it is not even the first card of the tarot, it is represented by zero, which holds both the beginning and the end—and is the chrysalis of an individual called to know themselves.

The Fool's correlation with the numeral 0 is highly symbolic, for it speaks to the infinite potential of empty space. The profound idea that 1 can only exist because there was first nothing, a void. If you seek a new beginning in your life, my love, meditate on this concept. Have you truly created a space, a nothingness from which the new can be born? To create this nothingness, you must be willing to accept your own ignorance, to accept your own "not knowing" of everything. When we do this, curiosity can return into our lives, and curiosity is the path that the Fool treads. After all, was it not a little bit of curiosity that led you here to me?

Never forget the Fool in your heart, my love. The part of you that is restless, seeking new heights and horizons to traverse, seeking to test the limits of who you really are. They will whisper things to you like "Why not?" and "What do you have to lose?" For the Fool has no baggage, no memory of wounds or identities that would inhibit their ability to follow the quest of their heart.

In every moment, the Fool is reborn—and so are you. All that is required is that you allow yourself to leave behind the weight of who you have always believed yourself to be and of who you have always believed yourself to become. Be here. Be ignorant. Be open to an adventure with no destination, where the excitement is in every step of not knowing . . . where *Der Weg ist das Ziel*. This is why the Fool appears to be almost dancing. They are in perfect rhythm with the flow of life, much like the final archetype of the major arcana . . . but you will meet them later.

Astrologically, the Fool has always been associated with the element of air, and aptly so, for they are the breath of life itself. The essence of consciousness as a force that propels us to discover ourselves. The first gasp that spells both our life and death, the bridge between divinity and the mortal realm. Do you feel yourself being formed and reformed with every breath? Do you feel how much potential is carried in the breath in your belly and in everything you will ever utter in this life by using it?

In recent times, the Fool has also been associated with the planet Uranus, which astrologically is the planet of superconsciousness. The stroke of genius. The spontaneous lightning strike of change that brings us into a higher state of awareness. Like the planet Uranus, the Fool is chaotic, unpredictable and eager for change. They are the power of acting on the odd thought that penetrates straight to the truth of your soul and defies the predictable and uninspired timeline of your existing reality.

Are you beginning to see how giant of a fool you are, my love? How much genius runs through your veins and you being completely ignorant of it? You are not foolish because you lack intelligence, you are foolish because you have the powers of a god and you don't even know it.

And is this not one of the great joys of life? To awaken to the superpowers that we always had within us, but had no idea how to use or control. Too many of us buy into our own foolishness: "I'm just a [insert limiting identity]," "It's just not me . . . ," "I could never . . ." We remain in our chrysalis and never even begin the quest to truly understanding ourselves. Everyone is born and will die a fool, my love, but foolishness that stems from the regret of not following your heart is the most punishing kind. Let the Fool clear your mind of all your doubts and fears from the past and future; remember that these spaces cannot coexist with the miraculous potential of your present. You are not defined by who you were and who you think you will be. You have the capacity to re-create yourself in every step, if that is what you so choose.

The Uranian aspect of the Fool is revolutionary, radical and unable to conform to any paths that are not of their own making. Is it not profound that such a powerful force of change and creation exists within your every breath? Is it not infinitely empowering to realize that you are of superconsciousness? That you have the capacity to think thoughts that could jump you into potentials that you never before thought possible for you and your life?

Look around you, my love, the Fools in your life will be revealed to you by the spring in their step. The carefree strut of a soul that is following the excitingly unpredictable path of their own making. Am I exciting you, my love? Are you not excited by the idea of having no idea of where you will be by the end of our journey together? Are you not liberated by the fact that your "not knowing" is a gift that allows you to transcend the chains of a preordained destiny? You are here, my love, you are infinitely here. You are being created with every step, every leap of faith. Will you leap into life with me now? Will you lead with your heart? Will you take the chance to find out what adventures await you? If so, let us continue!

IN A READING . . .

ASTROLOGICAL INFLUENCE—AIR AND URANUS: The element of Air represents movement, communication, new ideas and adaptability. Where is there a sense of a "change of wind" in the subject's life? The planet Uranus brings activation, unexpected breakthroughs and sudden shifts to the subject's experience. Surrounding or clarifying cards may give more information as to what expression this breakthrough will take. Uranus illuminates the genius and pure potential of a subject. Reflect on where in life they are now ready to experience radical change and liberation.

UPRIGHT (DIRECT): New beginnings. Breakthrough. Leap of faith. Liberation. Being born again. New adventures and experiences. Starting again. Divine intervention. Freedom. Spontaneity. Sudden burst of freedom.

REVERSED (RETROGRADE): Plans coming together. Yearning for freedom. Hesitation. Fear of a fresh start. Returning to simple things. Rediscovering your inspiration. Restlessness. Hiding new plans. Change of direction. Preparing for your great escape. The element of surprise.

#1 ◆ THE MAGICIAN

MAJOR ARCANA

Astrological Correlation: Mercury

Awaken, my love, to your magician consciousness. As we step into the unknown, brimming with possibility, we also come to realize our ability to have creative control over our reality. The desire to not only be in this life, but to create. In the Magician, you will find the part of you that is able to manipulate reality by mastering and interpreting the universal forces that flow through everything that finally manifests in this physical world.

"What in the hocus pocus?" You may very well say. How? It is simpler than you may think. Attention. Whatever becomes your field of attention, my love, automatically instructs the forces of the universe to assist in attaining or creating whatever it is you are focusing on. There is a powerful truth in the phrase "Be careful what you wish for" because your spells will always work out based on where you have been directing your attention . . . and we are not always conscious of where we have been directing our attention.

The Magician represents our capacity to categorize and interpret information correctly and our ability to focus on what matters—and what will always matter to us is fulfilling our personal desires. That is why he wields the wand (symbolic of desire) and holds it up to the heavens. A gesture that affirms the importance of recognizing our individual willpower in this life. It is an incredible phenomenon, but we seem to forget, my love, that we do indeed possess the gift of free will in this life!

Your ability to control where you place your attention in this life is the only testament you need to prove that you are free. Free to think as you please, free to focus on what you please and, thus, free to become who you please. When you become conscious of your Magician consciousness, you are able to see how much more of your life is under your control than you thought. The Magician cannot feel victim to their situation for they live with the knowing that at every point in time they have access to the tools needed to create the necessary changes in their reality.

A good Magician is not a master of magic in the way that you may think; they are a master of focus. A good Magician knows how to focus on creating the change that they desire regardless of what "unpleasant" or "unwanted" circumstances are currently coexisting in their physical reality. It is focus that creates mentality—and mentality is what will bring you closer to what you truly desire.

Astrologically, the Magician is correlated with the planet Mercury, which rules your mental faculties and is responsible for your capacity to interpret, translate and process information so that it may better help you understand yourself and the world around you. Mercury is also responsible for your capacity to recognize duality, to recognize that the only way something can exist is because it exists in relation to another thing.

Indeed, it is your Magician consciousness, my love, that allows you to discern the function of everything that exists within you and outside of you for they are two sides of the same coin. It is the profound realization that "As above, so below," in that the macrocosm is always speaking to and reflecting the microcosm and vice versa. That what is within you will always be shown outside of you and vice versa. That your focus is constantly being informed by where you are focusing within you and vice versa.

Are you witnessing the magic in these dualities, my love? Are you beginning to feel how much control you really have over the circumstances of your reality? Is it not empowering to realize that your personal willpower, the evidence of your free will, is what allows you to direct and communicate with the forces of this universe, to bend everything to be in accordance with your self-realization? That there can be nothing that exists purely outside of you for it is your self-consciousness itself that creates reality and, thus, nothing that is not in some way under your control? You do not give yourself enough credit for how influential you truly are, by virtue of possessing a will that is free.

This is what separates you from every other organism on this planet. It is a blessing (and a curse, remembering duality!) that you have the choice in being able to direct your willpower toward realizing the truth of who you are or in letting it be directed by everything and everyone around you. Do not forfeit your divine will, my love! For it is only you, with your unique mentality and desires, who has the capacity to materialize everything that you want and are in this life. To be able to affirm "I am, I am, I am." And to witness the magic of YOU reflected in everything around you.

Is that not a great miracle of this life? To recognize the beauty within you in something outside of you? Is that not the magic of creating? To say, this . . . this here, holds an aspect of me, it has brought me closer to the whole of who I truly am.

Now that you are aware of the power of your attention, my love, you have become acquainted with the power of your will. The Magician passes their wand, their baton to you, the promethean fire of self-knowledge. To assist in your quest to know yourself individually outside of the superconsciousness you came from. To create your individual mark as an expression of the godly force you didn't even know you were made up of, my foolish little love. Hold your wand and hold it firmly. Your will will be tested in this life because that is the only way it will grow strong and confident in asserting "I am, I am, I AM."

IN A READING . . .

ASTROLOGICAL INFLUENCE—MERCURY: The planet Mercury brings knowledge, tools and awareness to the subject's experience. Surrounding or clarifying cards may give more information as to what specifically the subject is attempting to manifest, create and gain control over. Reflect on the subject's field of attention and what they are currently charging in their life through their focus.

UPRIGHT (DIRECT): Newfound awareness. New knowledge. Aligning forces for a powerful manifestation. Successful alchemy. Spiritual graduation. Converging different points of focus into one direction. Adeptship. Alignment. Creative potential. Newfound motivation and willpower.

REVERSED (RETROGRADE): Recovering old knowledge. Rediscovering willpower and motivation. Reevaluating what you desire. Learning in private. Studying and evaluating your unsuccessful attempts at something. Work in progress. Shift of focus. Resolving a powerless situation. Returning scattered energies back to you.

#2 ◆ THE HIGH PRIESTESS

MAJOR ARCANA

Astrological Correlation: Moon

Beware, the path ahead is saturated in darkness. Do you see why I told you to hold firm to your wand? We cannot proceed unless we talk to the High Priestess, unless we pass through her initiation. For she holds all the secrets of your soul, your subconscious and your psychic knowing. She is the cosmic rite of passage through which all your desires are brought up from the depths of your being and into conscious awareness. You cannot avoid her. You cannot deceive her. She is wisdom and truth through and through. Her eyes are trained to navigate a world without light, without the need for conscious understanding. She is a master of the subconscious realms. It is her duty to make you aware of the deeper needs, the core truths that operate even behind what you will consciously want and desire in this life.

Here she is, on the fringes, never direct. She vanishes when you invoke her, for she does not speak in the language of your conscious mind, only through the emotions behind everything you do. Ignore her, she will grow stronger. Deny her, you will walk a road divorced from the truth of who you are. Do not worry. She is patient, patient for you to finally become still and listen inwardly. To realize that your willpower is only as strong as your awareness of your own subconscious. It is she that makes you aware of this realm of dreams, shadows and inner knowing. She is the High Priestess.

Many have a perfectly capable willpower and ability to focus upon what they desire, but few are able to align these desires with the core needs of their own vehicle. The High Priestess is responsible for the recalibration of your soul. She is the part of you that walks a path of complete alignment and commitment to your inner truth. This is not a conscious truth. It is much deeper than that and can only be described to you through symbolic language that rings deeply on all levels of your being.

The High Priestess' connection to your subconscious means that she holds the memory of everything that you have ever experienced and has, thus, been impressed onto your soul. This is a memory that transcends lifetimes, my love. The High Priestess will never ask you to know "why," only that you trust that you know. You know, my love, there are certain things that cannot be explained about the world and about who you are. You will realize these truths in moments of deep self-contemplation, where you catch a glimpse of your soul in the mirror. The truth of who you are that perhaps no one else has ever seen. And how could they, my love? You haven't even seen yourself. She will help you see yourself again and again. No matter how far you stray on this journey from the core needs of your soul, the High Priestess never forgets the way home for you.

And how could she? Your subconscious never forgets anything. It can only record and record and record, storing experiences and memories that inform everything you do and how you respond to your reality. Through this record of memories and experiences, the High Priestess divines to you the very patterns of subconscious that you have been operating from. All it takes for a subconscious pattern to develop is repetition and an emotional dynamic connected with what is being repeated.

Your subconscious automatically seeks out the most familiar behaviors that have always brought you a sense of emotional security, even if those same behaviors have now become maladaptive and sabotaging. Through the High Priestess, your patterns will be revealed. This is why she can only be heard in stillness, for stillness is always found at the beginning of becoming aware of and breaking a vicious emotional cycle.

The High Priestess has been associated with the moon, the celestial body that astrologically has always been connected with our emotions, sensitivities and subconscious cravings. You will never be judged for what you truly need in the presence of the High Priestess; all that she asks is that you honor those needs, that you give room for them to come up to the light and be realized or released.

Remember, you cannot bypass your own subconscious. You may be able to fool the entire world, my love, but in that silent conversation with your own soul, you will always confess to the High Priestess the truth of who you really are. And, in this intimacy, she will honor you with spiritual revelation, intuition and direction to rewrite what has been written in your destiny, so that you may take command over your life once again.

Yes, the High Priestess knows your destiny. You know your destiny. How? When your inner High Priestess looks at you, my love, she will tell you who you will be based on who you have been. If you are not happy with what you see, you have the choice to change that destiny by breaking the cycles that you have been repeating. Forget everything that you know, so that you may remember what you have forgotten, she will say. For only when you have begun to trust what you already know within beyond what appears to be logical on the surface, will you discover the deepest parts of who you are.

IN A READING . . .

ASTROLOGICAL INFLUENCE—MOON: The subject's inner emotional world and core needs are brought into focus. Surrounding and clarifying cards will provide more information on the unseen and intuitive knowledge that the subject has been picking up on subconsciously in their life.

UPRIGHT (DIRECT): Following the path of the soul. Stillness. Penetrating insights. Knowing the deep truth. Psychic revelations. Aligning with your deepest needs. Emotional intelligence. Being aware of what others are not yet aware of. Trusting your instincts. Connecting with past life memory.

REVERSED (RETROGRADE): Deep inner work. Evaluating deep-seated subconscious beliefs. Fear and hesitation around your own intuition. Remembering your true power. Spiritual growth. Cleansing from the influence of others. Learning to trust yourself again. Recovering lost knowledge. Reevaluating your deep emotional needs. Reconnecting with the self.

#3 ◆ THE EMPRESS

MAJOR ARCANA

Astrological Correlation: Venus

Behold, the Empress now seeks to make her presence known to you. How could we proceed on this journey of passion and desire without confronting the embodiment of Venus herself? It is she who bestows upon you your capacity to imagine, to love and to experience the abundance and sensual pleasures of this earthly world. Awaken your inner Empress, my love, and you will open yourself to effortlessly receive everything that you have fought long and hard to never lose.

Never would the Empress close her fist, never would the thought cross her divine brow that there would not be enough for her in this world, that she does not have a rightful place on this planet. You have a rightful place on this planet, my love. You are endlessly deserving and invaluable. The Empress represents the aspect of your nature that is deeply self-loving. She is the aspect of you that simply cannot settle for anything less than what you truly deserve for she is aware of who you are at your highest level of self-value. How could she give you any less, my love? How could she love you any less?

She is the Earth mother that endlessly provides for her children, for to witness your blossoming is the source of her joy and inspiration, the evidence of her love. A spoiling mother, your inner Empress cannot say "No" to you, my love. "What does your heart desire?" is her only question and her answer to you will always be "Of course, because I love you."

Witness her every time you glimpse yourself, your body in the mirror. What beauty, what endless perfection you are. You unfurling flower, yes, yes you are. Oh, to look at yourself and everyone and everything around you with an ounce of that infinite love and affection in the Empress' gaze as she marvels upon her children. Do you feel already how much more vibrant our journey together is becoming? Does the sun not shine a little brighter? Are the flowers not beginning to dance? Are you not filled with the love, reverence and gratitude of being alive? Of being here with me now? Of having the opportunity to love and be loved? Of being loved by this Earth for simply walking upon it? For simply existing?

Oh, how more than enough you are, my love, in simply being. Of simply blessing everyone and everything around you with your presence. When you can sit deeply in your true presence, you are always whole. It is there where you are able to show your unconditional love and affection for the sun, the moon, the stars. For your lover, your child and every other living being that wants to live, live, live like you, my love. That wants to love and be loved. That wants to be enough.

Oh, how else can I pour this from my heart to yours: You are more than enough in your presence. You can create worlds from the love in your heart. Your love, the softness in the center of your chest, is always your direct connection to the soul of this planet and to the divine mother, the Empress. She will return to you the kiss you blow to her in the wind with a sun that rises for you, with the trees that sway for you, with the love that surrounds you and the riches and pleasures of this world that will inspire gratitude in you.

With all of this, my love, you will open the doors to experiencing when you allow the pulse of a loving heart to deepen your connection to your mind, body and soul. Affirm "As I am, wherever I am and wherever I will be, I am deserving of unconditional love." There! There is a glow about you now, you blossoming rose! And all of your desires will come to you much more easily because of it, because whether you receive them now or later, the Empress has brought to your awareness the plenty that always lies in your present.

Love is always accessible to you, my love, and the love for yourself is a gift that no other thing will ever be able to give to you in this life. For to love yourself is to open yourself and, when you are open, you are able to experience the beauty that exists in all things. Is that not love, my love? To witness something for its essential beauty? To not seek to change it or demand of it but only wish that it comes to love its true nature, to know itself. For that which knows itself is always effortlessly beautiful.

The love from your inner Empress will beautify your world and your life. She will also make you aware of what pleasures in your life are more thorns than roses. When you connect with this level of self-love and self-value, everything in your life that is not fully nourishing your heart will be brought to your awareness. The Empress will gently point you toward aspects of your reality that are reflecting back to you your own lack of self-worth.

Allow yourself to be filled by her love, to realize the capacity for the universe to endlessly circulate back to you whatever it is you may have a fear of losing. The Empress' correlation with the planet Venus emphasizes her divine fertility and regeneration. She is the embodiment of the endlessly replenishing force of nature that will always give and give. When you recognize this force must also exist within you, you will begin to love and be loved in your most authentic expression. You will no longer love from a place of inner lack. Your pleasure will be in giving. When you are giving, you are able to see how much you are always receiving.

When you walk this journey hand in hand with the Empress, my love, no matter where you go and what you traverse, there will always be a sense of love and beauty. You will open yourself to experience the richness of your own creativity and your sensitivity to all the blessings this physical world can offer you will be heightened and they will be multiplied. Walk with me, my love, and notice the flowers that bloom with your every step and how your heart connects with the pulse of the Earth.

IN A READING . . .

ASTROLOGICAL INFLUENCE—VENUS: The subject's receptivity to unconditional love and abundance is in focus. Venus highlights the subject's quality of relationships and the overall harmony of their life in relation to their true nature. Reflect upon the subject's creative desires and their capacity to receive the quality of life that they truly are deserving of and have always imagined.

UPRIGHT (DIRECT): Harmonious, loving and exalted relationships. Fertile ground for the fruition of new hopes and dreams. Abundance of all things. Creative inspiration. Plenty. Beauty. The freedom to be as you truly are. Leisure. Radiance and charisma.

REVERSED (RETROGRADE): Protecting your worth. Finding more fertile ground. Reevaluating one's value and self-esteem. Reevaluating relationship dynamics. Glowing up quietly. Restoring leisure and beauty to your world. Not yet feeling deserving of the best. Coming to recognize your own beauty. Giving back to yourself.

#4 ◈ THE EMPEROR

MAJOR ARCANA

Astrological Correlation: Aries

Thunder, lightning, power, sovereignty. He approaches with a gravitas that bends worlds to his will. Will exalted. The Emperor sits on the throne of a will fully realized, of a self that has complete dominion over himself and, thus, the world around him. Notice the mountainous terrain of our journey, notice the peeling back of the verdant fields of the Empress. There is a stoicism here. For an exalted willpower requires discipline, control and reason over the wild forces of our nature.

Both the divine counterparts of the Empress (page 24) and the Emperor represent a kind of freedom we achieve from satiating our desires. The freedom of the Empress is the freedom to be, The Emperor's . . . the freedom to do. Your inner Emperor is here to preserve your sovereignty, my love. He recognizes his leadership and authority on all things regarding his own person. The Emperor does not seek out permission, confirmation or validation for each purposeful step he takes into his power.

There is a deep integrity and responsibility at the core of your inner Emperor, for with great power comes great responsibility. In fact, the level of his authority and sovereignty could never have itself been obtained if the Emperor had not developed a mastery over his free will. Do you feel the magnitude of your own autonomy, my love? Do you recognize the absolute freeness of your will by virtue of being an individualized aspect of a godly consciousness?

At no point in your life, my love, does your inner Emperor not possess a solution to the challenges and obstacles of your reality. You may not always like his answer, for his sternness and stoicism will always reveal to you your own lack of self-mastery, willpower and accountability as the primary problem in your reality. Indeed, the Emperor is a master of the most difficult battle of all: the battle against the self. He has seen wars. He has overcome himself again and again. He is graceful in his victories and humble in his defeat, ready to take the lessons of where only he has failed himself—regardless of who or whatever else there is to blame outside of him.

The Emperor sees no purpose in blaming or controlling the other for he knows that this behavior will only ever confirm back to him his own lack of control over his reality. To experience himself as a victim to forces out of his control is to stare his own death in the face, the death of his individual will. The end to his reign.

As long as you remain aware of your own free will, my love, at every point in your reality, your reign will be immortal. Allow your inner Emperor to define the limits of your reality, to say "No" to that which threatens your sovereignty, to that which could pose as an obstacle to your highest integrity and vision. Your inner Emperor emerges as anger, assertiveness and the deep desire for freedom. He will object when you disrespect your own boundaries, when you allow in that which could threaten the security and safety of your own being.

Why won't you fight for yourself? Why will you not fight for your own right to be in complete alignment with the truth of your inner being? The commands of the Emperor will push you into the truth of who you are, my love, but you must remember, the Emperor's path is one of confrontation. He will teach you how to battle. How to remain in dominion over yourself. For where you continually surrender your will to external forces will always point you to an enemy that you've allowed into the sanctuary of your own soul, to a place in yourself that you still do not have dominion over. To blame, to judge and to run away from the opportunities in your life, to assert and affirm the truth of who you are is only helping you run away from the self-mastery required to achieve the personal freedom and respect you deserve in this life.

The Emperor represents your ability to stand in the full presence and power of your "I am." When you still helplessly surrender to the wills of the things around you, when you deep down do not want to, you are restraining your inner Emperor from fighting for your freedom. And, goodness, does that make him angry.

Do you feel the passion and love that the Emperor has for you, my love? How deeply he wants to protect your freedom? How his joy is in seeing you whole in yourself? Oh, the rage the Emperor feels when he sees you in your disempowerment. How he wishes he could lift you up onto his shoulders and remind you of how you are always on the throne of your own world. That the highest and most accurate perspective of your reality can only be found when you are on top of yourself, when you claim full accountability and responsibility for the state of your reality.

When you affirm this, my love, you return all power that has been diffused into your reality back to you, and you rise, rise, rise . . . back into the throne of "I am, I am, I am." Never do you "lose yourself," my love, you can only forget the capabilities of your own power and autonomy. Never do you lose against something or someone, my love, it's only when you choose to claim the perspective that your personal power is not enough to bring you into your personal freedom. Never can you lose your freedom, my love, it's only when you believe that your independence and personal will is dependent on the will of something outside of yourself.

And, if that is what your freedom was based upon, you were not experiencing your true freedom at all. The Emperor will forge your individual path forward in this journey. He is the difference between passively observing the wins and the woes of your life and taking control, making conscious decisions that will force your reality to give you more of who you truly are and less of who you are not. He is the choice to choose the path that will lead you to the satisfaction of your own will—a will, remember, that is first and foremost selfish—and to choose against the paths that threaten the integrity of your inner being. More specifically, the integrity of your inner Empress, who is the keeper of the key to the most valuable jewel on this planet, a jewel worth more than kingdoms built from gold and rivers flowing with diamonds . . . the jewel that is your heart.

Astrologically, the Emperor rules the zodiac kingdom of Aries. The kingdom where the iron of our personal will is forged in the fires of challenge, resistance, pressure and conflict. The sign of Aries has always been associated with "the first light," the glimpse of the sun as it rises up from the horizon, the furious cry of the newborn as it affirms itself as an individual for the very first time.

For many in this world, my love, that cry they gave upon entering this world was the first and last time they ever allowed themselves to affirm themselves. Do not let that be your fate. Choose that now to not be your fate. Fight against the sublimation of your will. Fight against the dissolution of your unique light. There is no need to seek out becoming a ruler of another kingdom (and, inevitably, becoming ruled by it) when you know yourself to be the ruler of your own kingdom.

Let me tell you something to save you from the tragedy of the Emperor's journey, my love: The thrones that are yours to claim in this life will never ask of you to be anything other than the most authentic expression of your inner being. For anything other than you in your authenticity could never sit in your unique power. The sword in the stone, my love. You have thrones that only you can sit upon in this life by affirming the truth of who you are. You have swords that only you can unsheathe in this life because only you know how to wield them.

As long as you fight for a throne or a destiny that is not rightfully true to your inner power, it will resist you, reduce you and always ask for you to bend to its own will. In this way, you will never experience your true sovereignty, the vistas of your true freedom. You will look upon lands that on the surface are yours, but, beneath, yearn for their rightful ruler . . . because you, you are still yearning for your rightful throne.

Allow the Emperor to reveal to you the way to your true kingdom, the kingdom that was crying back to you when you first cried entering this world! The kingdom that is the coming home to your heart, the kingdom where you sit in the complete freedom of your "I am." Persevere toward it, my love!

IN A READING . . .

ASTROLOGICAL INFLUENCE—ARIES: The subject's ability to take the lead and assert who they are in their life is brought into focus. Reflect upon the subject's personal sovereignty, independence and ability to know and value who they individually are in their life.

UPRIGHT (DIRECT): Power through independence. Standing firm in your decisions and in who you are. Self-assertion. Receiving respect and authority. Taking control and giving commands. Ambition. Drive. Personal freedom. Knowing what you want. Overcoming all obstacles through your willpower. Not giving up. Finding dominion and victory over difficult circumstances.

REVERSED (RETROGRADE): Reevaluating your independence. Recognizing your individual strength. Recovering from self-defeat. Needing to do things for you. Taking care of yourself. Learning to assert who you are. Developing power in solitude.

THE ACE OF WANDS

MINOR ARCANA

Astrological Correlation: Fire, Aries, Leo and Sagittarius

Grasp your wand, my love! The wand that is your will, your desire, and your drive! It holds the source of your very life force! Hold it firmly for the remainder of our journey together for it will keep you moving onward even when the path home to yourself makes you weary and confused. Allow me to share with you some wisdom about this path of the wands, the suit of fire in the tarot and the road toward the realization and manifestation of your free will in this life.

The wands in their essence represent desire. The Ace of Wands is the gift of willpower that allows us to embark on the journey of following whatever it is that lights us up inside. This wand is our individual desire to realize ourselves and satiate our human need for personal freedom and expansion. To wield the wand requires courage, responsibility and focus. It is to say "I will myself into this existence" and "I command the universal forces to serve my personal quest to fulfillment."

The Ace of Wands is associated with the element of fire because acting from a place of personal freedom and passion ignites your inner fire. This inner fire is the source of your vitality, the spring in your step, the will to live and the will to create. Above all else, the Ace of Wands represents the will to fulfill your emerging desires and the free will to do so. When you find yourself feeling like you have no willpower, no motivation, often it is because you have lost a hold on this very wand. Meaning, you have lost a hold over your free will and with it your passion, desires and focus.

You are always focusing, my love. Even distraction is not a lack of focus: It is simply a focus that has been divided, and the more divided your focus, the weaker your will. With your incarnation, you came with the ability to direct and focus universal forces. To bend them to YOUR will. Remember, the primary function of your will is to serve the fulfillment of your individual, "selfish" purpose. To even begin to use the power of the wand, you must accept that it is selfish. You must accept that the wand only cares about you and your personal freedom. You must give yourself the right to be the painter of your own reality or more powerful wills will inevitably direct your life for you.

Where you do not take accountability, when you do not take responsibility for your own evolution, your fire does not simply become dormant within you, it is instead used to fuel the will of others around you. The wands are competitive. They are a test of will. The more you feed your personal will, the less you will be susceptible to being dominated by the wills of others. Use your will or be used. Direct the universal forces for your own creation or be directed.

To wield the wand is to ignite your free will. This is a choice. This is a conscious action. Many have wills, but few are free, for freedom requires one to take full responsibility for the state of their reality. Few have the courage to even be on a path of discovering what they truly desire, let alone attaining it. They drop their wand, too hot to touch, and give up on their personal freedom and the pursuit of their individual realization. A shame, my love, to abandon the tool that creates the path to all your fiery experiences, passions, adventures and exhilaration in this life.

Hold your wand and hold it firmly. Even when it burns, feel your courage strengthen with every desire you cast from your need to feel personally fulfilled in this life. The more you use your personal will, the more you will come to know yourself. And the more that you know yourself in this life, the more you are able to access deeper reserves of your power as a creator. Weak wills always correlate with a lack of focus and a lack of correct focus makes one subject to overwhelming feelings of powerlessness. These feelings brood in he who lacks self-knowledge, who is unable to focus on the power of will from within. For one who truly knows themselves has found the source of their power within them. True leadership is born from this very same place, for the one who has been freed knows how to make another free. Every good leader knows how to direct their wand. Notice how even the shepherd wields a wand that commands the sheep.

When the Ace of Wands presents itself, there is a birthing of a new will, a smoldering new desire or passion. Remember, we are only at the beginning of the suit of wands, my love, and so this burning desire within you may not be more refined or specific than the desire to be free, the desire to know yourself. The journey of the suit of wands is the journey of becoming self-conscious of your own will, of becoming conscious of what it is you truly want.

Notice that even knowing what you really want from your life is not information you actually begin with. You will discover what you want by discovering who you are, and you will discover who you are by pursuing what you want. How could you know what you want without also knowing who you are? You cannot separate yourself from what you desire. And, yet, how strange that we live in a world that attempts to do exactly this? We are forced to pursue things because they are the "norm," not because they reflect who we are within. There is no mystery as to why so many of us walk around with no will, with lives designed around things (if we were more honest with ourselves) we actually don't care much about.

When you have not embarked on a quest of understanding yourself as an individual, when you have not yet grasped the Ace of Wands, you cannot possibly come to understand what it is you truly desire. Grasp the wand, grasp it firmly. You need not know at this stage what it is that will satiate the fire in your belly, but wanting to find out is the most important desire you can focus your attention on in this life. You will never be punished, my love, for directing your focus on realizing yourself.

Challenged? Most certainly, for you are choosing to affirm yourself against a world that cannot affirm what has not yet been created. It is a worthy price to pay, my love, to discover the meaning of that fire that inspires you, that makes you feel alive. Honor it and you will receive a freedom in this life that very few possess: the freedom to be and do in complete alignment with who you truly are.

Astrologically, the Ace of Wands is attributed to all three of the zodiac signs under the fire element: Aries, Leo and Sagittarius. Aries, ruled by Mars, represents your primal will for freedom and survival and the inner fire that fights for your unique path in life. Leo, ruled by the sun, is the essence and expression of your spirit and is responsible for forming a confident sense of self and identity along your journey. Sagittarius, ruled by Jupiter, deals with wisdom, the philosophy of your life and the personal truths you are here to inspire others with. Harnessing the bravery of Aries, the radiance of Leo and the spiritual wisdom of Sagittarius, let us go forth and become masters of our own willpower!

IN A READING . . .

ASTROLOGICAL INFLUENCE—FIRE, ARIES, LEO AND SAGITTARIUS: The subject's courage, identity and personal philosophy is brought into focus.

UPRIGHT (DIRECT): Passion. New desire. New focus. Bravery. New sense of self. Sheer power. Confidence. Sexuality. New inspiration. Expressing who you are.

REVERSED (RETROGRADE): Reevaluating oneself. Holding back. Shift in passion. Questioning identity. The brink of realization. Rediscovering passion within. Taking accountability and responsibility. Inner strength. Hidden passions.

THE 2 OF WANDS

MINOR ARCANA

Astrological Correlation: Mars in Aries

What is that in the distance? It's the second wand, my love! The temptation of another will, another focus? Oh, but this won't do! Not with how selfish the wands are. They cannot compromise, only fight to the death! Their nature implies that the stronger will will always overcome the other, unless other forces can be applied to intervene.

In the 2 of Wands, you are presented with a dilemma. What do you desire more right now? What do you need to focus more on right now? The instant gratification or the long-term gratification? The desire for stability or the desire for freedom? The desire to stay or the desire to go? Many times, your desires are not even so clear, all that you know is that you desire more and you're eager to find out what that more looks like.

Astrologically, the 2 of Wands correlates with the planet Mars in Aries. This is the planet of desire, passion and drive in its home sign, emphasizing the point in our journey of desire where what we deeply want begins to conflict with what we currently have. Aries is a sign where new beginnings, passions and grand quests for personal glory are born. Meditating on this, you will realize in the 2 of Wands the deep desire to explore that which you have not allowed yourself to before. You will not be able to repress the yearning to test out the limits of your freedom. Mars in the sign of Aries desires nothing more than freedom. The freedom to choose. The freedom to have it all. The freedom to go out on a grand quest of self-discovery even if it only results in you coming home again, but, this time, without the inner restlessness of not having acted on your courage.

The 2 of Wands presents itself as a choice, but, really, my love, it is more so a confirmation that you are not yet at the destination of what it is you truly want or who you truly are. That there is more to explore. That by asserting what no longer ignites your inner fire you are opening the potential to what will ignite your inner fire. Yes, this is a choice. As I mentioned earlier, to wield the wand and your free will is a choice. How willing are you to discover yourself? How unwilling are you to live a life where unfulfilled desires exist as tormenting shadows in the periphery of your psyche?

In the 2 of Wands, you reconcile with this choice, only to realize it was never really a choice at all. Would anyone consciously desire to not experience personal freedom and expansion? Allow the 2 of Wands (as affirmed by the planet Mars) to push you beyond the confines of who you have accepted yourself to currently be. The 2 of Wands, with its fiery connection to Mars in Aries, is a very temporary position to be in. The inner restlessness contained within this card most often will force some kind of action or decision. Mars in Aries is too ready, too eager, too hungry for experiences that will develop a deeper sense of who you are.

There is an important note to make here when making decisions using your willpower. As an example, the desire to pursue being in a relationship as opposed to being single may be in the moment what you desire more, but if you are someone who has never allowed yourself the space to discover who you are on your own, your desire to be in connection with someone may not be coming from the desire to gain a deeper sense of who you really are.

The desire to discover more of yourself is not always the desire that is the most comfortable, exciting or easy to achieve. This is where your ability to discern, to make choices in the interest of your personal freedom and expansion, is of the utmost importance. You will always have the free will to choose, my love, and, the more you choose, the more you will develop a maturity around exercising the gift of free will. You will give yourself the capacity and freedom to fail. You will give yourself the opportunity to realize that although crossroads can be life-defining in the moment, all paths eventually will lead you home.

IN A READING . . .

ASTROLOGICAL INFLUENCE—MARS IN ARIES: The subject's bravery and ambition toward new endeavors is in focus. Reflect upon the subject's most self-invested desires and help eliminate doubts and fears regarding making certain choices. For, in the end, every path will lead to the one truth of who they are. Be bold!

UPRIGHT (DIRECT): New adventures. Choosing in the favor of freedom and personal expansion. Contemplation on what you really stand for. The world at your fingertips. Possibilities and opportunities. Carving out your own path. Discovering what is true for you.

REVERSED (RETROGRADE): Biding your time for something big. Building up courage. Reevaluating options. Reflecting on what you really want. Secret pathways opening. Opportunity you did not expect to arrive. Rediscovering your authenticity. Seeking out a deeper path in life.

THE 3 OF WANDS

MINOR ARCANA

Astrological Correlation: Sun in Aries

We have arrived, my love, at what I like to call "the shores of imagined potentials." This is the point where your desires begin to take the form of visions in your imagination. Your will to expand and discover the truth of who you are allows you to envision yourself beyond the horizon, beyond the physical and mental limits you had previously placed upon your current reality. There is a deep yearning that is contained within this part of the journey. There is a sense of something hopeful and exciting yet tantalizingly out of reach at the same time. Does that not sound like a bittersweet thing called desire?

In its essence, the 3 of Wands is the beauty and peace that can be found in the stretch of time and space between desiring something and attaining it. This space is what allows desire to incubate and mature, to surpass our expectations. It is the only way that we can remain pointed toward the continual unfolding of our true potential. When we look out into this distance, we feel the exhilaration of what could be. Whether things turn out that way or not is not the point. It is our willingness to dream and conjure creative solutions to where we find ourselves to be right now that holds the greatest importance.

In and of itself, the 3 of Wands does not present to you a solution, it only seeks to give your willpower permission to look beyond. There is a realization here that you are just beginning a voyage or awaiting confirmation that "Yes" this is your path, this is you stepping through a doorway toward what is meant for you.

The numeral 3 of this card speaks to the highly creative form that willpower takes in this card. There is so much potential and possibility that is opening to you at this stage in your journey, my love. What a blessing to not be locked onto a single goal, but to be experiencing the totality of what you could experience. The focus of the 3 of Wands is less on the practicality of who you see yourself to be and what you desire to experience and more on the contemplation of the "What if . . ."

You will face very strongly here both the yearning and detachment necessary for attaining what you desire. You will learn here to never give up on achieving your desires, but to learn to remain open to the horizons of how you could achieve them and how they will finally manifest themselves on the shores of your reality. Affirm here, that when there is a will, there is most certainly a way, because when you are unwavering in your focus upon what it is you truly yearn for, it is your will that will infallibly create a way.

The "shores of imagined potentials" will not ever ask of you to know what is beyond the horizon, only that you dare to dream, dare to envision. They do not hold you responsible for always knowing the way to your goal, only that you aid them through your inspiration and openness to create it with you and for you. Are you beginning to witness the beauty of wanting and not yet having? The excitement found there and that excitement being the sole evidence needed in knowing that you are pointed toward growth and self-realization? So often, my love, it is not that what people desire is impossible, it is that their attention and focus is not pointed on the what could be, it is addicted to what is, what is not, and what has been, and indeed that is all that will ever be . . . unless one dares to look out into the shores of imagined potentials.

In the 3 of Wands, your desires to mature begin to cultivate a vision. Seeing is experiencing what is, whereas having vision is our ability to experience through our yearnings, our desire, our excitement, the acquisition and realization of that which we do not yet have. A profound place to be, my love, to be at the shores of everything you both are and could be at the exact same time. The 3 of Wands is assigned to the sun in Aries, which reveals to us that embodying and consciously experiencing our personal freedom (sun in Aries) is not something that is somewhere in the distance or in some destination, it is found in simply being pointed toward the infinitely expanding horizon of who you are, my love.

Your very humanity implies desire and, for as long as you have desire, there will always be an imagined potential in the far distance. This is the territory of your expanding self-awareness and self-realization. Many in this world have made this process a curse, something to escape and become enlightened away from. Many have made an enemy of desire itself, seeing this process as one that can only be one of suffering and not one that validates to us the beauty of being a consciously expanding being.

Desire is not your enemy, my love, it is evidence of your humanity and infinite potential to realize the truth of who you are into this physical reality. This process is not a curse, it is a miracle. It is the process that has led to the creation of everything that has allowed mankind to surpass the predefined limits of our bodies and the forces of nature. The inconceivable inventions that our species have brought into this reality—both the beautiful and the destructive—all came from souls that cultivated a vision at the shores of imagined potentials. They were able to experience themselves and their reality beyond the scope of what was present in front of them. They focused on what could be and were driven by the desire to experience their fully actualized selves. By envisioning themselves at their highest point of personal freedom, they created a pathway, a practical arrangement of the undefined and infinite forces of consciousness that are available to us all.

Oh, the gift of vision, my love. Are you beginning to imagine where you could be by the end of our journey together? Heed caution in getting too attached to how it will unfold, but that excitement and anticipation you feel is not a lie . . . it is your heart witnessing something being defined in the infinite that it cannot wait to share with you in your physical reality.

Remember the sun in Aries with this card. Your desires are not something to escape from—they build your identity and a strong sense of who you are. We are beings that are deeply driven by desire. It is what makes us real and raw. It is what makes us committed to fulfilling ourselves in this reality so that we may fulfill the same desires in everyone around us. The only true suffering desire can cause is when you fail to see the connection between who you are right now and who you will be.

The very fact that you can envision yourself, my love, is all the evidence you need to know that you are in the process of commanding universal forces, that you are forming a reality that is personally yours. Every occultist will tell you, my love, that the physical world takes the most time to catch up to every other plane of reality, it's just the way it is. Still the airplane was created, the Internet, medicine and surgery. Still incredible athletes were forged, millionaires were made, dreams turned into reality, eventually. Vision, my love, vision, and a very stubborn commitment, remembering the sun in Aries, to realizing the most authentic version of yourself in this life.

IN A READING . . .

ASTROLOGICAL INFLUENCE—SUN IN ARIES: The subject's path toward self-actualization is in focus. Reflect upon who the subject sees themselves to be and who they see themselves as becoming.

UPRIGHT (DIRECT): Following your vision. New horizons awaiting you. Expanding your influence. Calling in a dream. Realizing more of who you want to become. Patience as paths toward your greatest desires are being weaved by the cosmos. Focusing on your inspiration.

REVERSED (RETROGRADE): Reevaluating your dreams. Seeking a higher perspective. Reconnecting with your true vision. Shift of vision. Feeling claustrophobic. Things happening for a greater reason and purpose. Resting from constant chasing. Appreciating the now. Focusing on what you can control.

THE 4 OF WANDS

MINOR ARCANA

Astrological Correlation: Venus in Aries

What a welcome reprieve for our journey. Four wands forge the foundation of a sanctuary here. There is a peace, a harmony, a celebration for what is rather than what we will at some point attain. How strange on this journey of the wands to come to a point of fulfillment? Where desire is satiated, if only temporarily?

Revel here, my love. Revel in the union of yourself with yourself. In the union of you with those whom you love. A celebration awaits you, a banquet, a feast for your senses and passions. You will find the Emperor and the Empress reposing here in perfect harmony. Where the kingdom meets the garden, where the individual will of man harmonizes with the force of nature. In the 4 of Wands is a harmony between masculine and feminine, asserting and receiving, desiring and experiencing.

The astrological correlation of Venus in Aries in this card presents the pleasure and harmony (Venus) that comes from establishing a strong sense of self (Aries). The 4 of Wands speaks of a joyous reuniting, a profound harmony between who we are and how we relate to others. Under this canopy, this fruitful sanctuary, is the reward of bridging the gap between the competing and individualizing aspect of desire and our desire for union and love from the other.

These two seemingly polar-opposite forces are at peace with one another here. We do not wish to be somewhere or someone else. We are not looking at what we don't have or what we wish we had more of. We do not even long to be further along our journey, for this reprieve nourishes a soul that tires itself out from desire. Look around you, my love, where else do you seek to be? Comfort, pleasure and peace are qualities that can only truly be weaved and experienced in the present.

Notice the figures in the distance, weaving garlands, here and now, consumed by the pleasure of the now. Notice how much more pleasure we are able to experience simply through bringing our awareness closer to the now. The vibrancy of the trees, the fruits and the sky are not something dependent on nature itself, it's our ability to experience nature, it's our awareness that heightens our senses and allows us to witness the beauty of life.

Indeed, my love, in this part of the journey, you will experience your heart connecting back with itself again, the most beautiful and profound reunion of coming home to yourself. Is it not a delight to know that home can be found not at the end of your journey, but along it? That you, an unfolding and blossoming flower, are here to be loved, experienced and nurtured in every step of your unfolding? That you are deserving of this. You deserve to seek sanctuary, my love. You deserve to be received and loved and warmed.

Can you open yourself to this? Can you allow in a present celebration of your journey toward everything you desire? Venus in Aries here brings a sense of completion and harmony to our quest for reinvention and self-discovery, even before we may feel like we're really there. What a blessing!

Oh, how tiresome this journey would be without these moments of reprieve, these moments of completion before we have truly completed whatever it is we are striving for. Do not skip this sanctuary, do not deny yourself this reunion with yourself. A reconnection with your sense of home is a reconnection with the truth of who you are. Nothing is more important than this reunion with yourself at certain points in your journey, for in this adventure of self-discovery and self-realization, we have a tendency to stray very far from ourselves—and we must—for it is in this desire to venture out and return home that we learn just a little bit more about ourselves.

Still, do not forget to return home every now and then, back to the sanctuary that grounds your constantly-seeking-desire nature. The richness of the 4 of Wands is found in the exchange of love and affection, of hospitality and generosity, of forgiveness, reunion and reconciliation, of pure celebration. When you find yourself being unable to celebrate purely, perhaps the strivings of your journey have exhausted your heart.

A heart that is not here is somewhere else yearning. It has flown into the realms of unforeseen potentials or in the desolation of the past and, all the while, you have failed to notice that the fire in the hearth of your soul has been neglected. You are no longer warm. A restlessness pervades your soul as you try to spark again what can only be found here, here, here.

Be here, my love, if only for this moment. There will be plenty of journeying, striving and expanding in this suit of the wands, I can assure you that. So, for this moment, reconnect with your joy and celebrate the existence of you being. As long as you can connect with that inner sanctuary that also can take the form of the people and the places that you love, you will never lose sight of the way back home to yourself. The light that is still on, the fireplace that still burns, the banter in the kitchen, the waft of something delicious in the oven . . . it is the domestic simplicities that will lead you back to yourself. Never forget that you deserve reprieve, my love, you deserve sanctuary.

Oh, how much of our journey is in the forging ahead with our willpower! And, oh, how many opportunities you will have to forge ahead! Rest a little now. Rest. I promise you that a soul that has allowed itself to recuperate keeps the spring in her step. The vagrant, the lone wanderer who rejects the hospitality of their own soul and of the love that is close and dear traverses great distances to find that they belong nowhere. Nurture the home within and you will find it without.

The wisdom of the journeys we undertake can only reveal itself when we have reunited again with our heart, with our inner home. In the sanctuary of rest, repose, love and affection, we are able to venture out into the world again with the fire in our hearts guiding us, not seeking the fire in our heart. Oh, to seek the fire, my love, is to live coldly. Loneliness, desolation, heart-wrenching solitude . . . the only friends of a soul unable to reunite with their inner fire. And your inner fire will always be restored in a space of safety and love.

IN A READING . . .

ASTROLOGICAL INFLUENCE—VENUS IN ARIES: The subject's ability to bring harmony to conflict, tension and old battles is in focus. Reflect upon where peace and harmony can be restored while also maintaining one's boundaries and sense of self. Whatever the circumstance, the outcome will result in love, passion and unity. Sincere intentions will bring sincere success.

UPRIGHT (DIRECT): Sanctuary. Safety. Grounded love. Passionate union. Resolution to strained affairs. Success in hard-fought battles. Celebration. Temporary rest and rejuvenation. Building a loving foundation. Committing to something that brings great joy.

REVERSED (RETROGRADE): Reevaluating foundations in life. Prioritizing your own happiness over maintaining other things at your expense. Seeking refuge. Yearning for the warmth of home. Resolving disagreements. Learning to share your space. Balancing individuality with commitment to others. Going to where you will receive love, support and stability. Rebuilding your stability.

#5 ◆ THE HIEROPHANT

MAJOR ARCANA

Astrological Correlation: Taurus

Observe, my love, where we found the celebration, we have also found the celebrant. Where you will find sanctuary, you will find a consecration of values that are built on a philosophy of unity, oneness, mutual love for fellow man and universally agreed upon or cosmic laws. The Hierophant is the keeper and translator of these laws. Their responsibility and duty to the moral integrity of mankind is of utmost importance. Their wisdom holds a direct link to universal truth, which allows them to teach and guide universally.

You hold this link to universal truth, my love, you are as universal as you are an individual. The Hierophant is the aspect of your being that has a complete understanding of universal order and is able to process cosmic guidance. The Hierophant has been referred to as "the higher self," or the part of our nature that is under the direct instruction of cosmic principles designed to keep us on a path of morality, integrity, love and higher awareness.

Indeed, abiding by certain core principles allows us to overcome the instinctual reactions and behaviors of our human nature that have a tendency to keep us trapped in cycles of suffering and spiritual desolation. The two followers that kneel before the Hierophant represent desire and intellect, respectively, illustrating to you, my love, how the passions of the heart and the thoughts of the mind both must bend at the knee of a higher wisdom. Both must be able to receive instruction from a higher source of awareness and that higher source of awareness, my love, is your inner teacher. What you are taught is simply a reflection of the inner teacher within you.

Be wary of losing contact with your own direct link to divine wisdom in exchange for the philosophies and ideas that you absorb around you. Remember that what you learn must always be examined by your own inner teacher. Not only will this allow you to divine deeper wisdom for your own unique path toward self-realization, it will allow you to filter out information that teaches you to be something other than the truth of who you really are. Your inner teacher, my love, can only teach to you the truth of who you are for that is all they really know. And it is more than enough, for in the truth of who you really are is the wisdom of the entire universe.

You, my love, are the individual expression of the wisdom of the entire universe. Do you feel it? Through this deep inner wisdom, this direct link to higher states of consciousness, you will expand your capacity to realize yourself in this universe. Many times, it will indeed require the assistance of certain mentors, teachers or resources . . . but your greatest teachers will never teach you—only your inner teacher can teach you—they will inspire you. Great guiders and wisdom keepers inspire you toward desiring and acting in the highest interests of your own being. Great teachers will inspire ideas, actions and desires within you that will align you on your path of self-discovery and self-realization. They will inspire your inner teacher to seek out more knowledge, more wisdom on your own terms. This is you being propelled along your own path of wisdom.

Through an awareness of your inner Hierophant, my love, you will teach yourself the most profound lessons of life. Every lesson you learn is a flame that can light a torch for another who has become lost in the darkness of ignorance and disconnection—as we all have and will fall into at some point or another. Remember that what is deeply true, what is in direct connection with higher wisdom, is always universal. If your light does not light up another, it is you who requires convincing of your own truth, not the "lost souls" around you.

The Hierophant has no need to convince others of their truth. It simply resonates in their presence, in every word. The Hierophant will never seek out others to awaken to higher wisdom, they will appear when one seeks to awaken. In this way, there is an aspect of initiation that comes with encountering the Hierophant. Are you ready to be granted the keys to the greatest questions you have, my love? Are you ready to receive divine instruction? To heed wisdom that can only be heard when both your desires and intellect bend at the knee, in awe of a deeper truth that rattles the core of your being? Do you accept the limited perspectives of your own mind? Do you accept the existence of a consciousness that supersedes that of your personal ego?

Oh, the humility that is required to bend at the knee of your own inner teacher, my love. Humility is the first lesson that your inner teacher will teach you, for without it is to be blocked from all levels of guidance that are above the narratives of your own personal ego.

Astrologically, the Hierophant rules the zodiac Taurus, the sign that is primarily responsible for the consecration of our personal values into this material plane. Aligning yourself with certain values and moral principles will bring purpose, meaning and stability to your life. A life without stability is not necessarily a life of being poor, it is a life that holds no firm values and, thus, is picked up by the wind and scattered here and there, believing in nothing for very long and falling for everything.

Furthermore, Taurus is a sign that is deeply connected to money and financial independence. Money will always follow in accordance with your values. Money that is scattered and spent purposelessly will always reflect a crisis of self-value. You will always struggle to make money when it is not in accordance with your true values. Awaken your inner teacher and you will awaken a path toward discerning your own core values. A great gift to give yourself, my love, is the discovery that true stability is found in a life aligned with the values of your inner Hierophant.

As you proceed on this journey of self-realization and increasing self-awareness, you may also find that what you once valued is no more. That what once gave your life meaning, stability and direction is no longer the source of your truth. Do not be afraid here, your inner teacher is responsible for consistently expanding your self-understanding and, thus, is always calling into question what you have become comfortable in knowing. Challenge your perceptions.

A great teacher is always a great student. Values do need questioning. Like the sign of Taurus, they have a tendency to become rigid, stagnant and, at times, dogmatic. Long-held values can become an excuse to remain in the comfort of a limited perspective of yourself and the world around you. When your values only seek to comfort you, instead of serving as a foundation for your expansion, they are no longer receiving direct instruction from higher awareness. They have become desires and thoughts that are rebelling against your own inner teacher. They will seek to continually convince you of something despite having extraordinary evidence pointing to the contrary. They will enslave you to knowledge and teachers outside of yourself, so that you will avoid confronting why your own inner teacher requires so much information, so much convincing.

Remember, my love, the truth of your inner being requires no convincing. Trust your wisdom, honor your values and humbly question the validity of what you know.

IN A READING . . .

ASTROLOGICAL INFLUENCE—TAURUS: The subject's moral principles, values and spiritual wisdom are in focus. The presence of higher institutions and support through important contracts may be available. Reflect on what wisdom the subject is attaining from their current experiences.

UPRIGHT (DIRECT): Profound lessons being learned. Attaining spiritual wisdom. Being guided by strong moral principles. Firm values. Trusting your ability and expert opinion on a subject. Validation from institutions and people in authority. Being respected for your values.

REVERSED (RETROGRADE): Reevaluating your beliefs and moral principles. Reassessing your position of authority. Questioning your reality, religion and other philosophies. Discovering your own point of view. Changing your opinion on a matter. Becoming more open-minded. Reevaluating your obligations.

#6 ◆ THE LOVERS

MAJOR ARCANA

Astrological Correlation: Gemini

Our journey complicates itself, for we have stepped out of the sanctuary of what is known. We are venturing now into territories where the truths about ourselves and the world that we developed from our beliefs and values are being tested and trialed. Our moral principles, our core beliefs, questioned, questioned, questioned! Why? Tempting desires accompany a will that is free, my love. It is in your nature to discover more of what you do not yet know. It is in your nature to step out of the predefined limits of your beliefs and to test the boundaries of the world around you.

There is something in you that is just not satisfied with being told who you are and how to live. There is a part of you that desires deeply to make and be responsible for your own choices. To carve out a path of free will so that you may experience a self-conscious realization of yourself in this life.

It is here, in the Lovers, that you will experience yourself as ruthlessly human, my love. A human with your own personal desires, needs, complexes, fears and passions. A human that yearns for union with another human. A human that simply wants to love and to be loved, to discover the meaning of love. To discover the force of life, sexuality and desire not only through yourself but in the merging with another. To become one with life. To know life. To be ruthless in life and in love with life. To face the consequences of that desire, to suffer the consequences of being a deeply loving, sensing, feeling and sexual being.

A choice, a temptation presents itself to you here, as the clouds part in the sky and you witness the angel staring down at you from above. You are the woman. You are the man. You are the angel. A triplicity in constant conversation. The desire to be, the desire to do and the desire to become spiritually realized. Oh, how these forces are coming together for you now. Oh, how departed we are from the wisdom of our core principles, of what we have written down and told ourselves will always be right, right, right!

There is no right or wrong here, my love. Only the unfolding of your self-understanding by pursuing desire. Can you handle this responsibility? Can you handle the capacity to choose in the direction of your self-realization by honoring what you desire more than what you have been told is the "right" or "rational" thing to do? It is here in the garden of the Lovers where the pure passion of desire supersedes everything that we have previously known. And what is at the root of desire? Is it not the need to discover more of ourselves? To become more conscious of what else exists in the undefined infinity of our eternal nature? If you are not learning more about your individualized self in this life, are you really living? Are the choices you make in life really of your own making?

Awaken here, my love, to the wisdom gained not through scripture or cosmic code, but through the unique unfolding of the choices you make in this particular finite incarnation. Choices made that have and have not been in spiritual alignment with the angel that—notice—oversees your dilemmas but never intervenes. Oh, truly it is a blessing to be overseen by a love that you cannot even fathom, to be loved by a force that respects your free will so much that it would never intervene in the affairs of your journey into self.

How could you journey into yourself otherwise? How else could you develop the ability to discern for yourself what is ultimately "right" or "wrong"? Is this not evidence of a highly realized soul? She who is given the choice to choose in every single direction and still ultimately chooses in the direction of love, in the oneness and goodness of all? Is not love to be able to give freedom? To see something as both its own individual expression and a part of you at the exact same time?

Oh, if you could feel a drop of this love that showers you from the heavens above, of angels that can only ever look upon you with a gaze of compassion and mercy. And what else could they feel but mercy? They know the suffering that comes from a will that is free. They knew you would transgress cosmic law, betray yourself, forget yourself and find yourself again. For how else could you become self-conscious of your highest powers? How else could you improve cosmic law? How could you consciously love everything you are unless you realized everything you are not? How could you consciously choose "right" if you did not allow yourself to choose "wrong" time and time again?

Oh, how the angels look upon your journey with awe and admiration. How they suffer when you suffer from your own choices, but know that this is the only way toward self-actualization. One of the most important choices you will ever make in this lifetime, my love, is the choice to forgive yourself. To forgive yourself for the choices you have made and will make in this lifetime. To forgive yourself for having a will that is free, that is seeking, at its root, only to know itself. To truly forgive yourself is to be able to forgive the choices of others in your journey, understanding that they, too, can only ever choose in the direction of their own sense of self-actualization.

These choices can sometimes hurt or harm others in the process, but it is not your responsibility to hold the spiritual judgment of another's journey. For to deliver spiritual judgment requires a perspective far departed from the personal ego, a perspective that only angels could possibly attain as they oversee everything and everyone from above. Let them carry this burden of spiritual judgment and retribution. These emotional burdens are a titanic and destructive load for the human heart, but are as light as another feather when carried by the wings of an angel.

Sometimes, the strongest desire of two individual wills is the exact same and this brings two wills into a union. Sometimes, this is no longer the case and union itself is no longer the highest expression of two individual wills. True love will always accept this, for to love truthfully is to love another in their individual path toward self-actualization.

It is in the Lovers where we develop the cosmic ability to hold I, you and we at the exact same time. All unions between two individuals that are spiritualized can mutually hold this triplicity. When a union is unable to hold this triplicity, it will ultimately fail, for separation on the physical plane is only ever the final manifestation of a union that is no longer united on any other plane of reality.

Allow the Lovers to guide you in making a decision of the highest vibration that you can muster at this point in your awareness. When this choice involves a shifting of timelines for not only your life but the lives of others around you (as it often does), you must be able to take into account what is not only best for you, but best for the other and the spiritual highest good of all (the most difficult, for it requires you to glimpse the perspective of the celestial beings that oversee from above). In taking action inspired by this triplicity of consciousness, you will find, ultimately, that they never contradict one another.

Alas, we will make choices that cannot uphold this level of consciousness. We are human. We are fallible. We are forgiven, but let us do our best to be discerning. To discern not only with our own eyes, but with the eyes of the other and the eyes of the angels above. To even practice this capacity is to be sure that you are on a path toward the fulfillment of your highest wishes and desires—and a love that transcends all things will be reflected back to you in everything you choose to love, my love.

The Lovers correlate with the zodiac Gemini and, indeed, it is this zodiac sign that is responsible for allowing us to experience discernment and duality. To be able to hold multiple perspectives together and experience the multifaceted nature in everything and everyone. It is in the essence of Gemini where we experience the freedom that comes from being able to choose. The joy of choosing in the direction of our expanding self-understanding, our ability to adapt and change our very perception of reality based on the decisions we make.

Yes, here in the Lovers, though the consequences of a decision may remain unknown, what is certain is that it will lead to a shift of perception. Nothing can be the same as it was beyond this point. For what has been seen cannot be unseen. What has been said cannot be unsaid. What has been understood can no longer be misunderstood. What has shifted in your very consciousness based on a conscious choice will residually begin to change your experience of reality. And what a freedom you will find there. Make the most important choice now, to choose in the direction of your self-actualization . . . and your unique path to fulfillment will open up before you, a place where not even I, my love, can know what treasures you will find.

IN A READING . . .

ASTROLOGICAL INFLUENCE—GEMINI: The subject's ability to hold duality and make conscious choices is in focus. Reflect upon where there is a powerful opportunity to bring about spiritualized relationships and to make decisions that will serve your evolution.

UPRIGHT (DIRECT): Making a significant choice for the highest good of all involved. Sacred union. Power in unity. A fated meeting. Integration of masculine and feminine aspects of your nature. Alchemy between people. Finding your "other half" (sometimes in yourself). Powerful relationships.

REVERSED (RETROGRADE): Reflecting on relationship dynamics. Evaluating if you are making the right choice. Needing more time to see things clearly. Resolving issues between your inner masculine and feminine. Finding wholeness in yourself. Letting a choice or decision be made for you. Overcoming your personal wants and desires and trusting the universe to find the perfect resolution.

THE 5 OF WANDS

MINOR ARCANA

Astrological Correlation: Saturn in Leo

Beware, my love, a group of quarrelling bandits has befallen us along our journey! Or is that a band of unruly youths play fighting? In any case, they are here to test your will and strength of character. For they also have free wills and they also have their own desires. So, what will you do? What will you do in a world that by its very nature will test your will? Such is the price you pay for being a being that is able to create their own destiny. You must find ways to come into the full expression of your unique light in ways that lift the freedom of those around you, not oppress them.

In the 5 of Wands, we encounter the part of this journey of fire where there is a conflict of interests. It could be between us and our environment; more often it is a conflict of interests within ourselves. When we are at war with one another, we are also at war with ourselves. Conflict itself is not the enemy, it is the enemy we make of ourselves and those around us. When we begin to demonize parts of ourselves or those around us, we isolate and fragment our being, which distorts our sense of who we are and allows drama, destruction and oppression to catch fire in our lives.

If winning a battle has thrown you out of the seat of your heart, my love, what battle have you really won? What have you really claimed when you have lost your most prized jewel in the process? These quarrelling bandits—so lost in their arguments, differences and egos that their willpower has become completely scattered—their attention is more on the fighting than on what they are really fighting for. For if they truly became aware of what it is they are fighting for, they would realize that they never had to fight to get it. Fights like these should only ever be in good fun, a play between the immature parts of our personality. Why do we fight, my love? Why do we argue? And, oh, how serious we can become in these petty squabbles! Are we not at our core attempting to affirm who we are? To say, I am here. I am here, why can you not see me? Hear me? Feel me? Understand me?

A burdensome task to try and control the free will of everything outside of you. They may not understand you, but you can always take the time to understand yourself. And if you truly heard yourself, I promise you that you would not so desperately seek that validation from that which is outside of you. What within you, is asking to be heard? To be affirmed? The truest essence of who you are requires no other source of light for it is a source of light.

You are a source of light, my love. You are an infinitely unique, individualized aspect of a godly consciousness. What do you have to fight against? To compete against? To "get ahead of" or "outsmart" and "outwit"? You are only outwitting yourself from your highest destiny. You are only outwitting your rightful place on a throne that no one else can claim.

There is a key difference if these youths in the 5 of Wands are fighting or playing. If they are fighting, they do not yet know who they are. If they are playing, they know themselves better than most. For some, the act of conquering and oppressing the other is the only way they have learned to express their identity. Yet, for as long as you continue to fight for what you desire, my love, you will always be fighting. For as long as you believe that there is not enough space for you to thrive as an individual, you will always be competing, comparing and denying yourself from experiencing the shining expression of your unique soul.

This idea is captured very well in the astrological correlation of the 5 of Wands. Saturn in Leo is assigned here, reflecting the challenges and obstacles you will face as trials (Saturn) in order to develop the most actualized version of yourself in this life (Leo). Here, you will push and pull against the limits of your sense of self. You will be challenged by the capacity for your environment to accept your emerging identity; sometimes you will be rejected entirely. See here that the sparring, the conflict of interests, the tensions that come up with this tarot card are all serving to refine your identity, my love.

Though the 5 of Wands appears as a very chaotic and disharmonious scene, this is the only kind of environment where the false layers of your ego can be peeled away and your inner light strengthened and better expressed. For do you really know yourself, my love, if you do not know how to be yourself in the presence of other egos, other identities, other souls on their own path to self-individuation? Pass the Saturnian trials of the 5 of Wands and you will build character. You will find yourself within the context of a world where others are trying to do the same. You will discover what truly separates you from other people, the inherent beauty that is your individualized expression of the one.

Welcome the resistance of this tarot card, for the resistance you feel is your identity being pressurized by the will of everything around you. Pressured until all that remains is the shining expression of who you really are. Confidence is something that naturally occurs, when you are able to play in the truth of who you are. Beings that do not know their individual core tend to fight for fear that there is not enough room for them, for fear that the other will control them (and, thus, they have already handed over their free will). Beings that know themselves see no need to fight among one another. They are too busy playing.

In the 5 of Wands, we see the first real test of our will against ourselves and others. Its astrological correlation of Saturn in Leo speaks to the push, the very real struggle to assert our identity, our light in a world of other lights also seeking to shine and radiate their power. In our solar system, we only have one sun. On Earth, every single soul is an expression of this godly force with their own force of attraction. It is through this push, pull and conflict against the world that we develop our unique signature, where we strengthen the power of our authentic selves.

The 5 of Wands is competitive, it is where we test the boundaries of how far our own light can take us. We fight for dominance, we fight for the freedom to achieve what our identity desires. In this battle, we mature our will, we learn where to push and where to surrender. In the 5 of Wands, we confront where we have become too attached to an immature ego that has become inundated with unnecessary battles that do not further its growth and expansion. In the same breath, it is only through these battles that we truly discover who we are and expand our zone of influence. Here, we develop boundaries around who and what we are so that we can feel more free, authentic, liberated and powerful.

Saturn's presence in this card implicates that this pursuit is not without its cost. There are those who will disagree with you, oppose you, be threatened by the advancement and expansion of your ego. Some of these oppositions serve to humble us, to mature and refine our will so that it still serves the ultimate good of the world. Other conflicts are opportunities to strengthen your light, to stand up where you would otherwise shrink back your power, and, in this back-and-forth, an increasing strength of character is always the result.

Relish in these moments of tension, of the pushback from asserting your light, for it is here in the fire that the very being that you are is being created. Saturn here bestows authority and power to those who have the audacity to become themselves in ways that also support the integrity of their soul. When the ego strays too far from its own integrity, its conflicts with others only reflect the conflict of interests within you. The resistance you face from others is a profound insight into the opposing wills within your own being. Time, patience and maturity is needed to understand whether your desires are helping you achieve a greater sense of who you are or taking you away from your inner truth.

The 5 of Wands is trial and error. Welcome all external resistance to your desires as guiding posts to unite closer with your essence. Honor the punishments as much as the allowances that Saturn delivers to your human experience. There can be no "wrong" in a reality where every trial and tribulation serve as opportunities to advance self-understanding.

The 5 of Wands is meant to indicate pressure, it is an invitation to be in the fight for the freedom to be as you truly are. Alas, no fight can last forever and already many now are out of breath. Only the most stubborn still stand their ground, alone, still lost in some idea of themselves. Others limp away bruised, humbled and matured. Let us, too, depart from this scene stronger in ourselves and back onto our journey of desire.

IN A READING . . .

ASTROLOGICAL INFLUENCE—SATURN IN LEO: The subject's ability to work through personal obstacles and stand in a strong sense of self and authority is highlighted. Reflect upon whether the battles that are being fought are worth fighting. How can a higher awareness about themselves resolve the conflicts that stem from a lack of self-acceptance?

UPRIGHT (DIRECT): Resisting the opinions of others. Integrating different aspects of your personality. Trying to feel seen and heard. Healthy competition. Building character and self-confidence. Growing under pressure. Being forged in the fire. Preparing for the real deal.

REVERSED (RETROGRADE): Taking accountability and no longer pointing fingers. Evaluating and working on your personality. Surrendering to who you really are. No longer keeping up appearances. Taking constructive feedback. Maturing. No longer being entertained by the same things. Being your own competition. Outgrowing situations.

THE 6 OF WANDS

MINOR ARCANA

Astrological Correlation: Jupiter in Leo

Do you hear the horns of victory? Horsemen are riding in with news of great achievements! Look, they're already propping you up onto one of their horses, for this momentous joy is incredibly contagious. I, for one, am very grateful for a steed at this point in our journey, for these little legs of mine have grown tired from preaching so much timeless wisdom. Don't flatter yourself, you say? Yet, the 6 of Wands is all about flattery! And who are these horsemen celebrating, you might ask? You, my love. They are celebrating you in your authentic expression. For you in your authentic expression is always a cause for celebration. A celebration of the miracle of life and of our capacity to shine as a unique expression of the one.

In the 6 of Wands, you will experience the glory, radiance and recognition that comes with self-realization. In this tarot card, there is a momentous validation and tailwind that fuel and bolster a sense of who you are. Be wary of letting too much of this amplification of your personal self go to your head, but it is important at certain points in your journey to experience the social rewards of shining the resplendent light of who you truly are. Without this external validation, we are unable to experience our own light through the eyes of another, which can be one of the most beautiful and empowering experiences that we can have along this journey of desire.

The 6 of Wands is a card of great affirmation. Where our sense of who we are is no longer exclusive to ourselves, but it is seen, respected and admired by our environment. You emerge victorious here, from the trials and battles against yourself and others. The tests of will that have refined a deeper sense of who you really are. You have won, my love. Not because you were a better competitor or fighter, not because you managed to "get ahead" of another, but because even through these tests you emerged with a heart that has remained open and true to itself. For a heart that has remained open and true can be the only victory that is truly victorious. What a blessing to be seen in your light. To be affirmed and validated for the person you have dreamed of becoming.

Experience here, in the 6 of Wands, a resounding "Yes!" from the universe. A resounding affirmation of you as a unique expression of the all. The astrological correlation of this tarot card is Jupiter in Leo, which speaks to the good fortune and personal expansion that always arises from an individual who has experienced self-actualization. And what does that self-actualization feel like? It is the feeling of carrying yourself into everything that you do. It is the feeling of experiencing and having others experience your unique creative signature impressed upon this world. It is the feeling of seeing the beauty of your own soul reflected in everything that you love and admire. It is the feeling of inspiring this same beauty and love in others when they witness you in your glory, in the embodied truth of your being.

Jupiter in Leo here brings to your awareness a sense of optimism, enthusiasm and confidence. How could you not be confident, when you are being celebrated for nothing more than what is inherently true to your being? How can you feel doubt, imposter syndrome or incompetence when you are only being asked to be who you truly are?

Furthermore, the Jupiterian 6 of Wands illuminates you as sage or guru (Jupiter) on the subject of what your light represents (Leo). Yes, you are a guru on the topic of experiencing your unique sense of joy! And this is a gift you will teach others simply by embodying yourself. Indeed, the 6 of Wands talks about leading by example. You are leading by being the example of a soul that is walking in their authenticity, in their highest truth. When you are there, you are automatically inspiring, magnetic and charismatic. You are automatically able to call others to aid in the expansion of your personal vision. In fact, they do not even need to be called. Simply by witnessing you in your element, many will be drawn to follow in your example, for in you they see the beauty of themselves, a profound resonance with the deep inner truths of their own being.

Oh, what an incredible contribution to give this world! To inspire self-realization within others through your own self-realization. Did I not tell you how contagious this joy really is? Recognize in the 6 of Wands the capacity for your personal ego and identity (Leo) to become a shining example of a universal truth (Jupiter). That you resonating your authenticity will always carry with it universal influence. Enjoy this glory while it lasts, because you must also realize that your personal identity is something that has the capacity to shift and evolve.

When we fail to connect with our unique inner light, it is here in the 6 of Wands where we may at times be overcome by arrogance and an overestimation of our abilities and experience. Jupiter in Leo here massively exaggerates the powers of our personal gifts and self-expression, and though this allows us to "fake it till we make it" and act in courageous ways, we risk falling off our own horse. We risk getting lost in the pursuit and constant re-creation of social, exterior validation rather than the continual expansion of our personal, inner truth. The first reflects a victory that will never fulfill the heart, the second a victory inspired by the courage of your heart.

So let us build momentum, my love, toward the ever-expanding potential of your individual self in this life. Let us shine, but be mindful of our capacity to burn too brightly and inspire love, beauty and courage in the hearts of everyone we pass along our journey.

IN A READING . . .

ASTROLOGICAL INFLUENCE—JUPITER IN LEO: The subject's potential for expansion, recognition and path toward fulfillment is in focus. Reflect upon where the subject's source of excitement and inspiration is moving them toward in their reality. Where is there an opportunity to increase their expectations?

UPRIGHT (DIRECT): A great victory. Riding the wave of success. Critical acclaim. Delivering great expectations. Being unforgettable. Feeling like anything is possible. A fruitful path of self-expansion and self-actualization.

REVERSED (RETROGRADE): Reflecting on disappointed expectations. Holding back grand plans until further confirmation. Reevaluating what is truly bringing you joy. Quiet victories. Needing a boost of morale. Learning to encourage yourself. Hidden support.

THE 7 OF WANDS

MINOR ARCANA

Astrological Correlation: Mars in Leo

Are you still holding your wand, my love? Are you still grasping it firmly? Don't get too comfortable! Challenges and obstacles still await you along this journey toward self-realization! Who are you? Who are you really? What do you stand for? What claims about yourself do you stand on? It is the answer to these questions that you are fighting for here in the 7 of Wands. The assertion of your personal sense of self and free will against the opposing wills of others. How confidently can you stand in the truth of who you are? Are you aligning yourself with your inherent radiance or are you trying to prove a false sense of self to the world around you?

Whenever we are attempting to prove, we are already admitting to ourselves subconsciously that we are fighting for something that we do not actually feel or possess. Make no mistake, the truth of who you are is confident and able to stand firmly in itself, but it is never from a place of "fighting," "convincing" or "proving." Pretending to be someone you're not will always feel like trying to keep your head above water. You will always feel like you are battling against everything and everyone around you—keeping something at bay. Keeping what at bay, my love? What is it really? I can tell you.

The only thing you are keeping at bay is a revelation around the truth of who you really are and what you really desire. A revelation that is oftentimes extremely painful for the ego, who is always seeking the higher ground and the "one-up" on everyone around you. A revelation that would force you to realize that these other wands you are supposedly fighting against, battling against, belong to no one.

There are no faces to these wands. Why? Because it is here in the 7 of Wands, where we get so easily caught up in the illusion of separation, in the illusion that there is an us against them, when it has and always will be you against yourself. The fuel you add to the fire of these conflicts, these exaggerated assertions around the simple and transparent truths of who you are, will only move you further and further away from yourself. When you are surrounded by conflict, you are always conflicted with yourself.

Notice this person, battling away at God knows what, so caught up in this fight for affirming something that they do not even realize that they are wearing a mismatched pair of shoes, they fail to notice the inherent dissonance within them that is fueling their apparently necessary skirmish against some invisible enemy. Only a resounding peace emanates when you are in the most authentic expression of who you are. This is not to say that people and circumstances will not continue to resist you and oppose that which you truly are, but they will remain as distant voices and their power will have no hold over you. Look at the higher ground you hold here, my love! What can really touch you when you are in your essence? When you are in such a sureness of yourself that you no longer so desperately require external approval?

Oh, and how I know how much validation can help! And you will be validated. When you are in your truest essence, you will be validated, even when you do not seek it! In fact, the only validation that truly satiates the soul is the kind that you receive without seeking. Is that not what validation truly is? To validate what it is that you have already found within yourself?

When you find yourself fighting tirelessly, whether it is with yourself or with the world around you, an opportunity is presenting itself to you to discover the essence of what really matters. The 7 of Wands (as with all of the 7s) brings spiritual revelation to those who are able to identify and dispel the false delusions that their ego is perpetuating. This is a tarot card that brings alignment, self-recognition and paves a path toward true inner confidence. The kind of confidence that resonates from within to without, not the other way round. A confidence that comes from a soul that knows itself to a point where there is nothing to truly fight for anymore. There is no more proving, convincing or battling to remain afloat. Everything that needs to be affirmed is simply embodied. There is no need for the isolation and jealousy that arrogance brings when you are in your irreplaceable essence. There is no need for convincing others when you are in your own personal conviction.

Allow the 7 of Wands to bring to you an understanding of where you are at in the embodiment of your personal conviction. This is a journey, my love, might I remind you? You will fight for your false delusions at some point or another. How else could you realize how much pain they are actually causing you? How else would you rid yourself of painful false aspects of your true identity unless they were so easily aggravated by everything and everyone around you?

Oh, and how serious yet ironically childish we become when we engage in these grand proclamations of "This is me, me, me!" And the beloved "My way or the highway!" Are we not all a bunch of angry children, my love? Angry at the world, angry at some god and, ultimately, angry at ourselves. Angry that we are still not seeing ourselves for our greatness. Quell the powerful tantrums of your inner child, my love, by promising yourself that you will see yourself. You will, now and forever, validate to yourself what already exists within you.

Astrologically, the 7 of Wands correlates with Mars in Leo, an obvious connection to how our will here (Mars) is focused on the affirmation and realization of our personal identity (Leo). More specifically, it is speaking to the maturation process of our personal ego, a graduation from constantly fighting ourselves and others to simply revealing the inherent beauty of who we are.

Though Mars can represent the immature, impulsive and generally insufferable parts of our personality, we cannot ignore his inherent desire to protect and preserve our individual free will. This protection will, at times, manifest itself as frustration and anger toward that which threatens your personal boundaries. It is up to you to temper the temper of this loyal warrior. Stand for the truth of who you are, but to attack another and to lift yourself above them is to stray very far from that truth.

When you are on the offensive all the time, you are protecting something that was never yours to protect. For what is truly yours does not need to be fought for. It naturally arises in endless supply from the depths of your being. So, let us continue on our journey, my love. Are you beginning to see how this journey toward what we physically desire is also a journey back to what we already have spiritually within?

IN A READING . . .

ASTROLOGICAL INFLUENCE—MARS IN LEO: Mars in Leo brings a passionate desire to self-express to the subject. The subject's ability to stand in the truth of who they are is in focus. They are developing a stronger sense of self by learning to express themselves with personal conviction. Reflect upon where in life the subject feels as though they are carving out their personal identity and where they can better affirm and validate themselves in the process.

UPRIGHT (DIRECT): Standing up for who you are. Asserting yourself. Expressing your authentic self. Defending your personal boundaries. Victory through recognizing your individuality. Having what it takes. Being proud of yourself. Expressing your raw truth.

REVERSED (RETROGRADE): Releasing the criticism of others. Releasing doubts and fears around who you really are. Reevaluating what you are fighting for. Learning to validate yourself. Developing a stronger identity within. Quiet self-confidence. Tempering your tantrums. Gaining self-awareness.

#7 ◆ THE CHARIOT

MAJOR ARCANA

Astrological Correlation: Cancer

And would you look at that, we have been lucky enough to strike upon a Charioteer along our journey together. Look at how they command their horses with such conviction and mastery. The Charioteer, in their essence, represents the inner alignment that is what actually gives rise to the external victories and momentum of our lives. And what is inner alignment other than awareness and mastery over the controls of your vehicle? The vehicle of your body and mind. The house of your spirit.

When you take the reins of the Chariot, when you are in complete vibrational accord with the instrument of your being, everything moves. Sounds delightful, no? The Charioteer will not fail to remind you, however, that it's easier than it looks. It is true that on the surface having mastery over one's inner world appears effortless. Yet, this is a product of a constant balance and rebalancing, a constant calibration and recalibration of the forces that are at work within the mind, body and spirit.

Indeed, the greatest challenge of efficiently operating the Chariot is to align the desires of the conscious mind with that of the subconscious mind. When these two "horses" are not working together, it becomes very difficult to have any control over your life. How can you have control out there when the forces within you are tugging in multiple different directions? As within, so without, my love, and, here in the Chariot, you will come to know and experience how deeply your physical reality is affected by your capacity to understand the mechanics of your own being.

The Chariot illustrates the sense of movement and momentum that is generated through a harmony of the mind, body and spirit. Notice that it is actually the third time this triplicity has presented itself to us along our journey so far. First in the Hierophant (page 46), then in the Lovers (page 50) and now in the Charioteer with their horses. Do you recognize the progression of this triplicity? The evolving capacity of your soul?

In the Hierophant, divinity came to you through a teacher, in the Lovers through the overseeing angel and now, in the Chariot, it has united with your very body and mind. It is no longer operating simply above you; here, divinity is operating through you. It's the product of a soul that has tempered the workings of the conscious and subconscious mind. And when this divinity is operating through you, you are in complete alignment and accelerated movement toward the realization of your highest wishes and desires. Do you understand the magnitude of this? The magnitude of the work within and its effect without? And so, what is this inner work, this inner alignment I am speaking of? What is the secret to the masterful control that the Charioteer has over their vehicle?

The astrological correlation of this tarot card will assist you here—Cancer, the cardinal water sign. It is your capacity to build intimacy with your emotional body that will give you the true control that you are seeking over the direction of your destiny. To be in alignment is to feel in alignment with every fiber of your being. To have every fiber of your being under the harmonious accord of who you truly are. It is the ability to experience emotional harmony within. Note that when I speak of emotional harmony, I do not for a second suggest that it is achieved through never experiencing emotional turbulence.

This is a numbing, my love, a repression. Repression will never guide the horses of your inner being, it will only make them restless and rebellious against your own will. You will be constantly pulling at their reins in a way that is punishing to yourself and, ironically, in this grasp for control over your own vehicle, you are subconsciously being led by the rebellion of your own inner desires. To experience emotional harmony is to be able to resolve the emotional turbulence that naturally arises within you as you grow, learn and move through life.

The Charioteer could have only ever learned to ride their chariot through riding their chariot. The manual is found in its operation. This is also true for every part of the vehicle you have incarnated with. It is your journey itself that leads to the mastery of the forces within you. No theory, no external blueprint or manual will ever compare to the understanding you will gain about yourself by building intimacy with the emotional tides of your own being. They are here to guide you, to bring you closer toward the home of who you truly are. They know home because they feel like home. They are of that home.

Mastery over the Chariot is a mastery over the intrapersonal forces that make up the entirety of your personality. It is to become aware of how every aspect of your personality is serving the unfolding of a greater destiny. Know that there is a divinity at the core of every aspect of your nature. As long as you continue to deny, dislike or disrespect any aspect of your personality, you will only be denying yourself of your highest potential.

It is only ever you that is truly getting in the way of your destiny, my love. To think otherwise is to make a gross underestimation of the powers that lie within you. Is it not infinitely empowering to realize that every time you experience a sense of emotional harmony in this life, you are leading your Chariot with perfect execution? That no matter how much time you have spent being emotionally turbulent, the second emotional resolution finds you and your inner waters are tempered, you are moving the fastest you have ever moved toward everything you desire?

Learn from the Charioteer that movement that is experienced within is not subject to the laws of space and time. Your emotional harmony collapses time. For a single action taken from a place of emotional harmony infinitely outweighs a thousand actions taken from emotional discord, from an inner vehicle that is pushed and pulled by the warring (and, in the end, sabotaging) forces within them. There is no comparison. Develop this awareness of how much you are truly moving within, my love, even when you feel like change has not yet found you in your physical reality.

By focusing your awareness on an inner alignment with your deepest core, you individuate your path. You will begin to respond to what feels harmonious for you and not what is generally harmonious for all. You will no longer seek to compare your path to that of another soul for you will equally understand that inner alignment expresses itself very differently among souls. Align yourself with yourself, and you will align yourself with a destiny that will take you to places and heights of emotional fulfillment you could not even conceive of, for it is a path that is not being followed, but is being created with every step of an inner vehicle that is attuned to nothing other than its own unfolding.

IN A READING . . .

ASTROLOGICAL INFLUENCE—CANCER: The subject's capacity to resolve emotional harmony within them is brought into focus. Reflect upon what factors in their life are contributing to a greater sense of inner alignment or feeling off track. Their current environment could be significant for their overall life direction. Surrounding or clarifying cards can point to the forces that their inner Charioteer is attempting to bring into harmony.

UPRIGHT (DIRECT): Emotional harmony. Connection of mind, body and soul. Conviction and alignment with overall life direction. In the driver's seat of life.

REVERSED (RETROGRADE): Resolving conflicting inner forces. Resolving emotional turbulence. Intuitively not on the same page with something or someone. Needing more time to feel on board with something. Returning to the source of what drives and fulfills you emotionally. Learning to master your inner world. Waiting for the moment to feel right.

#8 ◆ STRENGTH

MAJOR ARCANA

Astrological Correlation: Leo

How could we proceed further on this journey of fire without encountering the tarot card that encapsulates the cosmic purpose of desire itself? Are you not in awe? At how this woman with grace and compassion tempers the will of this powerful beast? This lion is infinitely more physically powerful than her, yet ultimately it is she that is more powerful than it, for she knows and experiences infinity itself. To know infinity is to become aware of the self that is beyond the wants, needs, urges, fears and distortions that come with your constantly evolving personality. It is to recognize your personal ego and individual identity as a layer of you, not the entirety of you.

In Strength, you are shown the essential distinction between cosmic consciousness and individual consciousness. You are shown your profound capacity to use cosmic consciousness to actually reflect upon your own individual personality! The first is eternal and is the you that has and will always exist in divine perfection. It is an essence. The second is developing. The human aspect of you is developing, my love, consecrating itself on this planet as its most authentic and exalted self.

This is a process and one that is filled with the trials and tribulations that are a part of our human experience. It is the maturation of the ego. The woman in this card represents your own cosmic intelligence exerting its power over the naturally exhibiting forces of your human self. It is exerting its power through restraint and direction that comes from a higher awareness. Is that not the essence of what true strength really is, my love? Power that actually increases under restraint and limitation? You are not a slave to the instinctual drives of your animal nature. You are a cosmic being with a will that is, first and foremost, free. So free that you chose to actualize your own divinity through an individual personality. You chose the courageous task to work your infinite essence into a finite realm.

It is in Strength where you will develop a symbiotic connection between cosmic will and primal will. The will to experience infinity and the will to experience individuality. These are not contradictory forces. Their harmonious melding is what always gives rise to a personality that is the embodiment of beauty, love, truth and joy. It is the process that is described in Strength that gives rise to the feeling of being embodied, of shining your inner radiance. Your inner radiance is a light that is paradoxically unique to you and universal to all. What words, my love, can I find to explain the magic, the beauty that is your soul's true expression?

Allow the tarot card of Strength to reveal to you your unique shining path to self-actualization. This is a spiritual process that occurs through the transformation of your desire nature. It is the difference between creating to live and living to create in this life. It is the difference between being motivated by self-preservation and being motivated by beauty. It is the difference between automatically reacting and consciously responding to the opportunities for evolution that we are presented with through life.

Allow the figure in this card, this avatar of higher consciousness, to present itself to you when you forget the infinity in yourself and in everyone around you. Allow her to temper your individual need to preserve a sense of who you are and recognize that what is of your true essence is immortal and, thus, does not need to be preserved. It will shine infinitely, no matter how many layers of your personal ego veil its expression. Know, too, that our essences can take on many different expressions and this can be easily observed in the very different personalities that populate this earth. What will be true for all, however, is that regardless of its "drama" or outer expression, our truest essence will always emanate a sense of grace, beauty, compassion and joy toward every other being on this planet.

Unrefined expressions of our personality—the aspects of us that cause harm, suffering and malice toward others—will always arise from unrefined desires. Unrefined desires are those that do not help us to realize more of our true essence. They keep us locked in vicious cycles of pleasure inspired from pain and pain inspired from pleasure. Addiction, greed and abusive uses of our sexual nature all manifest from our inability to point our desire nature toward realizing the beauty within us. That which cannot see its own beauty cannot have compassion for itself and what horrors emerge from our human nature when we cannot hold compassion. That which hates and harms others must hate and hurt itself—and to hate oneself is to live in a hell on Earth.

Allow this to inspire compassion within you for every single thing that has ever done you harm, my love. Let Strength turn every desire, every motivation you have into an expression of love, joy and beauty. An expression of the love, joy and beauty that is you in your divinity. Allow what satiates your body to be alchemized into what will satiate your soul. This is not about repressing your desires; it is about honoring them in a way that inspires more love for your own being. Nothing that will truly satisfy you is finite in nature. To always be subsumed by the pressures of what is finite is to become a slave to the very same animal instincts you are here to overcome.

When we are enslaved by what we deem to be lacking in our lives, our perception of reality becomes increasingly distorted and dominated by a need for self-preservation. It is these very same perceptions that create a world driven by the basest desires of human personality. A world where pleasure cannot exist without intense suffering, onto ourselves or onto those around us. Where is the beauty there, my love? Where is the compassion inherent to every soul? Where is the graciousness of a humanity that has chosen their base instincts over the desire to experience a love and beauty that exists in all things?

Every time you choose in the direction of what illuminates you from within, you are seeing more of who you truly are. This is a choice that requires courage and bravery. Fear drives our base urges and they keep us in fear. When you give over your free will, your willpower to the unruly and wild passions of your body and mind, the satisfactions you momentarily experience will always dwindle into the mere absence of pain. You will live only to avoid pain and it will always catch up to you. For nothing finite can ever replace the infinity you truly crave, the infinity that has and always will exist in the true expression of who you are.

And we will lose control, my love. Our personality is immature and developing. It does not enter into this world actually aware of its own divinity. Often, it is only through the deep suffering that we experience as a result of unrestrained desire that we seek out the source of true fulfillment. Having rampaged and ravaged everything around us, we inevitably realize that our insatiable gluttony will never be satiated by something in the finite realm—for its source is not of the finite realm. Its source is found in the harmony between the cosmic and human self. When you begin to experience eternity in your body, you are there, you are shining the radiant light of your soul.

Strength is a tarot card about overcoming the perpetual suffering of desire and it is through this overcoming that the shining light of who we really are is shown to us. We come home to ourselves, not in purely rejecting our animal nature and embracing our cosmic self, but by allowing the two to become aware of each other. To recognize that they both at their core share the same desire, to experience happiness, love, joy, peace and creation.

Astrologically, the Strength card is associated with the zodiac sign Leo. It is the sign of Leo that speaks of the unique light we are here to express and it is in the process that Strength describes where this is actually created. In fact, this card directly speaks of the process of creation itself on every level of reality. From the act of procreation to the birthing of a new creative project, magical things always unfold when desire unites with love, when the good of self seamlessly aligns with the good of all. When we lack identity, when we lack a strong sense of self, it is because the desires we have been fulfilling are actually not contributing to realizing more of who we really are. We are unwilling to sacrifice the vices of the ego that would end our cycle of pain and suffering.

Consequently, we will lack compassion for ourselves and for those around us and, tragically, others will sense that the light in us is simply not there. Our lives will become a race to escape the clutches of pain instead of the creation of love and beauty. Self-preservation will consume us and we will be driven by a gluttony that could never ever compensate for the infinitely abundant joy of a happy heart.

Oh, the importance of courageously following your heart, my love! Please promise me now that you will never forget the infinite nature of your soul. That you will never stop loving every aspect of your developing human personality with the compassion and higher guidance it truly deserves. Whenever you despair, whenever you feel at the mercy of desires that only ultimately create more suffering in your life, it is time to reconnect with what will remind you of the love and beauty that exists eternally within you.

IN A READING . . .

ASTROLOGICAL INFLUENCE—LEO: The subject's ability to exert awareness and grace over their instinctual reactions and perceptions is important for the progression of their reality. Reflect upon where a gentle strength can be used to bring out the best in themselves and others.

UPRIGHT (DIRECT): Leaning into compassion. Choosing to react differently this time. Seeing the good in all. Developing a strong character. Pursuing the right desires. Power in self-control.

REVERSED (RETROGRADE): Resolving destructive habits. Resolving deep emotions, shame, rejection and anger. Connecting with sexuality and sensuality. Recovering a surge of inner primal power.

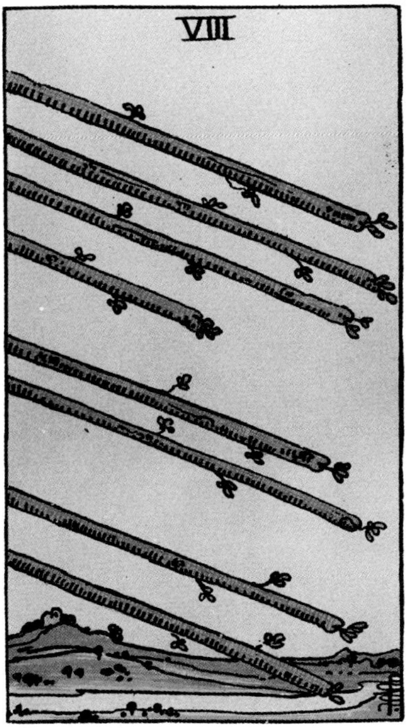

THE 8 OF WANDS

MINOR ARCANA

Astrological Correlation: Mercury in Sagittarius

Eight wands soar overhead! Do you know what this signifies? Nothing other than an accelerated momentum toward the fulfillment of your desires! Embrace the arrival of optimism, rapid progress and the effortless overcoming of obstacles and previous setbacks along your journey. What a welcome sight this is at certain points in the trying journey of the wands.

In the 8 of Wands, you will experience a rush of progress that could only have arisen after the more grueling test of willpower that we have witnessed with the 7 of Wands (page 61). Witness here in the 8 of Wands a confirmation that your attention is in the right place! That whatever you are intending or focusing upon is aligned with the path of your personal expansion. The 8 of Wands is a tarot card of great possibilities, opportunities and positive reinforcement. There is no sense of the "impossible" in this card. There is no stopping the flurry of wands that are moving with passion, alignment and complete conviction in their aim, your aim! Be convinced of yourself here! Be sure of your movement toward everything you desire!

The 8 of Wands is astrologically correlated with the planet Mercury in the sign of Sagittarius, where we see our mental faculties (Mercury) imbued with spiritual expansion (Sagittarius). What is expanding you in this part of your journey is the phenomenon of luck. And what is good luck other than the experience of successive moments where our affirmations about who we are are in fact validated by our experience of the world? Where our personal philosophy is in fact proven by our reality?

Discover in the 8 of Wands the magnetic force of every single belief that you hold about yourself and the world around you. The eight wands are arranged parallel to one another and, unlike in many of the other wand cards, are not opposing one another. These parallel wands are not in contradiction to one another. This is a powerful symbol for an extremely potent and powerful willpower—a will that has found the higher philosophy (Sagittarius) that all of its different desires are under the instruction of. Mercury (our lower mind) benefits greatly from understanding the macro perspective that the sign of Sagittarius governs. Mercury here is able to receive instruction from a path that is connected to purpose, inspiration and spiritual unfolding (Sagittarius).

Without this higher direction, Mercury (and, synonymously, our rational mind) tends to become scattered, unfocused and unable to translate information into personal inspiration. Information can only be useful if it allows us to access deeper parts of our personal inspiration. When what we learn does not connect to or fails to inspire us, we deny ourselves the experiences of momentum, ease and rapid progression that come with the synergy of the rational and imaginative aspects of our mind.

Both Mercury and Sagittarius speak of communication and, in the 8 of Wands, you will come to know the power of affirmation. The power of the word. To speak from your deep personal truth is to set these wands above us into motion. It is to activate and bend the universal forces that are freely available to you into focused direction toward the unfolding of your highest destiny.

Affirm to yourself here, my love, that you are moving in the direction of your highest reality. That you are in alignment with your highest reality. That everything that is unfolding for you is unfolding in a perfect execution of your personal expansion. That what is in accordance with your highest truth will always find you. That moving in accordance with that higher truth instantly places you on a path where luck, ease and opportunity are commonplace.

This is not to say that following in your highest truth will always be effortless in the physical, but the clarity and lightness it will give to your consciousness will allow you to approach your challenges with the divine knowing that obstacles can only accelerate your path to freedom and fulfillment. Do you realize the magnitude of this? That when you live by the affirmations of your highest personal truth all obstacles must submit to the unfolding and eventual realization of that personal truth? Your beliefs will determine the meaning and purpose that is extracted from everything you experience in this life.

This is a subjective realm for our perception of reality will always be unique to our personal philosophy of ourselves and the world around us. If we believe that we exist in a cruel world where we must also be cruel to be fulfilled, then we will live out this reality. Not because it is reality, but because it is the reality we chose based on a personal philosophy that has given us at some point in our life a sense of momentum.

See here in the 8 of Wands the immeasurable power of your beliefs. What beliefs are currently creating momentum in your reality? What aspects of your reality are they amplifying and expanding? Are the beliefs you hold about yourself and the world around you in alignment with your personal truth or are they a product of another's truth that has been projected onto you? What is of your personal truth will always grant you expansion, momentum and a sense of optimism for your life.

Pessimism, hopelessness, stagnation and close-mindedness are the residues of beliefs that are not truly yours. They are the fizzled spells of attempting to follow in the direction of that which you do not truly believe. When you lack momentum, optimism and perspective, allow the 8 of Wands to redirect you to the personal beliefs and philosophies that are energizing your reality. Your reality is constantly being energized by what you affirm about yourself. When you feel that your reality lacks energy, often it is because you are operating in ways that are not under the instruction of your highest personal truth.

And it is a blessing, my love, to feel this stagnation, for you will inevitably reconnect with that higher truth. When you lack motivation, direction or have a pessimistic view of yourself and the world around you, you have the opportunity to assess the beliefs that have become dead weight in your journey toward self-realization. Sometimes this requires letting go of certain expectations that are actually being perpetuated by beliefs that are not supportive of who you really are. Certain expectations and the pressure of the how and when often arise from a will that actually does not trust itself, that requires confirmation of its vision from the external before the need to have faith in itself.

When you operate from vision and not expectation, you will consistently remain inspired and in alignment with your highest will. Notice the difference here that when you are operating from vision you will find satisfaction in the pursuit of its realization. When you are operating from expectation, there is only joy in the realization of an apparent expectation.

Remember here in the 8 of Wands that these wands are in perpetual motion, they are not attached to a certain manifestation. Otherwise, this would ground them and destroy their momentum through the air. These wands are soaring because they are beliefs that are motivated by vision. They have no foreseeable end and, thus, they are truly free. Their capacity to create is endless. Your capacity to create is endless, my love, when you are able to consistently affirm to yourself the evolving truth of who you are. This is not to say that you should somehow empty your mind of every negative or pessimistic thought about yourself and the world around you and convince yourself of some utopian ideal. This is not realistic and can be a recipe for subconscious repression.

Instead, become aware of which beliefs about yourself and the world bring you a sense of optimism and inspiration for the future. Notice that it is the belief that gives rise to the optimism within you, it is not about forcing optimism within you. Beliefs that describe the truth of who you are will infallibly bring joy and optimism to your soul, to your inner being. Oh, what a delight your inner being experiences when you converse with it directly, when you express its truth. Let us soar with the beliefs that are in accordance with our highest will, my love! Let us ride the momentous wave of our vision!

IN A READING . . .

ASTROLOGICAL INFLUENCE—MERCURY IN SAGITTARIUS: Mercury in Sagittarius brings optimism, possibilities of travel and higher learning to the subject's field of attention. The subject's communications, voice and ideas are in focus. Reflect upon where a higher perspective will bring a rapid progression in their reality and help amplify the success they already have. Surrounding or clarifying cards may give more information as to what area of life or themselves is ready to experience acceleration and momentum.

UPRIGHT (DIRECT): Momentum. Acceleration of events. Far-reaching possibilities. Newfound optimism. Focusing on what is moving. Trusting your luck. Expanding your knowledge and understanding. Excitement. Spreading your truth. Spreading your wings. Being inspired.

REVERSED (RETROGRADE): Recovering your optimism. Reevaluating what truly inspires you. Resolving miscommunications. Hiding your excitement. Rapid, unseen progress. Opportunities being brewed for you. Returning to your passions. Picking up where you left off.

THE 9 OF WANDS

MINOR ARCANA

Astrological Correlation: Moon in Sagittarius

Oh, how far we have already traveled! Oh, the trials and tribulations we have faced. The battles we have won. The challenges we have overcome. Does this path of fire and desire not tire your soul? We are at the part of our journey where our fiery path of self-realization and self-discovery has tested every ounce of our will. Our fire burns low, conserving its energy. We seek refuge, sanctuary, a chance to recuperate and recover from a journey that has spent so much of our willpower.

It is in the 9 of Wands where you are given a chance to reflect upon the totality of your journey. To heal from the growing pains of a will and personality that are maturing. To reflect on everything you have learned along your journey. The journey that began with the inherent desire to "know thyself." The journey to carve out your individual will in this collective matrix. Take this wisdom, my love, if only for a little while, for as long as it serves your journey . . .

Beliefs are like batons: We borrow them, we hire them until they no longer serve our will. They are torches that guide our path through the darkness of our own ignorance until eventually their flame goes out. They must be exchanged for that which is more in resonance with our evolving personality. Our beliefs always guide our evolution and, as constantly evolving beings, our beliefs must also be ready to evolve. The figure you see up ahead is deeply rooted in their beliefs. And do you blame them?

Look how much they have achieved with their beliefs! Look at how well these wands guard and protect them! Yet, look at how "rooted" they have become in their physical reality. They are no longer the soaring 8 Wands of what could be, they have become fixed in what is and has been. There is no movement here, only a solemn stillness. There is a very real fear around whether what we already know will be enough to withstand what is to come.

Yet, this desire to withstand something is precisely the problem. To seek to withstand is to seek to experience life without motion—and to experience life without motion is to experience life without growing. To never allow yourself to be transformed by your experiences is to condemn yourself to living in constant fear of what is to come. For you will no longer be open to adaptation in your life, you will only seek to filter everything that comes to you through its ability to conform to what you have already known.

There is a time and a place to persevere in your truth, but remember that what is truly of your truth will never isolate you. It will never keep you in a perpetual fear of that which may challenge that truth. For your personal truth will always expand you and open you toward life, not retract you from experiencing it. Healthy beliefs keep you in motion, they do not keep you stagnant. Healthy beliefs allow your experience to be challenged, they do not keep you in a cycle of avoiding all discomfort. Healthy beliefs are concurrent with your present reality, they are not relics of your past. Healthy beliefs keep you in communion with others and have an optimistic view toward life, they are not overrun with suspicion and vigilance.

So much about this tarot card can be gleaned from its astrological correlation with the moon in Sagittarius. Observe here where our emotional security, sense of personal safety and inner foundation (moon) is being sourced from our personal beliefs and philosophies (Sagittarius). Notice that the resolve and perseverance that is coming from the figure in this card is not actually sourced from what they have known. It is coming from the hope that what is to come will contradict what they have experienced before. That the expectation for an incoming battle will not be fulfilled.

When you are tired, suspicious and vigilant, though so much of your mind is hell-bent on protecting yourself, is there not a part of you that truly wishes you were wrong? That seeks to be proved wrong? That secretly wishes that everything you have believed would no longer be validated by your physical experience?

Truly this is the cost of collecting so many of these wands across our journey. We have so much confirmation around what our will and the wills of others can achieve. Around what the consequences are for what we have once desired. What we gain in wisdom we also equally gain in a biased and close-minded perspective around our ability to attain what we desire.

It is in the 9 of Wands where we engage in this very delicate, sensitive and introspective process of separating true wisdom from trauma. It's where we become aware of the subconscious beliefs (moon in Sagittarius) that are re-creating a familiar pattern of safety and security in our lives; however, our beliefs were never meant to be the foundation of our emotional security, my love. They were always meant to keep us toward a path of inspiration, possibility and self-discovery. They were always meant to keep us inspired toward the unknown, not secure in the known.

By isolating themselves in what they have always known, the figure that we see in front of us is actually preventing their own healing. Like a scared, wounded animal afraid of trusting the hand that seeks to mend their suffering, they believe that it is no different from the hand that first punished them. Do you not seek to help this figure? Does not their wounded appearance inspire within you the deepest empathy, the deepest desire to heal them of that which torments them?

Yet, they mistake the tears in our eyes for a trick. Yet, these wands and their beliefs stand tall between us, preventing our ability to access their vulnerable core. Yet, they would rather remain in a state of chronic pain and discomfort than risk the chance to mistake that which heals with that which will hurt them. And, yet, what can really hurt more than pain experienced in isolation? Than pain that is never able to be alleviated from the experience of empathy and love?

A cruel demise to cast upon yourself, my love, to believe that what was once true must always be true. This can only ever be true for the soul that remains in the prison of what they have always known, that cannot bring themselves to question the perceptions that although once protected them, now only serve to perpetuate their pain.

IN A READING . . .

ASTROLOGICAL INFLUENCE—MOON IN SAGITTARIUS: There is a focus on the subject's personal beliefs that are underpinning their reality and providing them a level of emotional comfort. Reflect upon the subject's deeply rooted perspectives that are driven by a strong desire for emotional security. Where is the subject ready to challenge their limiting points of view?

UPRIGHT (DIRECT): Time of healing. Protecting yourself from further harm. Focusing on the essentials. Deep introspection. Consoling yourself. Wisdom through experience. Processing limiting beliefs. Bracing something until it is over. Stoicism.

REVERSED (RETROGRADE): Reflecting on deep emotional wounds. Reevaluating subconscious beliefs. Finally addressing what has been draining you. Reassessing your need for isolation. Shift of mindset. Restoring your optimism. Taking down emotional walls. Letting in medicine for the soul. Dropping resistance. A healing truth. The end of a grueling struggle.

THE 10 OF WANDS

MINOR ARCANA

Astrological Correlation: Saturn in Sagittarius

Oh, how far we have come on this journey of desire. How much we have focused our will and forged ahead despite all our obstacles and challenges. Yet, even these wands, brimming with vitality and the force of creation, must at some point be exhausted of their power. Our will must at some point become exhausted if we are to open up to a new set of desires. How quickly our single wand of passion and inspiration has multiplied and manifested everything we desire. Yet, with manifestation always comes a sense of responsibility and continued focus. For anything that is no longer fed by our willpower, focus and attention cannot sustain itself.

Our wands, our will, love to create. Our will needs to create, it is willed to create. Yet, the act of creation exists in every moment before manifestation. What is our will to do with that which is already manifested? Where lies the creative potential, the expansive possibility of that which has already been created? Exhausting indeed, my love, to exert the will to create upon that which has already manifested. Exhausting, indeed, to attempt to mold and move an object with the mind instead of an idea, a dream or a vision.

There is a lack of malleability in the physical world, there is a rigidness and a definitive nature to it that marks it as the finality of desire or the satiation of desire. Is it not impossible to still want something that you have already acquired? Is it not impossible to remain focused on that which has already manifested? Your will is always pointed toward your personal expansion and self-discovery. By the time you have satiated a desire in the physical world, your will is already searching for its next achievement, its next creative endeavor. For the will, in its essence, is insatiable. It has an insatiable appetite for self-discovery, for discovering the limits of its own power!

In the 10 of Wands, you will witness the exhaustion of your will. Not necessarily because you are lazy or lack perseverance (have you not persevered, my love, to acquire so many of these wands?!), but because your will has successfully manifested that which it had originally intended. What has already manifested no longer holds creative capacity and, thus, there can be no further expansion in pursuing that which has led you to this very moment.

The 10 of Wands marks the end of a cycle of manifestation that once began with a virile rod of desire, full of potential and bursting with possibility. When our will is focused on the pursuit of desire, it is charged with passion and potential, but when our will is focused on what we have acquired, it is no longer in pursuit of anything. And a will that is not pursuing anything must default to preserving instead of expanding, on surviving instead of unfolding, on maintaining instead of creating. This is a will that has allowed the forces of the material realm to disconnect it from its sovereignty, its infinite creative force. It has attached so deeply to the idea of what is manifested that it has lost its capacity to manifest.

Though the figure we see up ahead has achieved so much through the force of their will, in the process they have surrendered their free will to the manifested world. They are now led by the burdens and the struggles of the manifested world instead of the endlessly powerful force of their free will. An incredible irony, that with all of this manifested power they carry on their back, they have lost the greatest power of all, their free will.

There is no amount of power in your life that is worth being preserved by your will. To constantly preserve something is to instantly lose your power to that which was once a source of freedom for you. Nothing that is on your direct path of self-realization requires preservation, it is endlessly fed by the passion that arises from it being an expression of who you truly are. That which continues to be an expression of your divine "I am" and of your essence is infinitely sustained.

Remember that true freedom is not something that you should seek to find in the manifested world; instead seek it in she who has the highest capacity to create. She who has the freest choice in what to place her attention on. There is little joy or expansion to be found in glory obtained through something that we ourselves did not create. This point of the journey of desire is incredibly crucial. It is at this point in the journey, my love, that most fail, give up or, worse, continue on with an enslaved will.

All of these outcomes arise from a will that has exhausted its personal creative capacity, that has attached itself to what it has created instead of its endless capacity to create. Most of us at this point in our journey will not register the end of a cycle of manifestation and we will struggle endlessly to maintain that which is no longer being fueled by the life force of vitality and passion.

The exhaustion of our will is an essential gateway into a new cycle of virile desire and personal freedom. To opt instead to remain in the clutches of "what we have always done" is to reduce the infinite power of our creative free will to serve only the choice to remain enslaved. A terrible purgatory awaits the will that refuses its own renewal of life force. It will labor on, preserving and maintaining, serving everything outside of itself and neglecting everything (and its own power) within.

This is a remarkably Saturnian struggle, as represented by the astrological correlation of this tarot card with Saturn in Sagittarius. Here, what is primarily indicated is the struggle, limitation and restriction (Saturn) that we experience through repeating old cycles of creation that are now only serving an expired version of ourselves, an expired version of our self-understanding. The Saturnian influence of the 10 of Wands points us to the fact that the challenges and obstacles we face here are actually not new to us. They have circled back time and time again, each time weighing heavier and heavier on us until we are forced to reckon with the fact that our will is no longer creating, it is stuck re-creating.

Is that not what ultimately exhausts us, my love? That which we know we are doomed to re-create, repeat and redo time and time again. It is the knowing that we are no longer creating our future that actually exhausts our will. We cannot be truly exhausted by something that we don't know we will experience again. And if we know what we will experience again, this is another indicator of a cycle of manifestation that has reached its finality. There is no more unfolding, only the diminishing returns of fulfilling a desire we have already fulfilled.

The figure here is doomed with the Sisyphean task of creating that which has already been created. There can be no spring in her step, there can be none of the excitement and optimism that comes with the pursuit of an unfolding vision. She is far too weighed down by the accumulated "karma," the residual burdens that accompany sustaining that which exists in the finite realm. Despite the struggle and strife of this card, Saturn in Sagittarius here bestows great wisdom and maturity onto us at this point in our journey. It is a wisdom that is gained through processing the karmic consequences of what we have freely chosen to will into existence.

It is in the 10 of Wands that you will come to understand the true source of the desire you began with. It is here, in the density of the manifested realm, that you will master the harshest lessons of the journey through fire. It is here you will be able to drop the struggle of will toward something in exchange for invaluable knowledge of self. You will extract the immortal wisdom from your finite achievements. You will be ready to embark on a new level of personal freedom because of your newfound awareness of what has always burdened your free will. You will drop here the beliefs and perspectives that although once fueled you with life force and vitality now have become dead weight destined to re-create the past. Beliefs that re-create the past are always contaminated with a pessimism toward the future. They trap us in cycles of re-creation and make us doubt our ability to participate in the active creation of our reality.

Drop these wands here, my love, drop the beliefs and philosophies that have kept your gaze down toward the ground instead of on the possibility of new horizons. Drop the struggle and strife that has convinced you that you are a slave to time and to the finite resources of the material world. That you must perpetually suffer in order to experience the fruition of your desires. Drop the heavy cross that you carry, that tells you time and time again "Your fate is this struggle." You are not Sisyphus.

For as long as you have the ability to choose what you focus upon, you can choose to focus on the bourgeoning of a new freedom instead of an old, tired struggle. You can choose to realize how becoming aware of your lack of personal freedom is the very gateway toward truly understanding your path to freedom. That by becoming aware of the inner beliefs (Sagittarius) that have restricted (Saturn) your experience and perspective of reality, you can realize the inner truths that will always expand your understanding of yourself beyond the limitations of your physical world. By becoming aware of everything that you no longer are, you can become aware of everything you truly are. This is liberation.

It is a funny thing that the more we use our will to create what we desire in our lives, the more we forget about the power of our will. Instead, we begin to exchange it for the power of what we have received. A dangerous delusion to place your power in something you have willed into being instead of that infinite power that can will things into being. You will only experience the purgatory of the 10 of Wands if you choose to believe that the fulfillment of your desires must arise only from the exact same belief and way of being that fulfilled them in the first place.

We see here the struggle of a relationship that sources its power from preservation instead of mutual self-realization. We see here the struggle of labor that reproduces stability instead of actually helping one toward personal freedom. We see here the strife of maintaining something in our lives purely from a place of guilt, obligation and fear instead of inspiration and passion.

A cruel way to live, my love, to be led by the fears of the illusive material realm instead of the godly will that was the power that brought this world into being in the first place. These wands have been exhausted of desire, let us drop them here and venture deeper into the core of who you really are and what you can create.

IN A READING . . .

ASTROLOGICAL INFLUENCE—SATURN IN SAGITTARIUS: The subject's culmination of a cycle of creation is in focus. Reflect upon where in the subject's life they may be experiencing the need for a renewal of their willpower and how to unburden themselves from that which has already served its purpose.

UPRIGHT (DIRECT): Coming to the end of a long journey. The final stretch. True willpower. Carrying out final responsibilities. Temporary exhaustion. Yearning for ease. Being responsible.

REVERSED (RETROGRADE): Reevaluating the burdens and responsibilities that you carry. Being released of your long-term commitments and duties. Reassessing where you are re-creating suffering. Freeing up your energy for a new creation. Dropping that which no longer serves you.

THE PAGE OF WANDS

MINOR ARCANA: COURT CARD

Astrological Correlation: Mercury and Fire

And what is that darling figure doing? Don't they remind you of yourself when you began this journey of desire? Curious, optimistic, eager to explore who they are under the guise of exploring what is in the world around them. They gaze upon the wand of desire as if it is something to play with.

Indeed, this Page of Wands has the freedom to play with desire. They need not know where it will take them or what consequences could befall them—that nonsense will be dealt with when it arises. Look here, as this page turns to us now, their eyes glimmering with the grand dreams of a soul that has not yet experienced the consequences of their desire nature. A reckless innocence, is it not? A bravery not born through an overcoming of fears, but through a naivety in the unknown. Yet, it is a bravery no less!

Take something from this Page of Wands, my love, for when fear cripples your adventurous spirit, good fortune will always be granted to you for simply being foolish enough to venture out into the unknown. Why is it that luck has always been bestowed upon the beginner? It is because the beginner does not think like someone with experience. They have not yet experienced misfortune, failure, rejection or the possibility of things just not working out!

What a blissful consciousness! To not yet have a reference for failure! The beginner must base their prospect of success on faith, on the potential of the future, whereas the seasoned veteran will rely far more upon their learned ability, their experience of the past. You, my love, are a beginner at this particular incarnation of yours. Have you allowed yourself room in your life for failure? Have you allowed yourself to contemplate the possibility of your power? Have you allowed yourself the freedom to experience freedom for the sake of freedom?

There will be moments in your journey where you will have nothing to stand upon except for that which inspires you and draws your attention. Follow it. Naively, recklessly, curiously, follow your desire. How else will you ever come to know yourself? How else will you ever come to know the true limits of your power? How? Without the graze on your little knee? Without the overestimation of your current ability? Without the leaping before thinking? Without the pleasures of playing with a will that is free? Without the pain of playing with a will that is free? How will you come to better know the true essence of what moves you? Without a grand fall from grandiose expectations? Without a journey full of unexpected paths, obstacles and turbulences?

Look into the eyes of this Page of Wands and see your own spirit of adventure reflected back at you. It is a spirit of possibility, of the sheer power of "What if . . . ?" and "What will . . .?" And what you will come to realize is that what will happen is whatever you will to happen. Such is the exploration of this journey of desire. Like this page here, your wand of desire begins much taller than you. The more inexperienced you are, the stronger your desires will be because they are still fueled by the expectations of the ego. Only time, maturity and exploration will allow you to level out this bold, naive spirit with a mastery over which of your desires serve a higher will and which do not.

This is a journey of trial and error. This is a journey where maturity can only come through the experiences we face in our immaturity. Desire can only be matured by desiring. What do you seek to know about yourself and about the world? Go and seek it. Seek it in the most foolish, irreverent and recklessly naive ways! Seek it recklessly until you are no longer reckless. Better to first jump the gun then to never jump at all. Better to be disappointed than to never be excited enough to be disappointed. Better to live than to watch a life be lived. Better to will yourself into this existence than to allow yourself to be under a will that is not of your own choice.

Are they not a loveable little rogue, my love, this Page of Wands? Are you not a loveable little rogue, testing the boundaries of everything in your reality? Learning through touching the hot stove? And, oh, how you will be punished for it! Disciplined! Limited and matured by all the rules and the regulations and the norms of whatever society you have found yourself spawned in! Oh, how there will be so much time to learn the rules of whatever matrix you must be a part of! So, for a moment or two, my love, let yourself dissent. Let yourself find something out for yourself. Let yourself be told "I told you so."

Why? Because there will come a time where you will tell them so, you will tell them everything that they were never brave enough to find out. Now, let us leave this bold and brash youth, let us wish them all the best toward whatever they are desiring. Let us wish them good luck and they need not say it back to us in return. The very presence of this inspired little soul is an omen to you, my love, that good luck is always sprinkled along the path of they who seek to know themselves.

IN A READING . . .

ASTROLOGICAL INFLUENCE—MERCURY AND FIRE: The subject's passion for a new interest and endeavor is in focus. Their field of attention is on learning more about themselves. Reflect upon where they are ready to engage in playful exploration of themselves, others and the world around them.

UPRIGHT (DIRECT): Flirting with an exciting new possibility. Adrenaline. Beginner's luck. Unexplored horizons. Journey toward self-discovery. Playful curiosity. New philosophies, ideas and mentalities that inspire and motivate you. New ambition. Getting the green light.

REVERSED (RETROGRADE): Remembering your adventurous spirit. Recovering joy, playfulness and exploration in your life. Returning to your desires as a child. Keeping exciting news to yourself. Reflecting on your maturity. Thinking before doing. Waiting for more information before initiating.

THE KNIGHT OF WANDS

MINOR ARCANA: COURT CARD

Astrological Correlation: Mars and Sagittarius

How else could we hope to cross the remainder of this vast desert without the help of the Knight of Wands? See him introduce himself to us now! Look at how he rears his powerful steed onto its hind legs as if to make a statement! As if to affirm "Behold! Your knight in shining armor!" What a glorious display of will in action. There is nothing that can stop this Knight of Wands once he has focused his will upon a desire. Nothing can distract or derail him from his goal for there is nothing he wants more than to experience the passion and exhilaration that comes from pursuing his most powerful desires.

The Knight of Wands appears at points in your journey where there is no time to think, my love, only to want. Only to run with the adrenaline and excitement of your own desires. Reckless? Often. Regretful? Never. This fiery knight is in a state of constant momentum. His stallion runs on a fuel of passion, inspiration, sexuality, romance and the attainment of personal glory. His bravery and courage do not come from his naivety in the unknown (like the Page of Wands, page 85), they come from the certainty they have about what is still unknown.

Take this wisdom from this unstoppable knight that there are points in our journey where we have no choice other than to be certain about what is still unknown. Unless we are able to act in ways that affirm who we are before we have arrived at what we desire, we will be inevitably immobilized by doubt and fear. Witness this glorious steed on the verge of leaping in the direction of this knight's vision. Two hooves remain certain and grounded in reality, in what is, yet two hooves excitedly reach out into what will be.

Many may look upon this Knight of Wands and think "Oh how foolish! How irresponsible for this knight to be so sure about a quest to . . . where?" And the very same people will sleep that night affirming that tomorrow they will certainly rise. The very same people will behave in ways that indicate that they are certain that unpredictable tragedy will not befall them tomorrow and change the course of their reality. To live in this world, my love, is to board this fiery stallion and say, "Regardless of what befalls me in this life, I am inherently on a quest pointed toward personal victory and self-actualization."

Oh, how differently we move when we move from our personal inspiration and the desire to will our personal truth into this existence. How differently someone moves who is propelled by a vision rather than dragged by obligation! What obligation could this Knight of Wands have other than that which supports his own self-realization? When this tarot card presents itself, there is a complete and single-minded focus specifically on your individual path toward self-actualization. On your unique path toward . . . where? Toward yourself.

Barring it doesn't harm anyone, there is not a single desire you can have in this life that will not bring you closer to yourself. The very nature of acting on our personal desires, on being on a journey toward something we want, implies self-actualization. It is a journey that, at times, will and must appear selfish, reckless and rash to others. It has always been the case that the courageous be viewed as careless by the cautious.

And whether the cautious are ultimately right or wrong is not the point of the philosophy of the Knight of Wands. The point of your inner Knight of Wands is to preserve the courage and bravery of your heart. The heart can be reckless, it can be completely irrational! It is a path that will lead to pain, disappointment and reflections on what we could have done differently. Yet, it is also the only path where you will experience the blissful overcoming of failure. The exhilaration that accompanies new adventures, passions and unforeseen horizons. The magic of a journey where your heart burns with life and for life. The freedom that comes with being on a journey toward nothing and no one but yourself. To be ruled by nothing and no one but yourself.

This is the essence of the Knight of Wands, my love, how else can I articulate freedom itself? How else can I articulate the joy of knowing before you have become? Of seeing before you have arrived? Of living instead of waiting to live? How can you not be enraptured by the romantic and inspiring quest of this charming knight? So full of life that the recklessness of their actions is overrun by the joy of their vision.

This is a knight that happily fails, for ultimate victory is certain. Every time you take action from a place that is aligned with self you are embodying the Knight of Wands. The most special kind of victory is reserved for a soul that operates from the fire in their heart. Why? Because it is a victory not dependent on a certain attainment or destination, only the sheer joy of a heart that burns.

Now, we mustn't get too carried away into the sunset. Even though I am indeed charmed by this brave and passionate horse rider, I would do you no good to not also make you aware of their shortcomings. There are times when leaping before thinking will bring us repercussions. There are times where what we have been chasing or desiring was ultimately not aligned with who we really are, or when we come to realize that it is never what we really wanted.

Does this mean you should be slapped on the wrist and told "See how pointless your foolish and brazen quest was! See how you didn't get what you wanted!" No. Better to reckon with the consequences of your brave little heart, my love, than the consequences of a heart that has never loved, hoped, wanted or burned. Heed this: It is not any of the journeys themselves you embark upon that will ever punish you. For even that which results in disappointment grants an opportunity to realize more of yourself. It is the lack of courage to follow through in what makes your heart truly burn that hurts the most. To be deprived of your own courage is to be deprived of your own will to live.

Remember that your inner Knight of Wands can only run on the courage of the heart. It does not run on fear, doubt, shame, guilt, obligation, catastrophizing, future regret or any other poisonous sources of self-preservation. The courage of the heart will always overcome failure. In fact, under the instruction of the heart and not the personal ego, failure has no choice but to be morphed into opportunity for greater expansion and self-knowledge.

Oh, the whirlwind of passion and joy that you will leave in your wake on your journey to yourself! Do not despair when you fall, my love! All roads lead home if you allow them to. All frustrations and disappointments can be turned into new passions if you allow them to! For now, let us enjoy the wind against our faces. It is not always that we will be in the thrill of a grand passion.

IN A READING . . .

ASTROLOGICAL INFLUENCE—MARS AND SAGITTARIUS: The subject's inner drive and commitment toward a strongly held belief and vision is in focus. Reflect upon where the whirlwind passions of the heart and pursuits of freedom are ready to bring a new level of expansion to the subject's reality. Surrounding or clarifying cards may hint at the subject's motivations and intentions.

UPRIGHT (DIRECT): A fiery pursuit. Fueled by passion. Thirsting for freedom. Unstoppable will. Hell-bent on a mission. On the journey toward who you really are. Finding freedom. In the momentum of excitement and passion.

REVERSED (RETROGRADE): Reevaluating the purpose of your journey. Resting temporarily along a fast-paced journey. Momentarily slowing your pace and not rushing into things. Reconnecting with your spiritual direction. Redirection. Pausing for more confirmation. Preparing for a big journey. Getting yourself together.

THE QUEEN OF WANDS

MINOR ARCANA: COURT CARD

Astrological Correlation: Moon and Aries

And, so, we have finally arrived at her kingdom. Do you feel it? Watch now as the Queen of Wands approaches us. It is as if the energy in the air bends to her will. Presence, my love. The gift of this queen beyond all her other emanations is her presence. She has not said a word to us and, already, we are charmed. She has not communicated who she is for we already know.

The Queen of Wands knows that you know. She is the radiant force of self-realization itself. She is what we are able to experience when the light of our true nature is not only realized by us, but by everyone around us. Needless to say, this gives the Queen of Wands an effortless confidence and charisma. It is very easy to play a role when the character is based off of who you inherently are.

The Queen of Wands will appear at points in your journey to test the strength of your character. Are you authentic to who you truly are? Do you not realize the magnetic power of she who is unashamed of herself? And what does it mean to be unashamed? It is to own every one of your desires. To not judge yourself for what it is that you truly want. Shame festers in the individual that denies themselves their own desires. When we deny ourselves what we really want, we deny ourselves our own self-realization and, so, our radiant light, our radiant presence remains dim, remains hidden from lighting up the world around us.

Not in the presence of the Queen of Wands will you remain dim. How could she let you? How could this avatar of self-empowerment and the reclamation of who you truly are watch you bend at the knee in shame? "Up," she says. Just like it would do nothing on this planet any good for the sun to choose to hide its light for a day, no one benefits from you hiding the radiant essence of who you really are. "Up," the Queen of Wands demands of you now!

Meet her eye to eye as an equal. As a soul that shines with the pride of owning who you are. As a soul that can command this universe to obey your own free will. As a soul that understands her capacity to create a reality that is expanded and nourished not by conformity, shame and submission, but by the radiant light of your soul. The Queen of Wands will command you to stand in the glorious presence of who you truly are until every ounce of shame, fear and insecurity burns off of you. These shadows are burned away by the act of being yourself.

Allow your inner Queen of Wands to alchemize everything that you have ever been told you are not, could not, should not be into an unstoppable pride in everything that you are. True charisma and personal magnetism, my love, do not arise from exterior validation. Does validation help? Well, of course.

The Queen of Wands would never turn down a compliment, my love. Though, she knows deep within that her sense of self is determined by her and her only, not by the approval of others. She knows that it must be this way if she is to remain as the center of her own reality and not give away her power of creation to something or someone outside of her. She knows that she holds the wand of creation, that any validation she experiences is only a byproduct of the magic of her own unfolding.

The Queen of Wands will tell you that charisma and personal magnetism is forged in the absence of validation. It is forged in the fires of shame, invalidation, persecution and feeling invisible to those around you. It is the will to exist before the world has given you permission to. What power a light holds that has had no choice but to source its light from itself. What power a presence holds that radiates regardless of what or who has the blessing of witnessing her.

It is no surprise that the Queen of Wands astrologically rules the kingdom of Aries. The sign of Aries speaks to her independence and self-liberation from all that has attempted to control her. She is free from the projections of everything and everyone around her, for shadows cannot be cast onto light itself. She is embodied in the individuated truth of who she has determined herself to be. Aries here also emphasizes the highly passionate and sexual nature of the Queen of Wands—the queen of desire.

In this way, she represents the receptive aspect of the desire nature. Not the sense of going after and chasing what it is we desire, but the art of drawing what we desire to us. The art of seduction. The gravitational force of your presence. She is the law of attraction. She is what it means not only to desire but to be desired. Is it wrong to desire, to be desired? No, for the Queen of Wands will tell you that everyone seeks to be desired. Jealousy festers easily in the soul that shames their own desire to be desired.

Claim the powerful and indomitable will of the Queen of Wands, my love, and you will radiate magnetism, charisma, allure, sexiness and personal sovereignty. You will stop tirelessly pursuing your desires and, instead, have them tirelessly pursuing you. Your inner Queen of Wands feeds off of adoration and attention. These things help affirm the power she holds, but she should be careful to never allow them to become the source of her power. The source of her power is always from within, the strong sense of self that she has cultivated through standing in her personal freedom.

Embodying the essence of the zodiac sign Aries, it is the Queen of Wand's inherent understanding of freedom that naturally opposes her to the controlling forces of patriarchy and dogma. She is the witch (notice her black cat) that burns at the stake, affirming herself against the powers that seek to stifle her. She is the queen that wields the phallic symbol of the Wand, proclaiming to her masculine counterparts that "I, too, am free. I, too, possess personal sovereignty." That the truest test of an individual's masculinity comes from their capacity to honor the inherent freedom within every soul. To subjugate, to oppress and forcibly bend others to your will, is a sight that the Queen of Wands will burn for again and again to remove from the experience of every being on this planet.

Turn, my love, like a blooming sunflower, toward the radiant light of who you are. Follow it wherever you go and you will bring a little more warmth to those around you who have yet to realize the miracle of their own light.

IN A READING . . .

ASTROLOGICAL INFLUENCE—MOON AND ARIES: The subject's ability to attract what they desire and be desired is in focus. Reflect upon where in the subject's reality there is an opportunity to experience their inherent personal magnetism.

UPRIGHT (DIRECT): Being desired. Sexy confidence. Flaunting your talents and attributes. Star of the show. Attracting opportunities to you. Owning your self-expression and charisma.

REVERSED (RETROGRADE): Building back up your confidence. Recovering from a burnt ego. "Oh, no, you didn't . . ." energy. Reclaiming yourself. Falling in love with yourself again. Shift in style. Holding back until the great reveal. Learning to care less about what others think.

THE KING OF WANDS

MINOR ARCANA: COURT CARD

Correlation: Saturn and Leo

Now arrives the counterpart of the Queen of Wands (page 92)! And who could be a counterpart to the Queen of Wands, you may ask? Who could stand in the presence of radiant embodiment and not seek to quell her or be in fear of her, but instead hold her up higher to shine brighter? Like all of the kings in the tarot, you will come to know them by knowing their queen. Is someone not revealed by who happens to capture their heart?

As the divine counterpart of pure and liberated self-expression, the King of Wands represents the highest form of free will. The philosophy of the King of Wands would most certainly be "When there is a will, there is a way." It is his relentless will that has allowed him to ascend into the rulership of his own kingdom. The sheer confidence and perseverance of affirming "I am" in the face of every single obstacle and challenge that would threaten "you are not, should not, could not."

Indeed, the King of Wands represents the soul of the entrepreneur, the one who can move mountains with the power of their mind, with the might of their focus and attention. As the king of the suit of fire, he represents a self-discipline and mastery over the desire nature. Not in a way that would lead him to become ascetic, for the denial of desire itself does not always represent the mastery of it. Mastery is the ability to exert control, not to deny.

The King of Wands represents your ability to exert control over your personal will so that you may remain in complete authority and awareness over the direction of your unfolding reality. Harness his power to assert with confidence that you are the one creating your reality and none other will ever have the capacity to take that away from you, unless they are able to take away your mind. The King of Wands is completely focused on the wand in his hand, he holds his free will with extremely high dignity, integrity and responsibility. This is why he holds so much authority, for authority itself can only be maintained by he who has a command over his own will.

When you can command your own will, you are able to be responsible for the wills of others. This is leadership. Those who do not have a command over their own personal will will not be able to responsibly command the wills of others. They will not be able to responsibly handle power. The King of Wands is a leader because to be focused upon your own free will and personal vision is to be a leader in the process of collective creation in this physical matrix.

Do you understand the magnitude of that? That right now, through your personal will and focus upon your own vision, through mastering your focus and attention, you automatically become a leader, an inventor within the context of not just your own but everyone's physical reality? A great responsibility, my love. And what does the King of Wands want? Beyond all of his various desires, it is to perpetually experience the desire to desire. And who else to keep this king constantly desiring than the object of desire itself, the Queen of Wands? Bahaha! The King of Wands represents the aspect of our nature that will simply never be fully satiated.

Now, many looking upon this king would perhaps say, "Oh, what a cursed existence! To always want and want and never be satiated!" And they are deeply mistaken, my love. For the King of Wands is satiated more than most. To never be fully satiated is to be constantly on a path of satisfaction after satisfaction. There is a thrill, an adrenaline, a passion and a vitality for life that this king will always experience as a result of this temperament.

And when I speak of satisfaction, I am not speaking of a superficial soothingness of the personal ego, that perhaps the Page of Wands (page 85) might busy themselves with. This is a king, a master of the desire nature. At this point in his evolution, he has a grasp of what true satisfaction is. Ironically, he knows it is something that should never itself be grasped, for it is not something that can be found on the physical plane. True satisfaction, to a King of Wands, is the euphoric and spiritual experience of becoming. Of the consistent and constantly expanding alchemy of "I will" into "I am."

When you know that place, you will understand this (on the surface) restless and hungering king. When he takes the form of important people in your life, you will stop seeking to be what fully satisfies him and begin to share in the endless satisfactions of a journey together toward a greater vision. This is a selfish king. There is no other way around it. You must know, though, that the selfish will always be the most lonesome. More than any other kind of soul, they need to share their joys, celebrations and successes with another. The truly selfish are always the most truly generous. Is not true generosity the desire to share your joy with another?

The King of Wand's astrological rulership of the kingdom of Leo speaks strongly to his attributes of pride, generosity and passionate character. The sign of Leo is also one of the "fixed" signs of the zodiac, which lends it the responsibility of consolidation, structure and control. This gives the King of Wands a strong sense of identity and, at times, a stubbornness in vision. If the rigidity of his will and sense of self prevents necessary adaptability and fluidity at certain times, a King of Wands can find themselves on a road full of obstacles and little satisfaction. This a king that is indeed prone to ruling a kingdom of one if they choose to go without an essential foundation of humility.

What may surprise you is that our inner King of Wands becomes more insufferably selfish when he does not own his own desires. His repressed personal wishes will always eventually be expressed in bouts of anger, frustration and restlessness. And the frustrated soul, my love, has no room in their heart for anything outside of their own self-pity. A healthy King of Wands owns what it is they truly want. They do not make sacrifices. They are aware that their capacity to help others will always be proportionate to how satisfied they are with their own individual self.

There are few things more dangerous than a King of Wands who is not individually satisfied. At their darkest, this is the king who will punish the autonomy of others as a means to soothe their own inner inferiority. This is the king who will exhibit elaborate performances of "masculinity" to mask the self-pity and insecurity that pervades their soul. A King of Wands can only learn to exert their power with control when they know themselves. When they are set on becoming what they truly are not (the soul's compass highjacked by the ego's need for external approval), destruction is certain for everything and everyone around them.

Learn from this king that free will is something that requires mastery and self-discipline. It is the difference between becoming a brilliant creator or a brilliant destroyer. Call upon the King of Wands within you or around you, my love, when it is time to turn your "I will" into "I am." Despite the danger that comes with fire, the King of Wands will always be an irreplaceable catalyst toward everything you desire.

IN A READING . . .

ASTROLOGICAL INFLUENCE—SATURN AND LEO: The subject's ability to be in a position of leadership and command their reality is in focus. Reflect upon where there is an opportunity in their reality to take charge and assume full responsibility for what they desire.

UPRIGHT (DIRECT): Taking matters into your own hands. Leadership. Powering through. Giving commands. Going in your own direction. Doing things your way. Gaining respect.

REVERSED (RETROGRADE): Getting to the source of your frustrations. Recovering your self-respect. Learning to value your own opinion. Re-empowering yourself. Resolving old anger. Tapping into what you individually want and how to make it happen.

#9 ◆ THE HERMIT

MAJOR ARCANA

Correlation: Virgo

At some point in our journey toward what we externally desire, we will ask the question of what we internally desire. The Hermit represents the journey into the self that allows us to match these two things. You must, at some point, go on a hermit's journey, my love. You will never know yourself unless you at some point come to know yourself alone, for it is only alone that you can truly isolate what you want from what they want and, therefore, what you are and what they are.

The Hermit appears to wander and, indeed, this is what it is. A journey into the self is never about what happens outside, it's about what changes inside. It's about what is revealed inside. Though a Hermit will often be perceived as a recluse, ironically, he is the most well-versed traveler and has seen more than most. What many fail to realize is that the journeys that the Hermit has embarked upon have never had anything to do with their physical manifestations and had everything to do with following the lantern of his own inner light.

Heed, my love, where many use the world to learn about the self, the Hermit uses the self to learn about the world. There is an inevitable loneliness that accompanies this process, but it does not arise (as many would project) from the lack of individuals around them in the physical. This loneliness arises from the fact that very few will ever truly understand your internal journey through your life. Only those who have tapped into their own inner Hermit, those who have had no choice but to voyage deep into themselves, will truly be able to empathize. It is not a lack of people that makes the Hermit lonely, it is the fact that only another Hermit can ease their loneliness.

Indeed, the loneliness of the Hermit is internal, hardly ever external. It is always the internal loneliness that is the most painful, my love. There will be times where you may feel as though, in the vastness of your mind and soul, your voice is an echo that cannot be returned by anything or anyone. Yet, what joy, how simply filled our heart becomes when that echo—on some off chance—is returned. How it returns the spring to the Hermit's step. How the minutest validation of "You are on the right track" or "I am on the same journey" can propel us further along the path home to ourselves.

You are not alone, my love. The journey of the Hermit can seem that way—and it must—for in those vast stretches of nothingness and no one, you have no choice but to befriend the will within. You have no choice but to become the source of your will to live. You have no choice but to see the wholeness of who you are. To abandon everything you once desired for the desire to know yourself. To be in relation to nothing but yourself. How else do I articulate the feeling of yourself? How else do I speak of the blissful presence of solitude? The self that expands into the expanse of your physical reality? How much in the expanse of your world have you allowed for yourself to expand?

Notice how the Hermit uses their wand (their desires) as a tool for their journey, for their path that is being illuminated by their own light. They are not enslaved by their desires. They are not mistaking their desires for their internal light. They are aware of themselves beyond who they currently identify as.

To be on your own Hermit journey is to be able to deliver personal wisdom. It is to be able to put up a signpost at certain points along your path on the off chance that a distant soul may cross, as a guide for where they may need to practice caution or be encouraged. Are you aware of the wisdom held within your own journey? Are you aware of the wisdom that can only be uncovered by you on your unique path toward self-realization? To be able to speak from your personal wisdom is to be deeply steeped in the truth of who you really are.

This process of "steeping" is reflected in this tarot card. It is a process that requires two essential ingredients: time and solitude. The Hermit is shown as an elderly figure, because their wisdom is the product of lived experience. Lessons have been learned.

Maturity has slowly but surely replaced the gaiety of the immature soul. Do not be mistaken, the Hermit is more of an old soul rather than of old age. Age itself does not always imply wisdom. Age only implies that there has been more time and, therefore, more opportunities to gain wisdom in solitude. Time passed with no contemplation will not increase one's wisdom.

There are many who have lived an entire lifetime but have consistently failed to self-examine and, consequently, though they have aged in other ways, their wisdom will be that of an infant. Do not just listen to the elderly, listen to the wise. And who are the wise, you may ask? Those who can offer you personal wisdom. Those who are steeped deeply in the eternal truth of who they are. Have you noticed? Those who only spout wisdom from scripture and from gurus past and present do so because they have yet to develop any personal wisdom. They have yet to take that interior journey, the path of the Hermit. There is nothing inherently wrong with the wisdom of scripture, but it must be seen more as a tool than as a substitute for your personal path to wisdom.

When you truly walk this lonesome path within, you will inevitably encounter the one in all. You will be stripped of all the judgments and false identities that you have accumulated in order to survive in this world. When you come into contact with that essence of who you are, you will discover yourself both in your uniqueness and universality. You will recognize the importance of the path you have walked in this life and how, simply by walking it, you have made it that much easier for another who will navigate a similar journey too.

Question your path and learn to proceed in its mystery. The Hermit has only a few feet illuminated in front of them, they are only guided by the resonance within them. What is behind is done and what is beyond is unknown, all they know is to take a step one at a time with the highest awareness and wisdom they can muster at this very time. They proceed with the knowing that at every stage in their journey they will have the right amount of wisdom to take that next step. Allow what remains in the distant darkness to remain in the distant darkness. You will reach there in time.

Isn't it wonderful? The endless unveiling of deeper layers and dimensions of who you really are? There is a patience, an open-mindedness and an inner peace that can only be found along the Hermit journey. There is no rush here. There is no "busying" of the body in order to distract the mind and keep it from contemplation. There is no desperation to reach a destination or be rid of our loneliness through the loneliness of another. There is only a deep acceptance and devotion to the mystery of you, to the personal wisdom of a well-examined life.

Relish here, my love, the vast expanse of your endlessly unfolding inner world. As within, so without. Are you aware of the galaxies and stars within you as much as you are aware of the cosmos outside of you?

These concepts of self-examination and devotion are also key to the zodiac sign of Virgo, which is the astrological sign that is associated with the Hermit. Virgo represents the path toward purity and, indeed, the Hermit is on a quest to purify themselves from all desires that have estranged them from the deep inner truth of who they are. Sometimes, this will manifest in many as a renouncing of physical possessions or as a purification of their body and mind through alterations to their diet and a commitment to their health.

Too many, however, often get lost in the physicality of these experiences and their perceived martyrdom. They enforce self-control and discipline on top of deeply unregulated desires instead of addressing those desires themselves (which would require them to actually engage in true introspection). They forget that the entire purpose was to become more aware of the within, in order to bring greater meaning and simplicity to the without. The self-control and discipline of the Hermit is actually not enforced, it is what naturally arises from a soul that is aligned with their inner purity. It is what naturally arises from an individual who has nothing to hide or repress, for they have dared to traverse into even the darkest corners of their inner world. What will appear as a soul that has highly disciplined themselves is actually just the beautiful simplicity of she who knows herself.

Do not shy away from necessary periods of cleansing. Solitude, in its correct dosage, is always cleansing. It is always a necessary recalibration to the eternal truth of who you are. Are you at peace with yourself, my love? If everything around you disappeared, would the eternal presence of you be able to fill up that empty space? Can you devote yourself to yourself? So that you may be in service to others instead of constantly sacrificing for others?

I look forward to hearing the wisdom you glean from your experiences here. Introspect, contemplate, self-examine, but then remember to return to the world. Isolation too often becomes a false sanctuary for the wise soul. Food for the soul is mistakenly seen as a substitute for physical nourishment and indulgence in our basic human needs. Every person—young and old, immature and wise—yearns for love, affection and pleasure in this physical world. There is no nobility in completely denying yourself of these things.

And do not deny the world of the wisdom in your journey by hiding away forever. Know when to retreat, know when to return. You will learn when to retreat by losing yourself in others, you will learn when to return by losing yourself in yourself. Your personal wisdoms are the fruits of your soul, my love. When you hoard them all to yourself, they tend to rot and eventually poison the mind.

A tricky thing that both all the brilliance and all the madness of the mind festers in solitude. A Hermit is always a little brilliant and a little mad. And every step along their journey provides another opportunity for mad and brilliant wisdom. Let us help one another become a little more brilliant and a little less mad, then, my love, as we wade through this ice and snow.

IN A READING . . .

ASTROLOGICAL INFLUENCE—VIRGO: The subject's journey of self-development and their private journey into the soul is in focus. Reflect upon where there is the opportunity for deeper knowledge to be gained by going within.

UPRIGHT (DIRECT): A journey you must make alone. Releasing physical distractions. Narrowly focusing on your path. Progress will be made through solitude. A time of self-improvement. Finding a greater significance to your life. Strength and wisdom gained alone. Consistent routines and self-discipline.

REVERSED (RETROGRADE): Journey into the deepest parts of you. Resolving what isolates you from others. Needing time to reflect in solitude. Temporary withdrawal from usual routines. Deep spiritual work and learning. Reevaluating your entire path. Feeling called to something you don't yet fully know or understand. Being temporarily forced into reflective isolation.

#10 ◆ THE WHEEL OF FORTUNE

MAJOR ARCANA

Astrological Correlation: Jupiter

It seems you are at the point in your journey where you are ready to become aware of divine unfolding. You only need to look upon the solar system to witness the fact that our universe is constantly in motion. How could you ever escape this grand orchestration? How could you ever allow yourself to sink into the distortions of feeling "left behind" or as though there is no greater significance or force propelling you into your highest destiny?

Oh, to be swept up by the grand orchestration of the universe, my love. How else do I articulate that you are constantly in motion? Do you feel the weight of this in your soul? You, a single fragment of an inconceivable body of consciousness, spinning, changing, evolving through time and space. You, an aspect of a grand cosmic order endlessly organizing and reorganizing itself, expanding itself, expanding its own knowing of itself. You, imbued with the endless quest of self-discovery that began with the one consciousness, with the one seeking to know itself through all. You, a single soul carrying the power of universes birthed and reborn. You, a single cell among a titanic body of space. You, a body in which millions of cells play a role in your formation, forming, dying and renewing you completely in the span of nine months. You, energy in motion. You, unable to stop the flow of time and, thus, doomed to the blessing of eternal evolution.

Even if you did everything to halt the unraveling of your destiny, the momentum of the universe pushes you onward, even when you are unable to see how what is happening in your reality is contributing to your divine story. The consciousness of the universe itself is not yours to fully comprehend, but to glimpse. This, my love, to attain even a glimpse of your divine, unfolding plan is to see directly into the mind of God.

Do you feel it? The infinite intelligence that arranges and aligns every aspect of your reality to serve a purpose within another purpose—all encompassed by the inherent purpose you came in to attain self-realization. Yes, the universe does revolve around you. You, an irreplaceable center, a son of the sun, a micro spiral of the macro spiral. A being with its own gravitational pull, calling in everything that will allow you to expand your own understanding of yourself. The shifting of your reality is designed by you, for you, in direct response to your journey of accumulative self-understanding.

You cannot avoid your expansion even if you did everything in your power to remain in the pits of stagnation and misfortune. As long as this universe moves, it will move for you and for your evolution. The seasons will change, the moon will rise in place of the sun before being replaced once again. The cycles of the universe will cycle, for everything spirals on its own wheel, the wheel of life, the wheel of evolution, the wheel that spirals and spirals into higher octaves of itself as it goes back over itself and learns more of itself, the wheel of order and chaos, the wheel of fortune.

Astrologically, the Wheel of Fortune has been attributed to the planet Jupiter. Jupiter is the planet that is responsible for our personal expansion, spiritual evolution and the experience of living in our truth. The Wheel of Fortune is constantly turning in favor of our inner truth. The fortunes and misfortunes we experience are always serving our evolution, even when it is difficult to recognize from our limited perspective.

When the Wheel of Fortune is present, there is a greater alignment to the unfolding events in our life than we could possibly fathom or understand. It is where karma turns into dharma. It is where we see the consequences of our actions. The law of cause and effect and how it operates on the vibrational plane of existence.

Indeed, the esoteric meanings of the Wheel of Fortune tarot card are vast and various. There is no way to truly understand this card unless you have lived through the karmic cycles of your own incarnation. This card speaks of a very deep spiritual process, where one can become aware of how every single thought, action and event has contributed to their personal expansion and journey toward self-realization.

There is nothing that exists outside of the wheel. There is nothing that can exist outside of the gravitational force of the universe itself. When you become aware of this wheel—the wheel of life, the perfection of cycles—you can become a watcher of the wheel. To be a watcher of the wheel is to become aware of your place within the roulette of life. To become completely at peace with your natural place in this universe. To not be at war with the true expression of who you really are. It is to be connected to cosmic supply, the infinite beneficence of the universe.

The more you become attuned to the natural wisdom of your being, the more you will begin to receive the blessings from universal cycles that have and always will be destined for you. What appears as "luck" to many is quite simply a complete surrender and attunement to the natural cycles of the universe. It is to not ask for more or less than what is meant for you. It is to trust that you, in your authentic expression, will always have a place in this universal order and that many of your needs are here to be provided for you and "worked out" by forces that are beyond your conscious control.

When you can watch the wheel, you can begin to expect the "luck" of the universe, because your luck is the natural good karma awarded to a soul operating from their true nature. A soul operating from their true nature is in complete obedience to the highest principles of reality and, thus, always reaps a fruitful harvest. It is to be aligned with dharma, the overall "good" of the universe, and to its positive and self-improving expansion. It is to be able to recognize the true consequences of our actions and to develop the capacity to discern whether our actions are aiding the "good of all" or contributing to the downfall of our moral and personal character.

To the soul aligned with their dharma, misfortune can only ever be momentum that pushes them into paths in life that are more rewarding and fulfilling. To the soul only ever experiencing karma, a lack of accurate reflection on past actions and misfortunes can only ever lead to the re-creation of the same cycle of pain and suffering, again and again and again, until the cause and effect has been correctly discerned and overcome, until the individual has experienced an ascension in their moral or spiritual character.

There is nothing personal about this process, it is the only way that the universe can continuously facilitate its positive expansion and its positive expansion is its priority. We must do our best to make it ours, too, in our own infinitely unique ways. Do not be so easily flattered or fooled by the Wheel of Fortune when it presents itself to you in your journey. This card itself does not promise good fortune, it promises perfect consequences for your actions. It promises the perfect repetition of patterns that are contributing to your self-understanding and personal expansion. What is serving your personal evolution will continue to reward you. What is not serving your personal evolution will continue to "seemingly" punish you, until you gain the insight necessary to turn your karmic cycle into your dharmic destiny.

And it is that awareness, my love, that breaking of old karma, that is the greatest gift that this universe could possibly bestow upon you. For to break from karma is to end a source of suffering from the entirety of your incarnation. Connected to cosmic supply and the overall beneficence of the universe, let us turn the wheel of life!

IN A READING . . .

ASTROLOGICAL INFLUENCE—JUPITER: The subject's awareness of divine cycles is brought into focus. Reflect upon where there is the opportunity to surrender control and to trust the revolving wheel of life to grant the appropriate blessings for their journey. Surrounding or clarifying cards may speak to what aspect of the subject's reality this cosmic force is operating in.

UPRIGHT (DIRECT): Receiving what you need at exactly the right time. Trusting the process. Moving with the flow of life. Shift of circumstances approaching for the better. Divine arranging of people, places and things.

REVERSED (RETROGRADE): Understanding a past cycle. Resolving karmic situations. Preparing for a major shift. Stillness before the wheel of life turns again.

#11 ◆ JUSTICE

MAJOR ARCANA

Astrological Correlation: Libra

Just as law and order exists on this Earth, so does it exist in the fabric of the universe itself. As #11, Justice is a mirror tarot card of #1 The Magician (page 18). If you look closely, you may find many similarities. Instead of a wand, the figure in Justice holds a sword up to the heavens, demonstrating the importance of aligning our actions with a higher awareness so that we may have better judgment and discernment when dealing with the world "below" (represented by the scales).

Without aligning our own conscience with integrity, accountability and morality, our perception of reality tends to become incredibly distorted. We have no capacity to measure (noticing the scales) the weight of our words or the impact of our actions. When we are unclear of even our own motives, we lose all control over creating a harmony in our life and our reckless actions cause lasting damage onto those that fall victim to our internal chaos.

Justice represents the cosmic principle that propels us toward finding balance in this life, not just within ourselves, but within our relationships. The realization that there could be an overseeing force that must and will restore justice where there has been none is comforting to those with a clear conscience and haunting to those who benefit from the injustice of others. And what is injustice? It is to be aware of your own free will and still choose to act in ways that will lead to the suffering of others.

Where the Wheel of Fortune (the previous tarot card, page 105) speaks of blessings and mishaps that are beyond our conscious control, Justice speaks of the consequences that arise directly from actions we have chosen. Do you recognize the weight of the sword you wield? This sword represents every action you will ever take in this life and the consequences of those actions will bring you closer to your integrity or further away.

It is your responsibility as a Magician to be mindful of the incredible power that you hold over your reality. It is no small feat to possess free will, to have a choice in the matter of your destiny. It is so difficult to truly become aware of what we so easily take for granted. In the tarot card of the Magician, we became aware of our willpower and, in Justice, we become aware of the consequences of wielding such willpower.

We have the choice to do our best to act in accordance with what is ultimately right or to remain ignorant to that which tries to teach us an important lesson. And how can we be sure that we have done what is ultimately "right"? We have been able to assess where we ourselves are accountable and we have been able to carefully examine the evidence that either proves or disproves a point of view. We have attempted to see the "we" in the "I" and the "you," we have overcome blame and can witness the true motives of the people in our lives.

When true Justice is finally decided upon, it is never when we are overcome by wild emotions or driven by retribution. It is a place of peace and balance. It is a place detached from the subjective waters of the subconscious and grounded in reason. It is to make a decision that, at the end of the day, we know we are at peace with and can live with. To be able to face reality in this way is to preserve peace in your life and in your relationships. Numerologically, the number 11, that represents Justice, can combine to form #2. This reveals that #11 Justice is also a mirror of #2 The High Priestess (page 21); it is not a surprise that the matron of the inner voice is actually who instructs our sense of harmony and balance in the world around us.

Being of the age that you are aware of your own free will, are you ready to take full accountability for the current state of your reality? Are you willing to take accountability for the inner peace or lack thereof within your reality? Are you willing to take accountability for the dysfunction in the relationships and contracts that you value? This is not to say that others around you are not also responsible for achieving harmony in your relationships, but remember that Justice speaks of the actions that you can control. When you remain in the realm of what you can control, you remain in the objective realm of reason rather than in the emotionally charged distortions of blame and victimhood. When you remain in the realm of what you are accountable for, you can better decide for yourself if it is worth continuing a contract with something or someone or if it requires change in order to achieve more fairness.

All contracts and relationships fail when both parties can no longer find a mutually beneficial agreement. Justice is the objective recognition of where we draw the line between what I am responsible for and what you are responsible for as part of our shared agreement. This is a tarot card that deals with mutual reception, reciprocation, negotiation and the fair exchange of energy on all levels of reality.

Though justice in our physical world is indeed imperfect, you can be sure that it comes from a perfect expression of Justice on the nonmaterial plane. There is never a cause on this planet that will not have perfect repercussions. It is not for you to always know how those repercussions will unfold or be dealt. Perfect justice requires a consciousness that is perfect.

When you truly come to terms with cosmic justice, you can no longer hold resentment, retribution or any other emotional distortions of justice. Your conscience will be cleared of biased perspectives that only seek to contain you in the powerlessness of victimhood. Does this not give you great power? To recognize that no matter how imperfectly or unjustly an exchange of energy takes place in your physical reality, there will always be perfect compensation for all involved—this is cosmic law. To understand this on its most essential level is to understand the balancing mechanism of the universe itself.

It should be no surprise to you that #11 Justice is associated with the zodiac kingdom of Libra, the air sign that is known for its mediating, harmonizing and negotiating qualities. The planet Venus is the ruler of Libra, which also brings our attention to the idea that returning to a state of peace and justice also returns us to a state of beauty (remembering the Empress, page 24). That which is truly balanced is in complete harmony with itself and, therefore, will always radiate love, compassion and beauty.

Whenever Justice presents itself to you along your journey, know that there is a cosmic force of perfect justice that is operating in your reality. You are being asked to hold yourself and those around you with moral rigor. You are being asked to take action that will bring you into greater integrity with who you are and to be aware of the ramifications of letting yourself or another go unaccountable. It is important to note that observing injustice also makes you accountable. Do not absolve your responsibility as a witness of moral integrity by failing to act against injustice when you have the power to do so. Just as certain actions we make can bring us guilt and regret, so, too, can inaction.

It is true that actions do, in fact, speak louder than words. Actions and inactions will always betray an individual's integrity. This is why we utilize evidence in courtrooms to assert an objective perception of reality.

Taking accountability for what you can control in any given relationship, contract or circumstance will allow you to pass through an essential rite of passage toward deeper spiritual transformations later on in your journey. Here, Justice is one of the cards of the major arcana that presents itself as a gateway (noticing the two columns). Individuals who refuse to hold themselves responsible for the state of their reality cannot move further in their personal evolution.

For everything beyond this part of our journey can only be opened to she who can recognize that in whatever circumstance is being presented to her there is always an opportunity to achieve greater harmony and beauty. To wallow in the pits of what is unfair, unjust and often uncontrollable is to reject the law of perfect cosmic justice and to remain ignorant to the perfect compensation that is infallibly handed to you. Sometimes, that perfect compensation is nothing other than a lesson. A lesson that can be responded to with reason instead of raw emotion. A lesson that when responded to successfully will grant you an inner peace and a clear conscience that far outweighs the bitter pleasure of the most delicious revenge or retribution.

When you understand Justice, you will understand how to clear all karmic contracts to people, places and things that have burdened you. By knowing where you are accountable, you will know where you are not accountable—and you will be able to move through life taking actions that empower you rather than victimize you. If you're ready to weigh your conscience on the scales of perfect justice, my love, if you're ready to make peace with all that you have done, are doing and will do, in the name of the highest integrity you can muster, let us proceed!

IN A READING . . .

ASTROLOGICAL INFLUENCE—LIBRA: The overall karmic balance of the subject's experience and their relationship to justice is brought into focus. Reflect upon the subject's prevailing contracts in all forms in their reality and the importance of what is being balanced and exchanged in their life. Surrounding or clarifying cards may give more information as to what aspect of life Justice is pertaining to.

UPRIGHT (DIRECT): Important contracts being put in place. Significant relationships. The restoration of justice and equality in your life. Receiving blessings and consequences. Taking action in a formal and well-reasoned way. Trusting your perspective to be of the highest good for all.

REVERSED (RETROGRADE): In the process of completing past contracts. Resolving past injustices. Reevaluating the fairness of your current circumstances. Gaining further evidence to make a fair decision. Being deserving of something you did not receive. Reading the fine print and building up your facts. Changing your position on something.

#12 ◆ THE HANGED MAN

MAJOR ARCANA

Astrological Correlation: Neptune

Oh no! It seems that you've fallen for . . . a trap? Some lowly trick? Whatever the case, now you are hanging upside down! Did you expect that along your journey? Look at you, furiously thrashing about, working yourself up, wondering even perhaps if I have betrayed you? And why am I not rushing to release you from your plight?!

If you took some time to calm down, my love, you might realize that you are not dead, or dying, or even suffering. You're suspended. You're waiting. Waiting for what, you may ask? For me to stop being so sadistic and let you down? No, that's your furious little ego talking. You're waiting for divine illumination. You're waiting to remember who you really are. Now that's something worth waiting for. It's something worth hanging upside down for.

What you perceive as merciless, from your perspective, is, from my perspective, the greatest mercy of the universe. What mercy from the universe that at certain points in your journey you are suspended from further suffering at the hands of your own egoic desires and asked to look a little deeper into who and what you truly are.

The Hanged Man reflects the deep spiritual process that leads to gnosis—that is, direct insight from your cosmic self. Better to momentarily hang, my love, than to walk on feet ignorant of your true calling, ignorant of your path of least resistance and highest fulfillment. Do you not want a path of least resistance and highest fulfillment? Yes, but will I get you down already? No. You must linger here a little longer. Until this state of perfect surrender becomes the bliss that it truly is. Until you learn to stop struggling against the flow of your highest reality and allow in perfect insight.

And how could perfect insight have arrived with you walking as you were, so convinced of yourself and your own path toward pain and struggle? How could revelation strike without you first letting go of whatever you thought you wanted and how you thought it would come about? How could the bliss of your self-realization, self-remembrance and connection to the divine love of this universe come about if you were not (seemingly) temporarily suspended from the power of your free will?

Let the universe love you, my love. Learn this here, now, where you are forced to rely on something outside of your own free will, where you are forced to unite your personal will with the universal will, for that is the only way to experience the all within you. Melt, my love, soften, against the ebb and flow of the universe itself. Let yourself be caressed by a mercy that has, is and will always be available to you at all stages of your journey.

You are never exempt from perfect knowledge of who you are and where you should go. All that is asked of you is that you learn to surrender enough to receive this knowledge. All that is asked of you is that when you really don't know, you ask. This is not an easy process. We are impatient, independent and furious little children that are still learning to harness the true power of our free will.

It is in the Hanged Man that you will learn to go forth into a path of least resistance. It is here you will experience the breaking down of your will so that it may be replaced with something much stronger. There is a time and place to fight for your reality, but to understand who you truly are is never a fight, it is a surrender. What is left when you have let everything go but the endless void of your own soul? A void that is as much yours as it is the infinite cosmos' from where you and I have come from.

Whenever we refuse to surrender, we do not see ourselves as deserving of mercy. We have mercy for children and other beings that are innocent, ignorant and helpless. Do you not think that the divine views you in this exact same way? Though it may feel at times as though you are lost, this is never truly the case. Lost are those who do not seek, do not ask and do not stop. Lost are those who cannot even bring themselves to feel lost.

Be comfortable in your "lostness." If you know nothing else, know you are held. Surrender, give in to it. Trust that the only reason your path has blurred is because something clearer, brighter and truer to who you are awaits you. Time spent in surrender is never wasted. There is no waste in remembering your true power. Embrace the remembrance of your divine potential. Embrace your personal resurrection (noting the crucifix-like position of the figure in this card). And you most certainly will rise. Already, the yellow halo of gnosis is beginning to shine around you. For you have already begun to understand something very important: You have come here not only to discover yourself, but to remember yourself.

The Hanged Man has been astrologically correlated with the planet Neptune in more recent times; however, historically this card was simply attributed the element of water. Allow all of what you feel to be cleansed and released as you are baptized in the waters of the divine, in the waters of surrender. You will see yourself clearly and your disillusionment with reality will itself be exposed for the illusion that it always was. In the Hanged Man, we are cleansed of our fears, projections, expectations and delusions that only served to limit our ability to experience who we really are.

Neptune is the planet in astrology that specifically deals with our path toward transcendence, the transcendence of the physical vehicle and the resulting experience of divinity itself. There is a bliss, an ecstasy and a divine mercy that results when we become aware of ourselves beyond our body, and many have attempted to replicate this spiritual experience in the form of drugs and alcohol.

Indeed, certain substances can be used as gateways to reach this consciousness; however, it has more to do with the individual rather than the substance itself. Those who truly seek shall always find. Those who only seek to escape have not yet begun to truly seek. Neptune, in fact, governs all altered states of consciousness and, thus, sleep is also included here. Sleep is a natural process where the conscious mind is steeped in the waters of the subconscious, flushing out unnecessary information and serving to recalibrate us. Notice that this process, too, is involuntarily and must eventually be succumbed to.

The planet Neptune also deals with themes of disillusionment, melancholy, retreat and isolation. It is not uncommon to experience any mixture of these when undergoing the type of spiritual process that the Hanged Man depicts. It is not easy to forget what we have always known. It is not easy to remember our joy beneath the compiling veils of grief, disappointment and sadness. Yet, it will pass. Yet, we will become who we are meant to become, for emotional distortions are veils—they can only dim the ever-burning light of your soul.

And would you look at that, with all my rambling you've managed to turn yourself around, into an elegant tree pose might I add. From where could such confidence spontaneously arise? Where else from but the light of your true self. Before you thrashed around with such little grace and now you need only one leg to stand with perfect balance. My, my, how confusing and remarkable you are. Shall we continue, then? Don't chase me with such a scowl! You'll thank me one day!

IN A READING . . .

ASTROLOGICAL INFLUENCE—NEPTUNE: The subject's extrasensory perceptions and capacity to surrender are called into focus. Reflect upon the subject's spiritual experiences of a loss of identity, an increasing awareness of the cosmic self and moments of surrender that are assisting in bringing a newfound perspective on themselves and their reality. Sleep, dreams and altered states of consciousness could also be highly informative and relevant during this time.

UPRIGHT (DIRECT): Acceptance. Surrender. Dissolving resistance. Dropping the struggle. Openness and receptivity to spiritual awakenings. On the brink of powerful realizations. Giving up control and embracing flow. Temporarily transcending the limited perceptions of the physical body.

REVERSED (RETROGRADE): Profound insights and spiritual knowledge. Recognizing a completely new perspective. Finding alignment of the body with the soul. Remembering past lives or deep emotional memories. Sudden awareness of your cosmic form. Being reborn. Bliss.

THE ACE OF CUPS

MINOR ARCANA

Astrological Correlation: Water

The Ace of Cups presents itself to you opening the suit of water, the second suit in the tarot. Through the journey of the wands, we discovered the power of our will, but now . . . are you ready to pursue the calling of your heart? Are you ready to become receptive to your imagination? To make all of your dreams and wishes come true? Are you ready to taste the elixir of life that brings you into union with the cosmos?

What word could describe this miracle from the universe? This gift that endlessly replenishes, endlessly sources itself within itself and within just a drop encapsulates every dream of man, every yearning, every affection? Love. There are no other words that can draw out the meaning of this card other than love, the force of love in all of its forms, reflections and fluidic expressions.

The Ace of Cups signifies an inner opening of your heart that allows you to receive on a new emotional level, to receive with a newfound depth. Indeed, the suit of cups represents emotional experiences. They cannot simply be understood intellectually, they must be experienced through the heart. The Ace of Cups is the key that opens the suit of water, it is the bottomless chalice that holds every facet of the emotional experience. The joys, the sorrows, the miseries, the tragedies, the longing, the nostalgia, the grief, the darkness, the ecstasy, the transcendence, the sense of fulfillment and our dissatisfactions. All of these expressions and more deepen our understanding and our ability to experience the miracle of love.

When we drink from this chalice, we are embarking on a journey of discovering the wisdom hidden within the heart. We are asked to become receptive to ourselves, to our heart's desires, and only then can we begin to become receptive to the hearts of others. The Ace of Cups is a card of yearning, a yearning for something that we cannot possibly yet understand but only feel. As an ace, it is but a seed, we lack wisdom. We still don't fully know what our heart is truly wanting, but we know what we are being moved by—we are being moved by love. Love for ourself, love for another . . . love for life.

Remember, that the Ace of Cups that begins your initiation into the suit of water is for you to drink. It is a single cup that is for your nourishment. Your dream. Your love for yourself. The root of all the love you can ever experience in this world can always be sourced within you. Oftentimes, our journey through the suit of cups is the conscious realization that what you have been yearning for has always existed within you. Yet, we must yearn, we must love, we must face disappointment, heartbreak, loss and grief . . . for these are the emotional journeys that make life worth living.

The heart can indeed be foolish, yet to reject its yearnings is to deprive yourself of the dream you are here to bring into fruition. The cup you uniquely hold is the very substance of your soul. Within it is contained every emotional memory you have ever experienced from this lifetime and other lifetimes. Do you feel the magnitude of that? Do you feel the depth of your own heart? Do you not feel compelled to pour all of this love and wisdom into those that would receive it? Love love, my love.

Know this: Without a connection to the waters of your own emotions, to the ebbing and flowing of your own heart, life is but a barren wasteland that no one should have to roam. When the Ace of Cups presents itself to you along your journey, welcome home your heart's desires. What is it that you yearn for? What in the vast imagination of your soul are you ready to bring into fruition? Are you ready to open yourself up to receive?

Receptivity is one of the key qualities that defines the suit of water in the tarot. Without first opening within, you cannot hope to receive from without. And what does it mean to open within? It is to open the gates to the vastness of your imagination, creativity and the yearnings of your heart. It is to open yourself to the memory of who you really are. To be able to open from within is to be able to be gentle, compassionate, empathic and intuitive. It is to be able to become a vessel, a channel for divine inspiration or the emotions and experiences of another who seeks to be understood. It is to be able to listen with not just your ears but with your heart, to listen to what resonates with your soul.

When we lack depth within we cannot hold another. If you do not have emotional capacity for your own soul, how do you hope to also have capacity for anyone else in your reality? On the other hand, some of us give and give, filling the cups of others and neglecting our own. Yet, in doing so, we are truly helping no one. Giving and giving is the antithesis of receiving and, thus, is not a form of unconditional love. For love that is truly unconditional is always replenishing. When we are moved from unconditional love toward someone or something, we are replenished by loving them. It is not an obligation, it is a pleasure to love.

We begin with pure hearts, my love, but through our journey toward self-realization, our experiences reveal that loving and dreaming is more complicated than we first thought. To work toward regaining the purity of our heart is one of—if not the highest—milestones in the suit of water. It is to return the waters of your own subconscious to crystal clarity, to cleanse ourselves of all distortions that prevented us from giving and receiving the love of our own soul. So, let us discover the love that is within your soul. Raise your cup and affirm "I receive, I receive, I receive."

IN A READING . . .

ASTROLOGICAL INFLUENCE—WATER: A portal opens to a new dream and the experience of love in all forms for the subject. Reflect upon their imaginations and their deepest heart's wishes. Surrounding or clarifying cards may provide insight into what this new beginning will bring.

UPRIGHT (DIRECT): New love. New dreams. Opening of your emotional world. Blossoming of the heart.

REVERSED (RETROGRADE): Reevaluating your hopes and dreams. Bringing out repressed sensitivity and creativity. Seeking out a deeper emotional connection to life.

THE 2 OF CUPS

MINOR ARCANA

Astrological Correlation: Venus in Cancer

Shall we share this moment? Shall we drink to us? To the shared joy of two souls connected by the heart? The second cup in the suit of water introduces the receptivity of another to the love in your heart? What holds more pleasure, my love, than two souls that are bound by the heart. Whose heartbeats are synchronized? Who can feel one another's ebbing and flowing? The 2 of Cups represents spiritualized union. It is the meeting of two souls that are opened within or that are opened within as a result of their union. They have become vessels for one another. In this way, they are mutually nourished and evolved by all exchanges of their energy.

Have you experienced this? The alchemy of two openly loving souls? Of two souls only interested in fulfilling the other? For they are already so individually fulfilled by the pleasure of their union. The result of this kind of union is always a mutual ascension, for both are alchemized and transformed by the other.

The number 2 always introduces the idea of a mirror or reflection. In the suit of water, this manifests as a mirrored emotional experience. You will find that certain individuals along your journey toward self-realization have very similar emotional memories to you, that their lessons are your lessons, and vice versa. You will find certain individuals who just seem to get you, who, because of their own emotional experiences, have an innate and unspoken empathy toward you. This is because you share a great deal of emotional memory with them. Some of these individuals you encounter may even have subconscious memories with you from previous lifetimes.

To experience the 2 of Cups is to experience a mutual, unconditional love and empathy that dissolves the illusion of separation. This is not an experience where someone simply "understands" you or "can sympathize" with you, this is someone who seems to know you. Do you believe in soulmates, my love? Do you believe in the sacred meeting of two souls who are meant to serve one another's spiritual evolution?

It is this connection that is depicted in this tarot card. Remember, the primary purpose of a soulmate is to serve the growth of your soul—not whatever your personal ego wants. The meeting and parting of soulmates is arranged by factors that, oftentimes, are beyond your control. Unconditional love is being able to surrender to love, to surrender to the highest good of that which you love, which often requires letting go of control. It requires letting go of your personal need to feel "completed" by another and realizing that your soulmate has only highlighted (through their presence) the part of you that will complete you.

Remember, they are a mirror, never the source of your own happiness and fulfillment. The source of your own happiness and fulfillment has always existed within you; soulmates help us remember these parts of us again. All the love that you will ever receive is mirroring the love you have found for yourself. This can be a difficult lesson to learn and we will do everything in our power to avoid looking at our own reflection. We will blame the other for what they are (or are not) doing until we come to terms with what we are (or are not) doing for ourselves.

In the 2 of Cups, just as you are facing another, you are ultimately facing yourself. As a being that is of the age and mind where you can operate from your free will, you will find that when you are deceived by another, you have often already deceived yourself. When your boundaries are disrespected by another, you have often already disrespected your own boundaries. Others will see you as you see yourself.

Cherish your soulmates. Not just for who they are, but for the lessons they bring. You cannot ultimately control whether they will remain in your life forever, but their lessons will. Too many of us become so enraptured by the idea of uniting with someone that they become our "happily ever after" instead of their true purpose in helping us toward our "happily ever after." As long as you are in your individual body—your individual vehicle (refer to #7 The Chariot, page 65)—your individual journey never ceases, my love. Not before you meet the loves of your life, nor after! In fact, it is the continuation of your individual journey that actually allows your relationships to expand, evolve and find new ways to love the miracle that is you.

So, celebrate your union with individuals who see you. Never will you experience such an acceleration to your spiritual evolution and self-understanding than when you are in union with another. See union for what it really is and you will be able to take the best from love and be the best lover you can be. Union is alchemy. Two forces combine to improve one another. Two hearts come together to learn how to love even deeper and to facilitate the growth of the soul, even if that means they must eventually grow apart. Better to grow apart than to stop yourself from growing altogether. To stagnate yourself within any relationship is to stagnate the other in the process.

There is a tugging and pulling here, an ebbing and flowing as two souls continuously regain harmony with one another. In a relationship with two mutually loving and self-reflecting (not blaming) individuals, this process of joint evolution spirals the two upward into higher levels of bonding, intimacy and shared purpose. In dynamics where there is a great imbalance and an inability or unwillingness to self-reflect, the two will instead circle back to the same patterns until they can see one another (and themselves) clearly. Some will attempt to avoid the same patterns in their relationships by forgoing self-reflection and simply changing who they are in union with.

This process fails to recognize the other as a mirror and, ultimately, re-creates the exact same emotional pattern with a different individual. For if you yourself don't transform, your mirrors and reflections will not either. Our capacity to transform within (accessing deeper layers of our self) directly correlates to our capacity to build intimacy with others. It is always a deepening of intimacy with the self that calls in more intimate relationships. It is your relationship with intimacy that must deepen if you seek to change the quality of your relationships, not necessarily the individuals themselves.

Yes, the 2 of Cups indeed describes the process by which we develop intimacy with one another. Our capacity for intimacy is our capacity to transform through what we fear the most. Intimacy is what remains when we realize that offering our cup—the substance of our soul, the essence of our vulnerability—has not killed us. Oh, how risky it is to be vulnerable! And how much richness, growth, liberation and power is on the other side of that fear!

Astrologically, the 2 of Cups is assigned to the planet Venus in the sign of Cancer. Here, the planet responsible for harmony, union and relationships draws from the subconscious, feeling and emotional powers of the moon (ruler of Cancer). This association reveals that we are attracted (Venus) to those that we sense will fulfill our subconscious and most intimate desires (Cancer, the moon). Your soulmates will make you conscious of your subconscious desires. You cannot form a strong emotional connection or attraction to someone unless they in some way speak to the language of your subconscious mind.

And, as we'll learn (refer to #18 The Moon, page 246), our subconscious can be a double-edged sword. If all that we have instilled in our subconscious are patterns of unworthiness and low self-esteem, our "soulmates" become those who will mirror this back to us until we learn to see ourselves in a different light. If we have come to a point of high self-love within our subconscious, our soulmates will become those who will raise our self-love to even greater heights.

Remember, in the alchemy of relationships, subconscious desires are amplified and multiplied. What was already good will get even better and what was bad often gets worse until we can become aware, reflect, learn and grow. Oh, the complexities and joys of union! Have I scared you? Excited you? Follow the heart, my love, and do not shy away when destiny's hand moves you and another together. Learn from your unions. Learn what brought you together, learn what grew you apart. Learn where you failed one another and you will learn where you have always failed yourself. Learn how you love and how you felt loved and you will learn how to love yourself. What is that? You'd prefer to never have to deal with another, to save you the trouble?

Sorry, my love, but every pulse of your heart is a compass that brings you closer to those who want nothing more than to love you, for the heart yields no greater pleasure than witnessing you experience love in all its forms. The heart is the strongest muscle, after all, and it will take every ache, every yearning, every thorn of grief, betrayal, past hurt, abandonment and rejection and alchemize it into its eternal truth. You deserve to be loved.

IN A READING . . .

ASTROLOGICAL INFLUENCE—VENUS IN CANCER: The subject's emotional and intimate relationships are in focus. Reflect upon where there is the opportunity to develop deeper self-awareness while in union with others.

UPRIGHT (DIRECT): Love. Soulmate bonds. Alchemical relationships. Spiritual growth with another. Bringing different aspects of personality into harmony. Expanding your heart.

REVERSED (RETROGRADE): Reevaluating intimate relationships. Reflecting on your roles in relationships. Working on resolving inner conflict. Taking accountability in your relationships. Resolving blockages with intimacy and vulnerability. Accepting repressed desire for deeper emotional intimacy with another.

THE 3 OF CUPS

MINOR ARCANA

Astrological Correlation: Mercury in Cancer

The glasses clink as we exchange words of affection, affirmation, celebration and encouragement. Among friends and among good company, we find the third cup in our journey toward the realization of our heart's desires. In the 3 of Cups, you will experience the echo of your heart in those that admire you and believe in your dreams. Here, support is rallied for the mission of your heart and soul. This celebration of the substance of your soul is a ritual that amplifies what you are creating and manifesting.

Where the 2 of Cups (page 120) represents an alchemic ritual centered around the exchange of energy, the 3 of Cups represents a ritual that ushers in a process of creation and expansion. Join us in this ritualistic dance and celebration that opens a portal to whatever it is you seek to bring into your life.

The 3 of Cups is a card of shared imaginations and affirmed dreams. Is it not a blissful feeling when others share in the excitement of something in your life? Is it not endlessly uplifting to have your emotions and perceptions validated, understood and seen by those who support you? To have those who will cry when you cry, who will rejoice when you will rejoice? Who can share in your imagination and, thus, amplify the fruition of your dreams and for all involved?

One ambitious individual will be hardworking, yet three ambitious individuals working together will not have hard work. This is not simply because they are able to share their physical workload, it is because they are able to share in the like-minded imaginations of a future built on success, achievement and excellence. Find those that will amplify you in your highest vibration. You are in your highest energetic vibration when you are most aligned with the joy in your heart. Surround yourself with those who will lift you higher in your joy. Surround yourself with those who share a like-minded imagination with you. For whoever you celebrate or commiserate with, you are manifesting with, my love.

Just as good company can expand your joy and celebration of life, negative, pessimistic and envious company will inevitably pollute your subconscious and only serve to expand misery in your life. Remember, your subconscious mind is highly susceptible to what you and those around you are constantly affirming to it. If all you are saying and hearing from those around you are affirmations that reduce you or that lift you up by constantly reducing others, you are in the company of enemies, not friends.

Be wary of petty gossip and commiseration—this rarely exists in a vacuum. It is likely present even when you are not present. When people are brought together by the suffering of themselves or others, they are always brought apart by the same forces. Misery, indeed, loves company and many celebrate together and even bond not over their shared joy, but their shared suffering. To share in the misery of others instead of working to lift them up into recognizing their true power only perpetuates a hive mind of suffering and victimhood. Victim consciousness adores others who share the same imagination of powerlessness and perpetual suffering. Feeling comforted in your powerlessness is not something to feel comfortable about.

The 3 of Cups, in fact, speaks of all surrounding factors in your environment that are contributing to your subconscious programming. Words, people, places and things are all affirming oftentimes implicit ideas that are influencing your imagination about what is and what is not possible, acceptable, permissible, good and/or bad for your life. If you seek power, surround yourself with those who understand power. If you seek powerlessness, you will not have to look very far to find good company. Share in the imagination of those who speak to your heart's desires, and you will come together to celebrate and create more of the joy of life.

It must also be said that there will be times in our lives where we or someone we love truly is suffering. Someone who is suffering is not the same as someone who only seeks to suffer. Someone who is suffering deserves good company to lift them up into celebrating who they really are. Someone who is addicted to misery does not want to be uplifted. It is up to you to use this discernment in your personal relationships.

As long as you have good company, there is always a reason to celebrate your life. Sometimes, we may find ourselves in a phase of life where we are lonely or feel that we have no support. Consider, though it can be harsh, if you are someone who has become addicted to misery or if you have not simply found those who share in your imagination. In times where you feel alone, notice that the three figures are united by their chalices. When you are on the path of following your heart, it is always a path where others will eventually follow you. You must know this, that if you raised your cup high enough, the substance of your soul, for the world to see, how many would simply adore you. I mean, look at you, my love.

The astrological correlation of the 3 of Cups is Mercury in Cancer. This is why I have focused so much on how the ideas and words (Mercury) that we speak and hear are constantly suggesting imagery to our subconscious mind (Cancer). Mercury, our mode of communication and expression in empathic and sensitive Cancer, is what allows us to share in the imagination of others and to share what is truly in our heart. Mercury in Cancer, here, is the intimacy and almost familial bonds we are able to create by allowing others into our personal subconscious. To hold up, like these three chalices, to the light what we have hidden about ourselves, whether it be due to shame, fear of rejection or any other circumstance that causes us to withhold the substance of our soul.

In the 3 of Cups, our essence is celebrated and validated by those who honor our vulnerability. There is nothing in the shadows. We find through opening ourselves that our feelings are not so uncommon. That it creates a portal for others to open themselves too. Due to the adaptive nature of Mercury, it is also important to consider when this card presents itself if what you feel and think is a reflection of your internal compass or of external factors and people around you. Pay close attention (Mercury, refer to #1 The Magician, page 18) to what you are manifesting from your own subconscious when you are with others. Are you holding your chalices up to the fruitful happiness and fulfillment of all involved? Are you able to share in one another's imagination and experiences with empathy and understanding? Or do you find that the visions of those around you are vastly different to that which lies in your personal heart?

Sometimes, coming to terms with where you are simply different than others is the greatest lesson you could have taken from their company. It is not personal. The heart must follow where it will hear the echo of its own pulse. Our hearts grow, mature, change . . . so do our dreams and what we find fulfills us. It is no coincidence that when this happens, we may require a different environment or different company. Sometimes, those who celebrated who you were will not always be those who celebrate who you become. Worry not, my love, from the infinite fountain of love that streams from your own soul, there is no shortage of people who will celebrate you in this life. Let us toast to that!

IN A READING . . .

ASTROLOGICAL INFLUENCE—MERCURY IN CANCER: The subject's emotional and social environments are brought into focus. Reflect upon where the subject may or may not be experiencing the emotional support of like-minded and emotionally available people.

UPRIGHT (DIRECT): Feeling emotionally connected and supported. Shared joys and successes. Relating with others. Feeling validated and loved for your creativity, personality and ideas.

REVERSED (RETROGRADE): Reevaluating your connectedness to others. Resolving where you feel out of place or misunderstood. Restoring camaraderie in your life. Focusing on being surrounded by good people. No longer feeling emotionally connected to the same people. Change of social circle.

#13 ◆ DEATH

MAJOR ARCANA

Astrological Correlation: Scorpio

Did you expect Death to come so soon in your journey? Are we ever ready for the onset of nonnegotiable transformation in our lives? And is that sun rising or setting in the distance? Well, it depends upon if you see Death as an ending or a new beginning. Welcome to the cosmic law of transformation that urges on every single being on this planet toward evolution. It is nonnegotiable, we must evolve.

You are at the point in your journey now where you are ready to confront Death and learn to wield its powers. To live is to die and to die is to have lived. Death is always left in the wake of life and new life in the wake of death. The death process is the promise of change and the antidote to purgatory. Just as it brings an end to that which we wish would go on forever, it also ends that which we can no longer bare. We must have it both ways.

Heed this and never forget it: What no longer has the capacity to grow in its current form must transform. This is cosmic law and you will see it reflected in every aspect of this reality. It is the only way that the universe can persist in its perpetual evolution. And you will not have to wait for physical death to experience the process described in this tarot card. For within a single incarnation, you will die multiple times, for you are subject to the inner transformations of your being. And your inner being undergoes its transformations on its own accord. It knows when the next step of evolution is necessary in your journey.

By the time your exterior reality transforms, you have already been changed within. This is because all external transformations originate from an internal transformation. As within, so without. It is the transformation of the inner parts of your being that allows you to breathe new life into your physical experience on Earth. This is an incredibly profound process and it is at the center of all psychological and spiritual work. To be able to facilitate the death process with the conscious knowing that what is being "lost" is only being transformed into the next stage of evolution eliminates so much unnecessary suffering.

Universally, we have been taught to fear death, to do everything we can to prevent an integral process of our nature. We attempt to avoid endings at all cost, which only causes us to prevent new beginnings. We fear change and so we cling to situations that are uncomfortably comfortable. If you want something to change in your life, my love, you must be willing to at least temporarily let it go. Nothing has room to change in the firm grasp of fear. Embrace the death process on all levels of your reality when it arrives on its white horse (oftentimes unannounced). You must accept that everything in your life has the capacity to and will eventually transform.

There is a common misconception that what does not die is immortal. No, my love. What does not die is not living. What is immortal understands the laws of death and rebirth, it seamlessly accepts transformation and, thus, goes on perpetually. Only that which allows its form to change can be immortal. This is why the snake has always been understood as a symbol for immortality, because its form is constantly dying and being reborn. Unsurprisingly, the snake is one of the forms that represents the zodiac sign Scorpio, which rules this card.

You are no different, my love. The desires, thoughts and psychology you had when you were a child are (hopefully) different to your much-older psyche now. What you once wanted and, perhaps, were even attracted to could be very well different now. We change all the time and we don't even know it until we look back and see that our problems today are different from the problems we had back then. Where are you seeking to experience transformation in your life? Are you willing to allow things to fall away so that only that which is immortal remains? So that that which must change can finally change? All change that occurs in your physical reality can only happen because you have called it in, whether you are aware of it or not.

When #13 Death presents itself along your journey, you must understand that you are undergoing significant internal shifts that cannot be reversed. You are changing now. And you cannot outrun the white horse of Death. All that has been ordered to change must change. To resist this process, to attempt to overpower Death itself, is to suffer in purgatory on Earth. There is a reason why people say that souls that do not pass peacefully in death remain stuck between worlds.

The only way to have true power over Death is to accept powerlessness over Death. It is a tragic thing, my love. Those of us who are driven to end their lives prematurely too often lack the support and resources to overcome the inner transformation that has been calling and calling from within. You cannot outrun the white horse. There is no way around it, only through it. You cannot open your eyes and take your first breath in a new world if you are not willing to take your final breath in the old skin.

And, oh, how much liberation, freedom and power lies on the other side of every single transformation that you will be brave enough to undergo. The process of transformation destroys the old limits of your reality and always brings a new, unforeseen horizon. I need not mention the new limits that a butterfly feels when it first beats its new limbs.

Astrologically, #13 Death has been attributed to the zodiac kingdom of Scorpio. The zodiac sign Scorpio is of the water element, emphasizing that the process depicted in this part of your journey is first and foremost vibrational and emotional. It is the shift in the emotional inner realms of the subconscious and the spiritual illumination that follows, which leads to the exterior transformations represented by this card.

Scorpio is a "fixed" water sign that deals with our deep-seated urges and desires, and #13 Death emphasizes that this journey of transformation will require a deep internal self-examination. Scorpio represents the aspects of our being that we prefer to keep hidden from the world around us. These are the parts of us that are intense, actively seeking out emotional extremes and are deeply sexual in nature. Indeed, it is our instinct to repress that which we fear we will not be able to bring under our control. The questions that Scorpio asks of us penetrate the deepest aspects of our being and force us to become intimate with ourselves.

Know that every transformation you undergo in this life will bring you a greater intimacy with your personal being and every being on this planet. To have faced your own fears is to be able to show others that there is nothing to be afraid of.

The connection of #13 Death with Scorpio also brings to our attention that what often parallels a need for change in our life is what we are no longer willing to repress. Consider, what are you no longer able to hide in yourself? What do you truly desire? What are you no longer willing to hide about the truth of who you are? We will instinctively repress that which brings us shame, guilt and fear. #13 Death is the process that liberates all the power that these petrified emotions locked away for you so that you could access it when you were truly ready.

Oh, how boundless your power is on the other side of transformation, my love. To be able to say, "Here, here I stand on the other side of what almost destroyed me." Affirm to yourself in the moments where the soul beckons for deep change that "I remain open to bringing forth from the depths of my being all of my repressed power. I liberate myself now from the heavy emotional attachments that bind me to shame, fear and pain. All that is changing is good, for it confirms that I am ready for the next stage of my evolution." And, so, let us proceed to the next stage of your evolution, my love, and let the breath of new life sweep through that which gracefully decays.

IN A READING . . .

ASTROLOGICAL INFLUENCE—SCORPIO: The subject's ability to accept nonnegotiable transformation in their reality is brought into focus. Reflect upon where in the subject's life there is the opportunity to embrace rebirth and the resurgence of life after something is allowed to change. Surrounding or clarifying cards will give additional information on the nature and purpose of what is transforming.

UPRIGHT (DIRECT): Nonnegotiable change essential for the soul's evolution. Rebirth occurring in one or multiple aspects of life. New life after a period of stagnation. Good and needed change. Purging the unnecessary. Unimportant elements of life simply falling away. Moving toward your deepest desires and no longer settling. Sacrificing something for the better.

REVERSED (RETROGRADE): Getting to the root of your deepest desires. Reevaluating what you should keep and what you should let go of in your life. Deep inner transformations. Seeing yourself in a completely new light. Transforming yourself privately. Processing and letting go of deep emotional attachments. Cutting cords from the past.

THE 4 OF CUPS

MINOR ARCANA

Astrological Correlation: Moon in Cancer

A moment to rest and reflect, for this journey in bringing the imagination to fruition is not always easy. Let us rest against this tree and contemplate our dreams, our desires. On what we have and don't have, on where we are satisfied and where we are unsatisfied. Let us take some time to honor where in our lives we simply feel discontent. And as chance would have it, right here, under the silence of this contemplative tree, the fourth chalice! The chalice of contemplative emotions.

We need not act right away, we need not know for sure how we truly feel or what it means. All that is asked in the 4 of Cups is that we reassess our emotional foundation. This is a quiet card that invites us to look within and, more importantly, feel within. It is a reconnection with your softness and a reconnection with the true source of emotional security that has always existed within you. Notice, the astrological correlation here of the moon in Cancer.

Here in the 4 of Cups, we are sensing and feeling (moon) the source of our insecurity (Cancer), which almost always stems from a subconscious pattern that once protected us. From one perspective, in the 4 of Cups, our memory of the past (moon) hinders us from being open to receiving the chalice that is seemingly being gifted to us from the divine. Our mental energy is so focused here on what "always happens" or "never will happen" that none of our imagination is left to envision what really could happen.

Notice that this is also the first card in the suit of water where the cups are actually touching the ground. Here, our imagination has actually brought something into fruition and we are now being tempted to compare what has happened with what will happen. If things did not work out as we expected last time, we lose faith in trying again in the future. If things did work out as expected last time, we are left dissatisfied with how this time doesn't match up with the past.

We are caught with comparing our present reality with what we have already created. This is the life of a dissatisfied soul—re-creating patterns of security by forgoing what the heart truly desires and envisions. This is a pattern of psychological self-protection (moon in Cancer). Your subconscious just wants to protect you in the comforting womb of what has always been. Yet, you have come in with the will to create in the now, my love. You have come in with the ability to bring whatever you envision into fruition.

From another perspective, the magically appearing chalice in the 4 of Cups is what you are actually willing into existence through you recognizing your own dissatisfaction. To recognize your dissatisfaction with something is to be focused on your satisfaction and be working toward building a stronger emotional foundation. That is more than many would ever dare to feel within. By facing your dissatisfaction, you are calling in new imagery and suggestions to your subconscious mind that will lead to your overall fulfillment.

These suggestions will appear in the mind's eye oftentimes as spontaneously as that magical cloud in the 4 of Cups. Grab them when they arrive and plant new seeds in the garden of your subconscious mind. Be aware, my love, that the gift of the 4 of Cups can also be its downfall. The high degree of passivity in this card can tilt us into the comfortable discomfort of a victim complex, where we begin to subconsciously reject all goodwill from the universe—constantly reaffirming our victimized subconscious mind.

Notice when you are drifting into the depths of negativity, pessimism and when you are paralyzed by the pain of the past and the fear of the future. This is no longer healthy contemplation; this is a maladaptive emotional foundation. When you are here, your heightened sensitivity, vulnerabilities and insecurities will try to keep you from pursuing or even envisioning your heart's desires. Affirm "My personal dissatisfaction is not the result of something external to me, it is an opportunity to remember what truly matters to me, and I open myself to following the joy that always can be found deep inside of me."

Though the 4 of Cups describes a very tender and, at times, emotionally taxing process, know that the heightened sensitivity and intuition (moon in Cancer) it brings will always result in being moved toward fulfilling your heart's desires. The process of reflecting and becoming more intimate with our own emotional states of being also builds a stronger emotional foundation within us so that we stop looking for that security in maladaptive patterns of behavior.

The 4 of Cups brings deep emotional insight and spiritual awareness. After all, even the Buddha achieved enlightenment sitting under a tree. And, so, my love, how much more will you allow me to ramble? So that I can keep resting here and complete our journey some other time? What is that? You accuse me of being overcome by the passivity that I just preached against? And when did you get so wise? I think I liked you more in your ignorance. Alright, alright! Let us keep chasing our foolish little dreams!

IN A READING . . .

ASTROLOGICAL INFLUENCE—MOON IN CANCER: The subject's inner emotional realms and ability to receive new opportunities are in focus. Reflect upon where there is a need for passivity and contemplation in order to better understand a potential source of dissatisfaction in your reality.

UPRIGHT (DIRECT): Calling in a new source of emotional fulfillment. Contemplation. Receiving spiritual insight. Incoming opportunity that will not require much action. Finding inspiration in the mundane. Finding new joys.

REVERSED (RETROGRADE): Getting to the root of your boredom or melancholy. Reevaluating what emotionally fulfills you in life. Processing the past. Slowly and emotionally pulling yourself together. Finding a stronger emotional foundation. Becoming more vulnerable with yourself and others.

THE 5 OF CUPS

MINOR ARCANA

Astrological Correlation: Mars in Scorpio

There, the fifth chalice! Oh, but it looks to have been tipped over and now that gloomy-looking hooded figure is despondently fixated upon it. Let out a soul-crushing sigh, my love, welcome to the 5 of Cups. It does not matter what the scale of your tragedy is, for in the 5 of Cups, even the slightest inconvenience will feel like the world is ending. A stubbing of the toe? Hide under the covers all day and draw the conclusion that the universe and everyone in it is against you. A friend looked at you the wrong way? Time to spiral into all of the reasons why you are the burden of all burdens to be around.

Astrologically correlated with the planet Mars in intense and brooding Scorpio, the 5 of Cups is the reservoir where you will go to purge the accumulation of your frustrations, losses, disappointments and anything else that makes you want to wrap up in blankets and be inconsolable. The emotional suffering and deep brooding that accompanies this stage in your journey toward your heart's desires is an extremely important part of releasing that which has subconsciously blocked you.

Mars in Scorpio here heightens, amplifies and aggravates our deep subconscious emotions so that we can become consciously aware of them and, therefore, release them. You cannot release the influence of that which you are not even aware of. When we acknowledge these deep feelings, we give ourselves the opportunity to realize that they do not represent our entire reality. The hooded figure in the 5 of Cups is fixated on their losses and they will be for quite some time, until someone slaps some sense into them. I mean, until they realize that the intensity of their emotions is not something that can actually be sustained.

Mars in Scorpio purges deep emotions like a powerful crescendo, reaching a climax of vibration before, eventually, all must settle back into the stillness of this eternal truth. Your natural state of being is peace. Peace is the ocean from which all other emotions are only waves. Peace is the only emotion that can be truly sustained. Yet, our emotional storms are very important! They recycle our waters and purge the accumulation of unwanted mental imagery, emotional attachments and emotions from the past that are no longer serving our pursuit toward what will really fulfill us.

Purge, purge, purge, my love. Mars in Scorpio is emotionally masochistic. He will not rest until he has listened to every song on that depressing playlist, until he has warped his entire reality into a tragic novella starring his poor soul. I mean, just look at the drama of that cape. It's a look, it's an aesthetic, but if you plan on wearing that every day my love, well, I wouldn't complain. I love a good cloak, but this isn't helping my point.

The point is, the 5 of Cups is your permission slip to purge what needs to be purged. To own your depth of feeling. Only by expending your emotional energy here will you finally free yourself from the more insidious and chronic feelings that keep you down for much longer. Better to give yourself the space to feel everything that has ever disappointed you and release it all at once now than to feel a little disappointment in everything you will ever do. The heightened intensity of emotion that the 5 of Cups depicts allows for this rapid healing of accumulated emotional baggage. Yet, as you undergo these emotional releases, you must still keep that voice inside of you that knows, knows, knows and never forgets: "I am simply purging right now, for I know peace, contentment and well-being to be the natural state of my being."

When you can remember those two chalices behind the hooded figure, you will always have an anchor to help you ground and process whatever it is you are feeling. It is not about "building a bridge and getting over it," it's about knowing that there is a bridge, but right now you're choosing to sob over a river and be melancholically beautiful. There is beauty in your intensity, and there is also great art, but do not fall into the trap of believing that it is your forever.

There are two forms of compassion you must give yourself when you are dealing with this part of your journey: the compassion to feel and the compassion to let time heal. And, oh, how much better you will feel, and how much more real you will feel, when you allow yourself to experience your emotions fully. When you're aware that they do not represent your entire reality, but are a lens to better process the deeper aspects of your subconscious, you will no longer be afraid of yourself.

Now, I do not mean to generalize this to those of you who are receiving specific medical treatment or therapies for mental illnesses. You may not be in the position where you can safely feel your feelings alone and that is okay. You never have to process anything without the specific support you feel that you need. Do whatever works for you, just don't forget those two cups behind you. And some secret wisdom here for you: When you allow yourself to fully process deep subconscious emotions, you will often find that the root that kept tying you to a certain toxic desire or emotional attachment will go away. Remembering Mars in Scorpio here, it is in the 5 of Cups where our inner drive and desire nature (Mars) undergoes a powerful transformation (Scorpio).

This means that the 5 of Cups always leads to the birthing of new and more fulfilling desires that are free from the murky emotional baggage of the past. This is why there comes that point where you throw off that dark cloak in a grand gesture and say, "I can't believe I ever wanted that anyway! Are you kidding me?" You may find that you no longer even desire what once tugged at your emotional foundation so easily.

This is the power of Mars in Scorpio, the transformation of desire. And, so, let yourself toss off that cloak and emerge from the fortress of blankets eventually, for there is still too much joy that awaits you further along this journey. I promise. Just give it a bit of time, okay?

IN A READING . . .

ASTROLOGICAL INFLUENCE—MARS IN SCORPIO: The subject's subconscious emotions and disappointments are brought into focus. Reflect upon the emotional experiences that the subject is now ready to purge and release in order to allow the blooming of new and fulfilling desires. Surrounding or clarifying cards may speak to the field of life that is experiencing a cleansing of old emotional baggage.

UPRIGHT (DIRECT): Emotional release. Taking your time to feel. Coming to a full acceptance of exactly where you are. Mourning the loss of something but excited for the new opportunities that will take its place. Planting seeds for a more fulfilling future. A healing sadness.

REVERSED (RETROGRADE): Resolving deep, intense emotions. An emotional experience that brings up old wounds in need of healing. Healing and processing the past. Taking your time to move on. Taking the time you need to grieve. Honoring how you feel. Waiting for a storm to pass.

THE 6 OF CUPS

MINOR ARCANA

Astrological Correlation: Sun in Scorpio

Oh, the bittersweetness of memory, my love. To cherish the roses of your past is also to be pricked by the thorns of yearning for what is gone. Yet, is it gone? Nothing ever really goes; it simply changes form. It has simply transformed (noticing the astrological correlation of this card to the sun in Scorpio). The child up ahead holds the sixth cup on our journey through the suit of water, this time in the form of a bouquet of flowers. A gesture of pure-hearted kindness, does it not hearken you back to days of childhood innocence? Does it not warm your soul? Perhaps it even makes you yearn for that innocence again. It is the wisdom of the 6 of Cups to realize that whatever it is you yearn for continues to exist within you.

As you may have learned through the suit of cups, all external experiences are reflections of the ever-evolving substance of your soul. Allow the warming breeze of nostalgia to rush through your soul, but do not grasp at it, recognize that those feelings have never and will never leave you. For the warmth of your heart is the essence of who you are, it has the capacity to endlessly create that warmth again and again in your lifetime.

Feel the past, but do not seek to bring it back. Your heart does not exist in the past, it only exists in the now. There is nothing in the past that can be the source of your joy, it can only remind you of the joy that exists within you now. The longing you feel is the longing to reconnect with the sincerity of who you really are. This is why you are seeing the innocent love of children in this card. Memories of who we were as innocent children always reconnect us to the essence of who we really are. Yet, we do not usually desire to regress into our child selves. Instead, we learn to integrate that pure essence into who we are becoming. To understand this is to regain purity, innocence and joy in your relationships. It is to be able to love and be loved in a way that heals you in every passage of time.

It is the 6 of Cups that describes the powerful ability of the heart to heal the past through the experience of love and joy in the now. To be able to look back at your past and actually feel gratitude, love and compassion, no matter how difficult certain circumstances may have been, is to know that you have transformed. It is to experience the purification (Scorpio) of your spirit (the sun). Our memory must, at certain phases of our journey, undergo this purification if we are to retain the innocence of our heart.

Try as you might, but a heart that sees its past through the eyes of loss, vengeance and suffering cannot hope to love or be loved purely in the present. Innocence is not something that is determined only by age, it is one's ability to purify memory. It just so happens that the older we are, the more we have to process, and, as we correctly do so, our innocence only deepens.

Remember, the deepening of your heart and the transformation of your spirit is a process that can only occur in the now. Transformation cannot be bypassed. Regressing to the past or reliving the past will only reconnect you to your heart's essence. To truly integrate this essence into you, it must be alchemized into the now. To understand this is to overcome some of the most soul-sapping affirmations, such as "Those were the good old days," "I'll never feel like that again" or "That was the best part of my life."

No, my love. The best part of your life is right now, for all the joy you have ever experienced is recorded in memory and is, thus, present with you right now. It is available to you now, for its source was never found in anyone or anything outside of you. You are the one that makes you feel a certain way because you are solely responsible for the command of your own inner vehicle (refer to #7 The Chariot, page 65).

Are you seeing the true power of your memories? The bitter and the sweet? Do you see how the joys of your past can be bridged into your present? That the memory of your heart is perfect and pure, able to alchemize all experiences into gratitude, love and compassion? There are no words to describe the magic of this process. The return of your childlike glow, the uplifting and radiant light of your soul.

Notice how freely and easily children share their joy. They want to share their joy, for when they are joyous, they are overspilling with the essence of who they are. Notice how easily children forget and forgive. Does it not inspire the deepest desire to protect that innocence within them? For the purity we have as children is not yet conscious, which means we are also subject to naivety and a lack of discernment. Do not mistake naivety for an innocent heart. Naivety and a lack of discernment is a sign of emotional immaturity, the latter is a sign of great maturity—for the heart has deepened and transformed through alchemizing (Scorpio) the pain of the past.

The 6 of Cups, as reflected in its correlation with the sun in Scorpio, illustrates the rebirth (Scorpio) of our innocence (the sun). This is one of the primary spiritual purposes of nostalgia, for we are always nostalgic for the times where we have experienced the authenticity of our spirit, the purity of our joy. The painful aspect of this is also having to come to terms with what we feel we have now lost. Yet, there is a great beauty that will fill your life now simply by remembering that innocence.

The sun in Scorpio also illuminates and purifies the shadowy recesses of our subconscious and deeper urges. You cannot love openly and, simultaneously, assume the worst intentions of everyone around you. You cannot feel your childlike glow and, simultaneously, operate with a hidden motive or agenda. Allow the 6 of Cups, the experience of an innocent heart, to cleanse your memory. To reawaken your ability to give and receive love. To deepen your capacity to experience and rekindle intimacy in your life.

I can promise you, my love, that the best is never behind you. When you're at peace, when you're done with looking back over your shoulder, shall we continue on this journey toward the fulfillment of your heart?

IN A READING . . .

ASTROLOGICAL INFLUENCE—SUN IN SCORPIO: The subject's deep desire to experience innocence, joy and love is brought into focus. Reflect upon where there is the opportunity to reconnect with the simple desire to love and be loved. There is also the opportunity to heal the past and psychological wounds through bringing light to a current circumstance.

UPRIGHT (DIRECT): Purity. Experiencing unconditional love. Childlike joy. Friendly encounters. Reunions. Reliving past memories in a healing way.

REVERSED (RETROGRADE): Healing through remembering good times. Reconnecting with childlike joy. Keeping your childhood dreams. Making peace with the past. Forgiveness.

THE 7 OF CUPS

MINOR ARCANA

Astrological Correlation: Venus in Scorpio

Watch out! There seems to be a snake in that chalice of water that would quench you of your thirst. And beware of that cup of glimmering jewels, their gleam conceals the rust rotting them from within. Where are we, you ask? The land of all your hopes, dreams and deepest desires. Here, they fester and fuel the power of your imagination, bringing you closer to your heart's desires but also further outside of the realm of reality. Your imagination is full of possibility, my love, because it is completely unbound by the laws of space and time. The seventh cup lies somewhere here, among other conjurings of your imagination. There is a power in these fantasies, however, as they allow you to experience your deepest desires without having to manifest them into the physical realm.

Fantasizing is not in and of itself a destructive process, for it is only through our imagination that we dare allow ourselves to transcend the perceived limits of our physical reality. Nothing begins as a delusion. A delusion is only that in the imagination that you are not actively working to bring into fruition, into your reality, and that has not at all been vetted by reason. Delusions can often also be dreams that we, for whatever reason, have chosen to neglect.

In the vast dreamscape of the 7 of Cups, we become consciously aware of both our dreams and our delusions. What differentiates them? Dreams lead to the actualization of your heart's desires in the physical world. Delusions pull you away from that, for they have no interest in turning fantasy into reality. This would dispel them; it would kill them off in your consciousness. It is not a far stretch to imagine some of these chalices as hijacked abodes for the ghosts and demons of your own mind. These forces thrive in your mind, they are killed by reality. Nothing that your heart truly desires, my love, is killed by the facing of reality. The facing of reality excites your true desires because they want nothing more than to complete the process of physical manifestation.

The 7 of Cups is the quintessential card of imagination. It is neither positive or negative. The number 7 itself can only be achieved by adding an even and an odd number. Number 7 The Chariot (page 65) in the tarot speaks of the balancing of these "positive" and "negative" forces. The number 7 is between worlds. The 7 of Cups is a filtering process between imagination and reality, between what you think you want and what you really want. So, what does your heart truly desire? Oftentimes, we can only discover this by actually going for what we think we want! Cue everything in your life that "ended up not being what it seemed."

Sometimes, we can only move through the creative paralysis of the 7 of Cups through the process of elimination. This is a question about what you truly desire and your deepest urges, explaining the correlation of this tarot card with Venus in Scorpio. You will be surprised how often we disguise our own motives even to ourselves. The tricks we experience in the external world often happen because we already tricked ourselves.

Venus in Scorpio here also combines #3 The Empress (page 24) with #13 Death (page 128). On a deeper level, this reflects the rebirth of your creative imagination (Empress) through the transformation of your desires (Death). On a more mundane level, what we once valued in our life is now changing. It is selecting desires that reflect our new values that helps wade us through the murky waters of old temptations.

Heed a bit of truth in this land of illusions and deceiving appearances. Illusions are always disguising something. They are trying to hide something, for what is beneath does not (for whatever reason) feel loved or ready enough to be seen. Illusions love to disguise what we are just not yet ready to accept in our reality. Illusions fade with self-acceptance. They are vapor. They cannot persist in the physical.

A blessing to know this, my love, for what does not fade is always of the eternal substance of your soul. Have I confused you? Clarified you? I can barely see you in this realm of smoke and mirrors! If you don't already, you'll have to trust your heart's compass to venture beyond this point!

IN A READING . . .

ASTROLOGICAL INFLUENCE—VENUS IN SCORPIO: The subject's hopes, dreams, fantasies and fears are brought into focus. Reflect upon the subject's highest wishes and ideals and discern as to whether the actions they are taking in reality are supporting these dreams coming to life.

UPRIGHT (DIRECT): Choosing what is closest to your heart out of many options. Many possibilities and potentials. Deep imagination. Burst of creativity. Navigating between what you want and other people's perceptions of you. The sky's the limit (or, rather, your mind is).

REVERSED (RETROGRADE): Reevaluating your options. Waiting for an opportunity that will feel more solid. Not being pulled by anything in particular right now. Giving time for your inspiration and imagination to return. Keeping your dreams and hopes to yourself. Unlocking hidden fantasies.

THE 8 OF CUPS

MINOR ARCANA

Astrological Correlation: Saturn in Pisces

Oh, how far you have come, my love, on this journey toward what your heart desires. Already, so many of your imaginings have turned into realities. They are lined up here, all the dreams that you have crystallized. Yet, there is a sense of an incomplete artwork. Yet, a certain gloom descends upon all that stands before you, as if anticipating the completion of a jigsaw puzzle only to find that the final piece is missing. So, what will you do, my love? What will you do with the looming dissatisfaction that threatens your personal fulfillment? If only you could just be happy with this incompleteness, if only what you thought was the destination of your heart was the destination of your heart.

Alas, you have reached the eighth cup, the perceived abandonment of success and the return to the path of the soul. What happens when your heart is simply no longer in the same place? When you have emotionally moved on? Remember, by the time you voluntarily abandon or move on from a certain situation, you have already emotionally moved. Your soul has already begun to traverse what is beyond the horizon, even when you are actively resisting it in your physical reality. Though the decision to move on from what dissatisfies you in your physical world is voluntary, on the emotional level, this is actually an involuntary process.

It is in the 8 of Cups you will become aware that at certain phases in your life it will seem as though forces beyond your control guide you back toward the path of your highest good. It is the somber and disciplinarian Saturn in the soulful and wandering sign of Pisces that correlates with this card. What is reflected through this astrological pairing in its essence is spiritual discipline. It is your ability to commit to the greater cosmic cycles of your life that will reveal to you your level of spiritual discipline and maturity, to be able to forfeit your attachment to all that you have created so that you can progress into a new level of your purpose and fulfillment.

This is a sign of great spiritual maturity and evidence of a soul that sources their strength not from the finite ego, but from the eternity of their soul. It is to be able to be perceived as "stepping down" in order to "step up" to a new level of self-realization, purpose and meaning in your life. One of the most challenging lessons (and, indeed, in the Saturnian 8 of Cups there is always a learning of lessons) is recognizing that you cannot control the compass of your soul. To resist or repress the evolving imagination of the soul (Pisces) is to live soullessly. It is to turn everything that once gave you emotional fulfillment and satisfaction into heavy burdens (Saturn) that take and take and give diminishing returns.

We suffer in the 8 of Cups when we don't know how to gracefully let go. We resist against a path that would bring us to higher levels of emotional fulfillment and completeness, sometimes out of familiarity, sometimes out of fear, but always out of a constricting attachment to a dream that no longer truly fulfills us. The more you must grasp at a dream, my love, the more evanescent it becomes. Like a bubble, it pops when enough pressure is placed upon it. The 8 of Cups presents itself as a test of faith in the perfect cycles of life and a trialing of the integrity of your soul. As with all cards that involve the planet Saturn, there is a karmic element to the 8 of Cups that signifies the breaking of a cycle.

In this part of your journey, it is the breaking out of creating and re-creating what your heart no longer truly desires. It is the pulling back of the curtain to realize that there is so much more to what you could have imagined. That there is so much more joy, fulfillment, magic and happiness that awaits you if only you would stop restricting your own mental imagery.

In this way, the 8 of Cups represents a quest into a new layer of your inner world, which always results in the exploration of unknown territory in your physical reality. The only way you could have proceeded on a path of unknown territory is if you were first able to imagine that something more exists beyond what you have experienced time and time again.

This is the 8 of Cups, my love. Just as it is an abandoning of what has already been created, it is a journey to meet the part of you that has already felt the beauty, joy and happiness on the other side. You are not here to live in disillusionment. You are here to use disillusionment as a tool to follow the compass of your soul.

Many live in fear and denial of their own melancholy and personal dissatisfaction with life. They learn to gaslight their own intuition and keep playing a world of appearances and false illusions. Yet by taking themselves at face value, they consequently live shallow lives that are devoid of any real meaning beyond the preservation of self. When your sense of emotional fulfillment and personal satisfaction can only be maintained by consciously resisting disillusionment, you are remaining ignorant to your highest good and purpose.

The 8 of Cups is a melancholic card. There is no way around grieving what is fading away. Yet, to be able to recognize the spiritual significance of your emotions and experiences is to be certain that you are on path to everything that your heart truly desires.

And how difficult it can be to leave the eight cups behind! By this point in your journey, you have invested so much of your imagination, your emotions and the essence of your soul into mastering (Saturn) an aspect of your reality. Yet, what you may not realize is that the true mastery here is invisible to the eye (Pisces). You are mastering the cosmic flow of your reality. To be in constant resistance to where the tides of our life and our own emotions are taking us is to be in constant resistance to the dharmic purpose of our life and our personal sense of emotional fulfillment.

The presence of Pisces in this tarot card raises themes of surrender and a retreat from that which is no longer quenching our spirit. The motive behind this card is, first and foremost, emotional and spiritual in nature. Logic and practicality may say otherwise about how you feel. The intellect may convince you that it would be a "waste" to not proceed with something—even though you are no longer emotionally present. The mind may come up with endless calculations about how "nothing is all that bad" and that the issue is more to do with your lack of gratitude, a chronic inner restlessness or always chasing the "grass that is greener on the other side." Notice how these perceptions gaslight your own intuition and keep you playing in the world of appearances where everything "should be what it is." Yet, Saturn in Pisces will reveal to you here, my love, that nothing is ever as it seems.

The 8 of Cups forces us into asking deeper questions about the fulfillment of our soul. It is a quest to no longer be afraid of feeling aimless or lacking in direction, for these are temporary states of being that through surrendering to them allows us to discover a deeper sense of purpose. It is to commit ourselves to our own personal contribution to the overall good of this universe. Is this not true wholeness and completeness? To feel that your existence serves the completion of the entire universe. That, in your surrender to everything that you are and love, you are seamlessly attuned you to your highest purpose.

Take the lessons from your experiences and shuffle onward toward the callings of your soul. And always, it will call, for it is already where you are seeking to be. The journey toward the center of your heart and the unlocking of your eternal nature is not for the faint of heart, that is why so many numb themselves to the slightest sign of disillusionment instead of allowing it to expand them.

See the mountains ahead. The journey will try and test your obligation to the unfolding mission of your soul. This is not a mission that you will ever truly consciously grasp or that anyone can foretell for you. It leads you on just beyond the edge of your consciousness, calling, "Remember, remember, remember."

So, let us answer the call of your soul, my love. Let us trust that there must be something significant up ahead, that we will find all the answers that we are looking for because we are committed to seeking them. Be bold enough to inquire into the nature of your lack of fulfillment and you will uncover realms of possibility that you could have never imagined and vistas that surpass the beauty of everything that you once told yourself you would never go beyond.

IN A READING . . .

ASTROLOGICAL INFLUENCE—SATURN IN PISCES: The subject is exhibiting spiritual discipline by learning when to move on for their highest good. Reflect upon what area of life the subject is being challenged to surrender control from and continue toward finding what will truly fulfill them.

UPRIGHT (DIRECT): Making the mature decision to move on. Following your spiritual path. Emotionally detaching. Clearing old baggage. Prioritizing what you know in your soul to be true.

REVERSED (RETROGRADE): A final goodbye. Closure. Tying up loose ends. Planning your escape. Recovering an old dream. Needing more time to emotionally prepare.

THE 9 OF CUPS

MINOR ARCANA

Astrological Correlation: Jupiter in Pisces

And as we reach the wise number nine in the suit of cups, we come to find the secret to fulfillment. Sit with me here for a little while on this humble wooden bench. Have we not ventured so far, accomplished so much? Let us contemplate a little while and melt into the ambience. Can you find the deep gratitude hidden beneath everything that is?

The nine cups you see before you actually do not represent anything to do with physical achievement itself. It is the sense of having achieved and finding the bliss of personal satisfaction. It is a feeling, a state of being. One woman reaches the highest position in her field of work, yet she may not feel this resounding satisfaction. Another displays her artworks for the first time at a local market—she sells only one canvas—she could not have been more satisfied if she tried. What is the difference?

The astrological correlation of the 9 of Cups with Jupiter in Pisces will tell us much here, for Jupiter in Pisces is the realization of one's highest path to fulfillment. Jupiter here exalts the imagination, meaning we are more likely to perceive that our highest wishes and dreams can and will be turned into reality. The woman that received the highest position in her field did not receive her highest wish—it was someone else's. The woman who sold her first artwork brought one of her most fulfilling dreams to life. There is nothing more fulfilling than to be living your dream, my love. To witness the images of your inner vision (Jupiter in Pisces) be brought into life. To allow another to witness the truth of who you are beyond the illusions of appearances. The artist understands this process naturally, for to display their work is to allow others to peer into the contents of their heart.

Will you share with me the contents of your heart, my love? The 9 of Cups is the experience of art as life and life as art. It is the art of living. You do not need to be a painter in order to experience your artistry in this life. Your artistry can be found in everything that you have had a hand in creating in this life—that is, every moment. One of the greatest joys is to be able to marvel at your own creations, to be in awe of the infinite inspiration that is always flowing through you, whether you are aware of it or not, and your capacity to bring your inner self to life. A mother marveling at her children playing by the beach is an artist. A lover coming home to a bouquet of flowers left by the love of his life is an artist. A chef taking a moment to cook herself a meal after working for others all day, exhausted yet gentle on herself, is an artist.

It is in the 9 of Cups that the experience of deep gratitude, appreciation and love allows us to transcend, even if only for a moment, the wheel of time. It is the experience of eternity in a moment and a union of the heart with all that exists. Relish in those moments. In a world where we are so often fulfilling desires—and we must, for our path of self-actualization beckons us—these moments of complete contentment and satisfaction become the sweet nectar of life. The enjoying in and sharing of miracles. A momentary capturing of the magic that flows through every moment. This space of transcendental love and expansion of the heart is always available to you. For every moment of your life, captured as a single frame, is evidence of the miracle of your soul, the miracle of your perspective.

When the 9 of Cups presents itself to you, know that your dreams are here to be fulfilled. Expand your inner vision and connect to the moments where you feel that you are in love with life. No matter how brief they may at times be, they exist. And, remember, a single stroke of joy is enough for you to learn how to turn that stroke into streaks and then into forms . . . and, before you know it, masterpieces forged from the joy of your heart and soul will be created all around you.

Do you recognize the eternal inspiration in a single moment of your happiness, my love? How else can I describe to you how infinite you are? If only in a moment you have enough love in your heart to dissolve time and space? Let go of arriving at this place or someplace where you will "feel fulfilled," let go of arriving at a sense of satisfaction. You don't need to arrive, you're either sitting on this humble wooden bench or you are doing something else. You're either perceiving the magic behind the moment or getting caught up in the living of it. Live, live, my love, and we must. And there will always be plenty of living to do, but sink back a little sometimes. It's there that eternity finds you. It's there the art of your life reveals itself to you.

There, you will discover the vastness behind whatever glimmers on the surface of everyone and everything. So, show me the art of your life, miraculous soul. Show me what makes you happy. There is no greater blessing that you could give me than to be in the presence of you in the joy of your dreams.

IN A READING . . .

ASTROLOGICAL INFLUENCE—JUPITER IN PISCES: The subject's highest wishes and personal sense of fulfillment are brought to attention. Reflect upon what the subject perceives to be their "happy place." Where is there the opportunity to take their dreams to the next level?

UPRIGHT (DIRECT): Fulfilling success. Personal satisfaction. Acclaim for your artistic and spiritual achievements. Feeling like you have everything. Having something to be proud of. Respected by many.

REVERSED (RETROGRADE): Restoring faith in your creative and spiritual pursuits. Reevaluating what you need to feel individually fulfilled. Resolving feeling disconnected from your success. Resolving self-sabotage. Preparing a masterpiece behind the scenes. Being on the verge of bringing your dreams to life.

THE 10 OF CUPS

MINOR ARCANA

Astrological Correlation: Mars in Pisces

Here, in the 10 of Cups, we have reached the grand finale of your heart's desires. A rainbow arcs above us symbolizing completion, harmony and the glorious return of light after a long-weathered storm. Two actors raise their arms as if bowing at the conclusion of some fantastic drama. The drama that is your life and, more specifically, this chapter of it. A joyous, happy ending for all involved. Like all great tales, all the plot lines of your life and those involved seem to converge at this point and find their resolution.

There is a sweeping peace in the 10 of Cups that promises the idea that "everything will make sense in the end." And, does it not always seem to make sense in the end, my love? The epic drama that is your life, with all of its emotional turbulence, surprising turns of events, leaps of faith . . . its joys and sorrows, somehow all converge to bring higher wisdom, clarity, peace and fulfillment.

The 10 of Cups, the rainbow at the end of the storm, is the reminder that all emotional experiences are ultimately transitory. Even the closure, clarity and satisfaction found in this card is temporary, for like all the number tens in the tarot (another form of the number one), endings pave the way for new beginnings. There will be new dramas as a result of new desires. There will be new emotional experiences that will build upon what your heart has already learned and is now ready for. The rainbow itself in this card is the perfect metaphor for the evanescence of dreams. We can appreciate their beauty, capture their memory, but, ultimately, we must be ready to let them fade into the light when the time is right.

The 10 of Cups is a card of quiet joy and quiet loss. Everything is perfect and, for exactly that reason, it must come to an end. There is no more growth here, there is no more potential for self-discovery. Like an amazing memory, it is a moment that we wish could have lasted forever, yet we are finally ready to graduate into entirely new experiences. At this point in the suit of cups, our sense of fulfillment and closure from multiple areas of our life will inevitably propel us to contemplate "So, what next from here?"

And, with the astrological correlation of Mars in Pisces, hidden within the peaceful resolution of the 10 of Cups is the seed of a new dream (Pisces) and a new drive (Mars). Mars is the planet that propels us constantly toward the unforeseen horizons of our personal freedom and self-realization. Mars is full of zest for life and actively seeks out experiences of tension and conflict that will allow us to feel heroic. In the dream world of Pisces, however, there is no more tension, no conflict and no resistance. Victory becomes imminent. Neither is there a single point of focus or goal that would allow Mars to activate its hunting sense.

So, it is here, in the 10 of Cups, that Mars has no choice but to experience, even if for a limited period, satiety. All immediate threats and conflict in the drama of one's life are resolved and erased in the 10 of Cups. It is here that we are able to drop the fight against ourselves or another (Mars) and come to a place of inner harmony (Pisces). There is no chasing here. Nothing to do, nothing to struggle for. That day may come again, but, for now, it is time to surrender thine individual will (Mars) to the divine (Pisces), to let a higher will show us the new path. Rainbows have historically been associated with messages and signs from higher powers as confirmation of one's path.

And here, in the 10 of Cups, you must recognize that your path is being confirmed, affirmed and divinely protected. Somehow, in some way, through the mysterious workings of the universe or otherwise—and as the heroic protagonist (Mars) of your own story—you must recognize that you are naturally oriented toward victory. You are naturally oriented toward the fulfillment of everything that your heart desires. You will and must have your happy ending, my love.

It is not personal, it is not me giving you empty platitudes, it is the only way for the universe to resume its expansion. Old stories must eventually come to an end. They are naturally structured to. It is usually our own personal, egoic intervention that prevents or prolongs the unfolding cycles of our life. All karma (or past actions) and unresolved conflicts are cleared by the conclusion of the suit of cups. This is an essential cleansing process that allows us to proceed and experience a new chapter of our life instead of a warped re-creation of what we have already experienced. This is also why two generations of family are illustrated here, representing the healing of one that heals a lineage.

Encapsulated in the finality of the 10 of Cups is a mastery of every lesson held within the journey toward the fulfillment of the heart. The power of union and shared imaginations, of receiving, of alchemizing pain and the nostalgia of the past, of discerning dreams from delusions, of developing spiritual discipline and of experiencing inner fulfillment and the outer realization of your dreams. All of this wisdom converges into the realization that all roads eventually lead home.

There is nothing left to say but congratulations, my love. Exit stage right. You have passed with flying colors. A journey that ends opens a gateway to a new chapter. A new cast of characters, a new array of emotional experiences, all perfectly woven to move you not only through life, but deeper into life. How endlessly, endlessly, exciting. The show must go on!

IN A READING . . .

ASTROLOGICAL INFLUENCE—MARS IN PISCES: The subject's passionate dreams are brought into focus. Reflect upon what the subject perceives to be their "end game." What does true and everlasting fulfillment look like to them?

UPRIGHT (DIRECT): On the path to your dreams. The promise of long-term peace and happiness. Nothing left to do but to enjoy. Celebrating the end of a long journey. Heading toward a safe and loving environment.

REVERSED (RETROGRADE): Shift of long-term dreams and future plans. Reevaluating where you really see yourself to be moving forward. Reassessing your commitment to your dreams. Focusing on your own idea of happiness. Feeling like you need to raise your expectations for your life. Manifesting through daydreaming.

THE PAGE OF CUPS

MINOR ARCANA: COURT CARD

Astrological Correlation: Mercury and Water

At the footsteps of the Kingdom of Cups, an adorable youth approaches us! It is the Page of Cups, they who possess an innocence of heart not yet weathered by the storms of life. And look how openly now they present their cup to us, as if to say, "To everything in this world I give my heart!"

Naive? Perhaps, yet a hint of magic seems to follow them everywhere they go as if divine forces have taken it upon themselves to be the protective eyes of this youth blinded by love. Blissfully unaware of both their stroke of genius and clumsy misfortunes, nothing seems to weigh heavy on this page's heart. Somehow, somewhere, they were struck by cupid's bow and now can't help but see the wondrous good and beauty in everything and everyone around them. Do you see that wistful, sparkling look in their eyes as they peer at something apparently mundane? A dangerous hope, yet heart-warming all the same. They see the potential in all things, they cannot help their foolish little heart from believing.

The Page of Cups is indeed the part of you that will never stop foolishly believing. It is their beauty and it is their bane. Whether it is the prospect of a new romance or any other endeavor that is led by the heart, the Page of Cups peers into the waters of their own imagination and utters the fabled words, "What if . . ." And, voilà, a dream is born. A wish in the form of a fish arises from the seemingly uneventful chalice that had been charged with oh so much hope and that is all the Page of Cups needs as confirmation—that a grand destiny awaits them.

Learn from this page, my love, the romanticization of life. Whether you choose to acknowledge it or not, there is a part of you that believes in the most "foolish" dreams. Your inner Page of Cups is the imagination shared by every child who has not yet been faced with the severity of responsibility and maturity. Your inner Page of Cups is the keeper of every wish you have ever wished upon. You may have forgotten them, but they have never forgotten what gives you pure, childish glee.

This part of you is extremely tender, vulnerable and does not respond well to scrutiny. Self-criticism is a sure-fire way to scare away this timid spirit. They want to share with you everything that you, for whatever strange and fantastical notion, have always loved. They are your inner genius, artist and romantic. Every time you believe in something, they will share a little more of their magic with you. Every time you believe in something, my love, you regain a pureness of heart.

To encounter a Page of Cups along your journey is always a mark of goodwill from the universe. This is the passing soul through which the divine delivers messages of heartfelt sincerity directly to you. This is a genuine offer of love and friendship, for what could not be genuine from the heart of a child? So, make a wish and, this time, don't let yourself forget it! You inner Page of Cups never ceases to expect something absolutely amazing to be right around the corner. Disappointment never weighs on their heart very long, for their hope is easily restored by the magical synchronicities that seem to follow them everywhere they go.

When you learn to see the world through the Page of Cups, you will come to realize how many things really speak to you. Be the imaginative child that "pretends" to interact with their environment. Some will laugh, some will shake their head, some will be concerned. Yet, they have forgotten the first language they ever learned, the language of dreams. In truth, they have no one to be concerned about other than themselves.

What is life, my love, without having a foolish little dream guiding your heart? So, let this adorable little page dream and let yourself dream. The more foolish the better. Offer your heart to another and witness their hopes with the greatest sincerity. When words elude you or a certain pessimism threatens a storm over the bourgeoning of a new dream, whether it be yours or another's, four words, my love, will always suffice: "I believe in you."

IN A READING . . .

ASTROLOGICAL INFLUENCE—MERCURY AND WATER: The subject is encouraged to follow the inspirations of their heart with curiosity and openness. Reflect upon where a new endeavor of the heart is ready to blossom in the subject's life.

UPRIGHT (DIRECT): Genuine intentions. An exciting dream. Natural talent in artistic and spiritual work. Playful, loving connections. A gentle love. Remaining open to possibilities. Trusting who and what feels sincere.

REVERSED (RETROGRADE): Reevaluating the sincerity of your intentions. Remembering your natural talents and gifts. Learning to be your own supporter. Calling magic, love and romance back into your life. Keeping a whimsical dream to yourself. Reconnecting with a good person.

THE KNIGHT OF CUPS

MINOR ARCANA: COURT CARD

Astrological Correlation: Mars and Pisces

And how else would we move through the Kingdom of Water, the kingdom of the heart and all of its fantasies and dreams, without being escorted by the Knight of Cups? He is the lover, the romantic, the unstoppable pursuit of the heart's desires. He is the embodiment of following your heart.

All of the knights you will meet along your journey here represent a certain momentum and, in the Knight of Cups, there is a great momentum toward your dreams, the chasing of your dreams. Do you know the feeling of being swept into a grand adventure, my love? Not because of anything fundamentally extraordinary happening, but because the Knight of Cups is able to romanticize his existence.

To the Knight of Cups, every moment can be seen as a step in the unfolding drama of life. The wins and the losses, the miracles and the misfortunes . . . all of this and more inspires the Knight of Cups, it does not deter or discourage them. The Knight of Cups, under the influence of his Martian nature, enters headfirst into experiences that will bring a depth of feeling and the experience of fantasy on Earth. He has a hunger for feeling and the magic of life.

Astrologically, I have attributed the Knight of Cups to the planet Mars and the zodiac sign Pisces to represent the heroic and fantastical quest of this knight in his single-minded focus toward the realization of his dreams. His role is as a harbinger of romance, good fortune and good news that even feels as if it has been sent by the divine. The Knight of Cups seems to always arrive as an answer from the universe, an answer to the soul who is seeking out the magic of life. Just be careful to not get too swept up in the fantasy of it all.

When the Knight of Cups represents an individual in your life, you must be aware that though fantasies can and do often turn into reality, they struggle to be sustained. A Knight of Cups seeks to explore and satiate the romance of the heart. Their greatest gift is not their stability, but rather the freedom of their heart. To experience their romance is to become aware of your own heart's desires, whether they are the individual who will ultimately fulfill them or not.

This does not matter so much. People come and go, my love, but to know how you like to love and be loved stays forever. To find a love for yourself through the love of another is a blessing that the Knight of Cups gives generously and effortlessly. For who better to show you the magic of your own soul than the individual who will idealize and romanticize you. Who, especially in romantic attraction to you, will look at you as if it is impossible that something so perfect could exist. How could you not fall in love with yourself there? Yet many of us, instead of taking the opportunity to fall in love with ourselves, we fall in love with being loved.

We see the Knight of Cups as a destination even when they are but a passing traveler on the journey of your heart's desires. The gift of love is a miracle, but the biggest lie that you will ever tell yourself is that it doesn't exist in infinite amounts in your reality, that only a certain individual could ever emotionally fulfill you or, worse, that no one could ever fulfill you! Embark on the quest of the Knight of Cups and activate the compass to your heart's desires! Affirm, "I am always rewarded through the bravery of my heart." That acting boldly on my heart's desires progresses me toward my emotional fulfillment in this life.

The Knight of Cups is a good omen. He is a form of cosmic assistance that will ferry you closer to your heart's desires. Do not mistake the knight himself for your heart's desires. They are a convoy, a guide that will bring you higher awareness and spiritual illumination. Be wary of getting lost and enraptured in the object of your love and affection. Remember, our true dreams are materialized when confronted with reality. Delusions, on the other hand, are killed (refer to the 7 of Cups, page 141).

And, so, while we are still on the back of this magic horse, being ferried toward experiences we could never even dream of, tell me, what is your most heartfelt wish? It is yours in spirit and so it will be yours in body. And since you have shared with me your wish, I shall share with you a secret about love. You will not find it in the beginning of a journey or at the end as some grand prize, but always along the way to something else.

IN A READING . . .

ASTROLOGICAL INFLUENCE—MARS AND PISCES: The subject's movement toward love, romance and their dreams is in focus. Reflect upon where in their life there is the possibility to embark on a magical quest of following the heart.

UPRIGHT (DIRECT): A fairy tale–like adventure. Bringing long-held fantasies to life. A journey inspired by love, creativity, romance and beauty. Romantic gestures. Poetic expressions of love. Being whimsically inspired by life. A powerful imagination. Being on the road to your dreams with no plans to stop.

REVERSED (RETROGRADE): Disillusionment that brings a shift in focus. Remembering what truly motivates your heart. Pausing along a quest toward your dreams to resolve emotions. Withholding a desire to express yourself romantically and whimsically. Tapping into your hopeless romantic again.

THE QUEEN OF CUPS

MINOR ARCANA: COURT CARD

Astrological Correlation: Moon and Cancer

If you don't look deeply, you will miss her or, worse, mistake her for your own reflection. For the Queen of Cups blends into the waters of life. Observe her grace. She is fluidity upon fluidity, perfectly attuned to the energetic vibration of everything. To look into her eyes is to be simply penetrated with love. She softens everything and everyone around her, for what could not help but be subsumed by the tranquility of her soul.

The Queen of Cups is the embodiment of emotional and psychic attunement. She is responsible for attuning you to the harmonics of your heart and all hearts that will beat alongside you. Your inner Queen of Cups is capable of perceiving the most subtle frequencies. She is the voice of everything you yearn for. Principally, the yearning to love and be loved. To be able to be receptive to the affections of others. To feel emotionally secure and supported by the people around you. She is the weaver of every dream, every longing, every poetic musing and muttering of your soul. The Queen of Cups is the keeper of your most tender and vulnerable wishes and dreams. She holds the record of every memory that has ever touched your heart and soul so that you never forget what it is that truly fulfills you.

Astrologically correlated with the cardinal water sign Cancer, she is the nurturer of all that is growing in your mind's eye. Your inner Queen of Cups provides the visions and psychic knowings that will guide you to the fulfillment of your emotional needs. As a queen, she is also attributed the Moon (celestial body of our subconscious mind) and, in the element of water, she will make you aware of the nonnegotiable needs that satisfy your heart and soul. Do you know what you need, my love? What hopes and dreams are carried in that wistful gaze of yours? In the exhalation of your breath? When you look up at the moon?

Your inner Queen of Cups will never reject what you feel. This is both her gift and her struggle. She is the merciful queen because she is at the mercy of the tides of the universe and her own emotional realm. She is the compassionate one because she gives the gift of compassion to herself. There is a yielding and surrendered quality to her that allows the slightest shifts in energy to be perceived. She is one with the infinite waters of consciousness, which grant her a natural, spiritual affinity and wisdom. Witness how her cape even blends into the waters of her environment, how seamlessly she influences and is influenced by what is around her.

This emotional fluidity grants her the gift of empathy, but also the struggle of overwhelming sensitivity. Your inner Queen of Cups requires emotional reassurance in order to halt the rivers of deep and murky emotions that can, at times, plunge her into a sense of powerlessness and helplessness. She benefits from knowing this above all else, all intensity of feeling is temporary and that emotions can be better processed when communicated rather than left to infuse and ruminate in the subjective waters of subconsciousness. If left unchecked in the vast waters of her imagination, the Queen of Cups is prone to seeing the potential in a situation or person even if it never translates into reality.

A Queen of Cups must learn to be secure in herself and how to emotionally fulfill her own needs, otherwise her dynamics with others can become tainted with her need to receive their affection. Affirm "It is a gift to be able to see the potential in all, but what I can see for another is only helpful if that individual is able to see themselves in the same light."

The Queen of Cups must respect her ability to recognize the potential of every heart and ensure that she offers her healing to those that are actually seeking out their full potential. The attentive, intuitive and sacred love of the Queen of Cups should not be wasted on those that siphon or do not reciprocate her affections. Remembering the connection with Cancer, the Queen of Cups can be a highly sensitive and fragile soul. Heartbreak and unrequited love can shatter her world, yet she will always reform with greater strength and a deeper heart. She is what lurks beneath the surface of the world of physical appearances and mirrors back what others dare not see or feel in themselves. Whether you like it or not, you will feel what she feels. The truth of your heart will be revealed to her, for she is more familiar with your interior realms than perhaps even you are.

The Queen of Cups opens the floodgates to vulnerability and emotional intimacy, healing those who are ready to receive and eluding those who are ultimately fooling no one but themselves. Honor your inner Queen of Cups, my love, and she will honor your path with more than you could ever wish for.

IN A READING . . .

ASTROLOGICAL INFLUENCE—MOON AND CANCER: The subject's ability to attune themselves to their deep emotional needs and what they are yearning for is in focus. Reflect upon their most tender and vulnerable wishes.

UPRIGHT (DIRECT): Psychic insight. Manifesting your heart's desires. In a creative flow. Exuding love, affection and gentility. Success through following intuition.

REVERSED (RETROGRADE): Reconnecting with your softness. Reevaluating your heart's desires. Yearning to feel emotionally connected again. Reflecting on your intuitions. Intuitively holding back your heart to protect yourself. Venturing deep into your emotional and fantasy world for rich insight.

THE KING OF CUPS

MINOR ARCANA: COURT CARD

Astrological Correlation: Saturn and Scorpio

And who could be the king of the Kingdom of Water? Who could tame the tempestuous seas and swallowing waves? The all-consuming power of the emotional realm itself? There he is! Who is that, you say? You expected more of a pirate-looking fellow, hmm? More roughened up by the ebbs and flows of life? Yet, does his saintly looking face not impress you more? The fact that he has retained his composure, his countenance of peace and focus, amid the storms that surround?

The King of Cups has a remarkable discipline and control over the vast dreams and illusions of the imagination. He is a master at operating from a place of peace, centeredness, emotional maturity and balance. Notice how, differing from the blending cape of his queen (page 160) counterpart, the king's throne appears as a slab of stone that is completely unaffected by the swirling waters that surround. The impenetrable gray throne implies a balance between mind and soul, consciousness and subconsciousness.

Like a painter that has mastered a medium, the King of Cups' disciplined approach to the emotional realm actually allows him to bring forth complex creations into the world. There is a perseverance to accomplish all that his heart desires. The very same emotional control that limits his imagination allows him to actualize his dreams into reality. A King of Cups will complete his creative endeavor. He will achieve in reality what he visualizes. Not out of a reckless flurry of inspiration, but through the consistent presence of his persevering heart regardless of his shifting emotional state.

Your inner King of Cups is aware that inspiration, romance and the swirling emotions of life will always rise and fall. He knows that he may not have a control on how he will feel on any given day, but he is able to manage the consequences of those feelings. He is able to take accountability and full responsibility for the effects of his emotions on either supporting the highest good of his self-realization or hindering it.

A healthy King of Cups radiates emotional security because his emotions have been understood and examined by firmly held principles and goodwill. This is a spiritually advanced figure who brings a gentle heart combined with a strength of soul. There is no confusion around what he feels and why. He is not one to entertain the emotionally tumultuous dramas of life, for he knows all too well that it is always a lack of personal accountability that drives one deeper into crises spurred on by unrestrained emotions. Who is in the driver's seat of your own mind? He will ask. Do you govern the creative force of your emotions or do they govern you? Are you able to influence them or do they always seem to influence you?

Associated with the planet Saturn and the zodiac sign Scorpio, the King of Cups is able to sit in the seat of authority because he has confronted and made peace with all that had once sought to emotionally control him. He is not at war with his own emotions, neither does he repress them. Instead, he acknowledges their power and focuses upon coming back to a place of stillness and a centeredness of heart. Heed his divine wisdom and affirm "All complicated thoughts and emotions are ultimately consumed by the simple truth of my loving heart."

The King of Cups gives himself the space and time required to gain clarity and awareness over all that he feels. When he presents himself, there is a focus placed upon gaining emotional control over a situation and/or seeking out those who can assist us with this process. The King of Cups is an adviser, a morally conscious and spiritually aware individual. They have a great sense of duty and responsibility in bringing healing and awareness to all who seek it. Your inner King of Cups wields the great responsibility of keeping you in control of your own consciousness. To recognize your powerful ability to discipline and prioritize your heart's desires. To overcome unhealthy addictions and emotional patterns that siphon your creative and sexual energies so that you may be raised into higher levels of spiritual realization.

The King of Cups will remind you that though emotions come and go, the peaceful presence of the heart always remains. The more you place your attention upon it, the less you are likely to be swept up by the torrents of life. Oftentimes, it is not the crises themselves that wreak havoc on our lives, it is our unstable and volatile emotional response to them. Crises merely expose the strength or weakness of our emotional foundation. A King of Cups whose throne falters under the tempestuous waters of his emotions and the memories that fuel them will often show a lack of accountability and can become emotionally destructive to himself and those around him.

This is a soul that has no reign over his inner demons and whose emotional balance is replaced by emotional extremes. An unhealthy King of Cups shifts from emotional outbursts to emotional withdrawal and has an inability to maintain vulnerability. His stoicism is sourced from repression instead of a true mastery and acceptance of his emotional world—and it is only a matter of time before the crises of life expose his true emotional reality.

Learn from the King of the Cups in times of great emotional strife. You are not cursed, you are being given an invaluable opportunity to remind every aspect of your being: "With awareness of my mind, body and soul, I am in control."

IN A READING . . .

ASTROLOGICAL INFLUENCE—SATURN AND SCORPIO: The subject's capacity to master their own emotions and wield a patient heart is in focus. Reflect on where there is the opportunity to regain peace and composure over the storms of life.

UPRIGHT (DIRECT): Being emotionally in control. Exuding love, patience and kindness. Pursuing noble spiritual and creative ambitions. Sharing your wise counsel. Overcoming emotional obstacles. Being a pillar for others.

REVERSED (RETROGRADE): Regaining emotional stability. Recovering from inner demons. Overcoming personal insecurities. Building a stronger emotional foundation. Receiving counsel. Reevaluating artistic and spiritual direction. Needing more time to make a calm decision. Regaining your composure.

#14 ◆ TEMPERANCE

MAJOR ARCANA

Astrological Correlation: Sagittarius

An angel descends upon our journey now: #14 Temperance, divine grace! Do you recognize how infinitely supported you are by this universe? If you do not, you will know now, for #14 Temperance is the eternal balancing agent of divinity. Meaning that no matter how far you somehow stray from the harmony of your own being, balance will inevitably be restored.

Your inner being is naturally attuned to the frequency of you. The universe understands that you are here to experiment and explore with the powers of your being. The divine watches over you, tempering your experiences and guiding you toward your fulfillment, but never interfering with your free will (as with the angel in #6 The Lovers, page 50).

When the angel of Temperance presents itself along your journey, it is time to recognize that greater forces are at play in your current reality. You may not fully understand why things are moving in the rhythm that they are moving, but you can be sure that you are divinely protected in the process. There is a very good rhyme and reason to the flow of your reality whenever Temperance is involved, for the balancing agent of divinity is incapable of imperfect alchemy. Alchemy is one of the primary significations of this major arcana card. The ability to blend extremes is one of the most potent ways that we evolve our personality and progress spiritually.

It is the alchemy in #14 Temperance that allows us to develop the balanced perspectives of a mature personality. A mature personality does not operate in extremes. To be operating through the world in extremes is, oftentimes, a symptom of completely distrusting the balancing agent of divinity. It is to subconsciously affirm "I am alone in this universe." Yet, the angel of Temperance holds two chalices. One for you and one for the universe, for the perfect alchemy of your life is always the product of this sacred co-creation.

And, so, you must above all else know that when this angel descends upon your journey, all is well. And, yes, we perhaps wish things could alchemize a little faster! And wish this would be a little less awful! And wish that would take a little less time! And wish that person would be a little less infuriating! Yet, all is well. All is well, all is well and all is well under the divine instruction of #14 Temperance. Allow your inner emotional realms (represented by the waters in this card) to be balanced for you by the grace of the divine. Yet, you must also be conscious of your part to play in this very important ritual that will evolve your personality and bring you closer to whatever it is that you truly desire.

Pay attention, my love, to how you are responding to the circumstances of your life. Temperance emphasizes balance, moderation and a patient will in dealing with your reality. And, of course, in order to understand harmony, we first may need to experience extremes. As we adapt to new levels of our personality, new challenges emerge. Time, patience and a continual returning to the faith and love in your heart is essential in order to progress through the trials of character that #14 Temperance represents.

An alchemist's advice: The goal in this part of your journey is to successfully integrate extremes, not to simply choose one way or another. It is to extract the power in different aspects of your being and to bring them up toward a united whole. The circumstances in your life are perfectly designed to assist you in bringing out more of certain aspects of your personality that are currently requiring further integration. This can be an uncomfortable and challenging process. It can feel as though you are being "tested" by the universe and, in some ways, you are. The man who is afraid to speak up for himself will be constantly "tested" by his colleagues at work who never let him get a word in during team projects.

Under the divine instruction of #14 Temperance, this is an important alchemical opportunity that will allow this man to bring out the confidence and assertiveness inherent to his personality. In this way, the angel of Temperance is here to hold you as you struggle against who you are. No matter what you are facing in your reality, under #14 Temperance, never are you more held. You are held, you are held, you are held, my love. You are cradled and you are caressed—and you have more room for error than you may probably think.

This understanding is what actually underpins the sign of Sagittarius, which rules this card. The zodiac kingdom of Sagittarius is characterized by faith and belief in the beneficence of the universe. Any true Sagittarian will tell you that they simply do not fail. For even if they somehow did, Sagittarius will always extract the spiritual lesson from experience. And, in this way, something is always gained. The Sagittarian qualities of higher perspectives and spiritual expansion are deeply embedded in the meaning of #14 Temperance. Sagittarius also represents the natural laws of the universe—and #14 Temperance is one of them.

In its subtlest expressions, #14 Temperance describes the internal spiritual process by which one can become acquainted with the forces of the universe that flow through them and, by extension, the forces that form the building blocks of the universe itself. But, just for today, let us find peace and reverence in the knowing that this universe could never and will never leave you completely to your own devices. It is not the universe that shuts us out, it is we that shut it out and stubbornly battle against ourselves until we are finally too tired to further hurt ourselves.

Indeed, #14 Temperance represents one of the expressions of mercy from the universe, the gentle kind, like that of a wink of the sun's light as it appears for a moment between gray clouds. As if to say, "I am here, my love, I am here, I am here." Trust that the universe is always brewing and weaving things for you. It is allied with your expansion. The concept of divine timing is also attributed to this tarot card. Yet, there is a great misconception that divine timing is a passive action. That we must simply "just be patient," that it is to simply wait for "something" to happen.

Remember that the weaving of your self-actualization in this life is a co-creation. In truth, divine timing is the active tempering of your personality until you are ready to step into what the next stage of your path entails. It is to push a little bit here, and then to pull back again, and then to push a little bit more, and then to fall back again—trialing and testing our limits—and fine-tuning our vibration until, inevitably, harmony is restored where previously we were flung between extremes.

This is an active process that involves actions that bring a higher level of perspective and awareness (remembering Sagittarius) to your life and to your journey. Above all else, my love, when this angel descends, affirm "All is well, all is well, all is well."

IN A READING . . .

ASTROLOGICAL INFLUENCE—SAGITTARIUS: The subject's capacity to balance internal forces and accept the co-creation of the universe is highlighted. Reflect upon what the subject is currently alchemizing within them in order to bring about new results in their reality. Surrounding or clarifying cards may speak on which forces in their life are currently being tempered.

UPRIGHT (DIRECT): Alchemizing a new reality. Balancing your personality. Trusting in the divine plan. Meeting challenges as opportunities for growth. Divine protection.

REVERSED (RETROGRADE): Working on bringing harmony to deep internal forces. Reconciling opposing perspectives within you. Restoring your faith in the universe. Resolving final tests before a major breakthrough. Quietly brewing something powerful. Just a little more time.

THE ACE OF SWORDS

MINOR ARCANA

Astrological Correlation: Air

Behold the grand blade that descends from the heavens above, illuminating your path forward with clarity, truth and conviction. Witness your initiation into the suit of air, the suit of swords, where the obstacles of life are felled by the power of action and intellect. What could possibly stand in your way with this sword at your side? Indeed, it is only you who has the capacity to truly be an obstacle to whatever it is you desire. Your journey through the suit of swords will illuminate to you how truly powerful you can be, in both achieving your greatest desires and sabotaging them. Your capacity to create and destroy.

Wield the Ace of Swords and recognize the knowledge that becomes available to you with every action you take. The capacity for your actions to lead you to profound self-knowledge. To the self-examining soul, actions are taken in order to better come into alignment with our deepest inner truths. Your actions will always betray your innermost beliefs and the contents of your mind. Even the most deceptive soul acts in deceiving ways. You cannot escape what the actions you take in this life will say about you. You will also discover how what you say to yourself and others will influence your actions.

The Ace of Swords is as much a card of breakthrough awareness and action as it is a card of the power of affirmation. Affirm, my love, "I allow the sword of my inner truth to cut away all within the mind that seeks to deter me from the path of my highest good." Affirm, "I move forward decisively in the direction of my highest truth!" The Ace of Swords often represents a truth that cuts through all illusions and false beliefs. It is action that responds to no one's order but that of the divine will. And what is the divine will? It is none other than the highest truth of your being.

A man's family continuously reminds him of how it will be impossible for him to get a job now due to his unemployment over the last year. Instead of falling victim to these false projections, he affirms "I will only take action toward that which is of my highest truth." Due to the extra time he had available, the man had taken inspired action in helping neighbors with their gardening. Before he knew it, his actions inspired by divine will had drawn the clientele of the entire neighborhood, eager to provide remuneration for his services. The consequences of his inspired actions have now cut away the false beliefs that previously surrounded him. What can be cut down by the sword of divine will was never truth at all. Choose your truths wisely, for they will be the swords that will carve out your reality. Your inner truths will be sharpened by knowledge and intellect, your false beliefs will instead blunt the sword of your truth. A blunt sword does not strike its mark well. It is not precise, it is indecisive. You will always find beneath indecisiveness an array of false beliefs.

In the Ace of Swords is contained the highest levels of glory and success, which begins with the smallest inspired action. As with all of the aces, at this stage in your journey, you may lack the wisdom and knowledge to know where a certain idea or action will take you. You may still be uncertain about the consequences of taking an action or entertaining a particular way of thinking, yet what is certain is that you will develop knowledge that you previously did not have. The only reason we are even able to take action in this life is because in every situation we have a perfect level of knowing and not knowing. The greatest leaps we will ever take in our personal growth and evolution involve a great deal of not knowing, for, if we knew, we would likely never embark on a journey of self-understanding in the first place.

When the Ace of Swords presents itself, you are on the cusp of a significant inspired idea or action that will carve out new and unforeseen possibilities in your reality! Affirm, "I take action with what I do know to be true and remain open to learning what I do not yet know. Above all, I align my actions with the highest truth I can muster at this stage in my journey. I take action with the balance and karmic awareness of Libra, the inspiration of Aquarius, and the adaptability of Gemini."

And, so, are you ready to wield the Ace of Swords? Strike forward now with conviction. Let the beautiful integrity of your soul be revealed in every action you take!

IN A READING . . .

ASTROLOGICAL INFLUENCE—AIR: There is a particular focus on the ideas, convictions and inspired actions of the subject during this time. Surrounding or clarifying cards may speak more on what direction the subject will be taking in their reality. Reflect upon what they are now ready to express and move forward with conviction.

UPRIGHT (DIRECT): The first of many inspired actions. Breakthrough. Affirming yourself. New mentality. Cutting to the point.

REVERSED (RETROGRADE): Reevaluating your truth. Holding back important words. Reflecting on your actions. Patiently observing. Waiting for the right moment to strike. Getting clear on what you stand for.

THE 2 OF SWORDS

MINOR ARCANA

Astrological Correlation: Moon in Libra

A woman crosses the second sword of the suit of air across her chest. She wears a blindfold, as if desperate to not allow her biased perceptions to intervene with her deliberation, assessment and final truth. She yearns for an inner harmony, so that her next step can be taken with clarity and reason. Do we not all seek clarity and reason at some point or another, my love?

In the 2 of Swords, there is a deep yearning to create internal balance, to align the conscious mind with the subconscious mind. Here, under the waning moon, we evaluate both sides of an equation that pertains to how we should best move forward in life. It is a time of stillness, deliberation and mental simulation. We simulate here what could be by connecting our reasoning with our heart. You are blindfolded here so that you may become more aware of what you feel rather than what you see. The loss of seeing what is allows us to decide from the more subtle realms of our inner being whose role is to return us to a state of inner harmony.

The 2 of Swords will ask of you to be able to hold duality. Can you extract the truth from both sides of whatever is mentally conflicting you? Are you able to recognize that what ultimately creates choice is not the challenge of what is "right" and "wrong," but the challenge of what is "right" and "right"? So, what is "right" for you? What is the truth that speaks from a deeper place in your heart? The truth that is most close to your heart always comes from a place of wholeness, not inner division. A truth from the heart is gentle and open. It holds no pressure to be right, it needs no convincing, for it is what it is. It does not weave elaborate stories around itself. A deep inner truth will always place you back into your heart. False truths have a tendency to keep one stuck and divided in the mind.

Astrologically, the 2 of Swords is correlated with the moon in Libra, representing the yearning for union with others and your inner self. Honor this struggle, my love. It is a process. It is temporary, as long as you allow yourself to take small steps in the direction of where your heart yearns. In the 2 of Swords, as described by the moon in Libra, there is a strong emotional need for reconnection with yourself that often parallels a strong need for reconnection with others. Understand here that the indecision you feel about something is the sign of a strong reasoning mind, not a weak one. To make a just, well-balanced decision is not easy. It is hardly ever simple. And what is most challenging is that regardless of what we choose, we will have consequences to deal with. We will have to face the repercussions of what we have chosen.

Here is where the wisdom of the heart must be found. In the stillness and in the deliberation, for it is ultimately the heart that speaks of our deepest inner truths. Allow me to share with you the two ways in which the heart most often speaks its truth. The two swords ultimately become one when you understand that they are two sides of the same coin. The truth of the heart is always revealed to you through what it yearns for and for what it regrets.

When you have truly followed your heart, when you have acted from that place where the soul resides, you will no longer yearn and you will no longer regret. For the heart that has chosen in accordance with itself experiences unity, harmony and inner peace. This is the ultimate destination of the 2 of Swords and it is a process that you must be willing to experience through action. You cannot know if you will continue to yearn or if you will ultimately regret before you have taken action. You must be willing to experience these faces of the heart that ache, that feel incomplete, that desperately seek for you to find unity within so that it may be shown to you without.

It is the experience of yearning and regret that allows the heart to come closer to its center. Be blindfolded to your logic and intellect, for just this one still moment, so that the heart may inspire within you actions that will bring you closer to the harmony you seek. When you reason well, you will find that the actions you take are deliberate, purposeful and always result in greater clarity, not more confusion. Remember that the heart is gentle, tentative, feeling. It moves forward with complete awareness of its own truth. Actions born out of chaos can only create more chaos. Actions born out of the inner harmony that can be found within chaos will always steer you toward calmer waters. Let the mind communicate often with the heart.

And allow the moon in Libra of this card to remind you that the division you may witness in your external circumstances and in your relationships always correlates with a mind that is striving for balance within. A lack of inner peace will always manifest itself as emotional distress in relationships, for it is always in our encounters with the other that our subconscious imbalances are reflected back to us clearly. You are blindfolded here to help you resist the temptation of solely judging the world around you. Indeed, it is tempting to convict something outside of you as the culprit of your own disharmony, your lack of peace.

You are asked here the difficult task of resisting the projection of your own emotional discord onto the people that are highlighting it to you. Try as you might, you will never find unity within by casting judgment and dividing yourself from the people around you. If you sense imbalance in your relationships, first look within to gauge why you have put gold on the scales in exchange of another's wool. Balancing the dynamics of your relationships requires great intuition, it is not one size fits all. There is no point in offering a ton of gold to someone who finds more pleasure in a blanket of wool. It is not that they are not appreciating you, it is you who are failing them in their core needs.

It is in the 2 of Swords and its correlation with the moon in Libra where you will become extremely emotionally aware of your compatibility with everything and everyone in your external reality. When you are experiencing an inability to provide for what is required in a particular dynamic, it is time to find the heart again, to turn the discerning gaze inward instead of projecting blame outward. For the actions that truly come from the heart are never experienced with "not getting enough in return." The heart simply does not act with expectation for the pleasure is found in the action itself.

If you are unable to act from this place, you should not be questioning if something outside of you loves you or not. You should be questioning if you truly love that which you are taking issue with. This is not a judgment to place upon yourself—to judge yourself for not being able to love something or someone—but you must be willing to face that your heart is yearning for something or someone that it can give to without obligation. You owe this both to yourself and to the world around you.

In the 2 of Swords, you will discover the true subtleties of balance and justice. Recognize that you would not be indecisive if reasonable arguments couldn't be found on both sides of the equation. This is the art of fine-tuning the heart. The reasoning of the heart requires time, patience and compassion. Of taking action a little here, and a little there . . . making time for stillness so that you may better understand where your heart settles. Of course, there are times in this journey where we are not afforded the luxury of testing out both swords, of testing the weight of what part of ourselves we believe more.

Remember the little steps for they have little consequences. Balance is not found in extremes for extreme actions will always result in extreme repercussions. Yet, sometimes it is only through these extreme repercussions that we are hit hard enough to face ourselves. Extreme actions have a tendency to manifest when you carry with you a mind that projects blame and injustice onto everything outside of you and to nothing within you. Oh, and how quickly the mind can come to justice when it is condemning the other! How quickly, rashly and extremely it can behave when it can bypass the consultation within! Heed caution, my love, the harshest judgments you cast outside of you will always stare back at you in the reflective waters of your own subconscious. Self-righteousness is the furthest you can be from internal and relational harmony in life.

If you truly seek harmony, be willing to not always be right. A heart that is unforgiving and unyielding cannot make others feel seen and heard and, therefore, cannot deliver fair judgments. Whether it is with yourself or another, listen with the heart and then act with reason. Oh, how much easier life becomes, my love.

IN A READING . . .

ASTROLOGICAL INFLUENCE—MOON IN LIBRA: The subject's intuitive sense of balance in their life and their relationships is brought into focus. Reflect upon where the subject feels that they are weighing the pros and cons of committing in a certain direction. Surrounding or clarifying cards may give more information as to what in the subject's life is currently bringing up division within that is ready to be resolved.

UPRIGHT (DIRECT): Careful deliberation. Bringing an unbiased, objective and well-reasoned approach to a certain situation. Balancing the mind and the heart. Coming to a final verdict on something and on how you feel.

REVERSED (RETROGRADE): Weighing the pros and cons of something. Deep reflection. Reevaluating what feels balanced in your life. Needing more time to come to a balanced decision. Reading into the subtext of something. Becoming aware of unspoken agreements. Reevaluating people-pleasing tendencies.

THE 3 OF SWORDS

MINOR ARCANA

Astrological Correlation: Saturn in Libra

A rain descends and our hearts become heavy. You won't have to look far to find the third sword of the suit of air for it is lodged in the heart. There is a point in our journeys where our heart just . . . breaks. An inspired action somehow leads us to suffering. Our self-criticisms and the criticisms of others just get to us. A vulnerable part of us is pierced.

The 3 of Swords is pain. In all of its forms and its expressions, it gnaws at the heart with everything that could have been, and should have been, and would have been . . . if only. If only what? If only we had nothing to steer us toward what is truly best for us. Alas, the universe loves you too much to leave you in perpetual suffering. The Band-Aid must come off. We learn not to touch the hot stove by touching the hot stove.

The 3 of Swords is astrologically correlated with Saturn in Libra and you cannot avoid the karmic element of Saturn in this part of your journey, my love. Wherever Saturn goes, harsh lessons are taught and, in Justice-bound Libra, it is here where we receive perfect karmic compensation for exactly what we have done.

There are certain lessons that can only be taught through pain. Pain and suffering forces the development of self-knowledge. It is easy to witness those who never face their pain know very little about themselves. And they who know nothing of themselves cannot hope to change their circumstance. And can you blame those who avoid their pain? Who wants to suffer, my love? Is not the greatest knowledge the knowledge of how to end our suffering? How many of our actions are driven by the desire to just avoid pain? Yet, the 3 of Swords is the karmic accumulation of all the pain we have been attempting to avoid.

It comes up now to be confronted directly in front of us as a mirror (Libra). In our relationships and in our external circumstances, it must finally be dealt with. A blessing in disguise, to experience this grand purging. The release of all that which has been causing you suffering without your conscious awareness. Hidden blockages here are exposed and held up to the light of truth. The profound understanding of self that the 3 of Swords always results in allows us to truly overcome pain, to truly heal by confronting the source of our suffering.

Heartbreak is rarely the result of a single event. It is a heart that is saying, "Enough, enough, enough." It is a heart that has weathered the same pain again and again, possibly beyond lifetimes, and, finally, cannot hold the same burden much longer. Libra is a sign that rules all forms of contracts and agreements and, in the Libra-ruled 3 of Swords, there is a cutting of cords from that which has continuously been a source of pain in your life. For, surely, you do not deserve this pain? This rejection? This, for whatever reason, blockage in the attempt at following your heart's desires?

Heed this from a fellow soul that has suffered: Be thankful for the pain that strikes in one blow. Its sharpness allows it to often be addressed directly. It is the pain that slides in slowly, just enough for you to care, but not enough for you to do anything about it, that slowly kills the soul. Confront that which wounds you, my love. Better to feel the sting of the antidote than to suffer with the poison from that which you avoid. Pain is best worked through, not avoided. Otherwise, the mind tends to develop extremely intelligent ways to keep you from feeling that pain.

We will hurt, but we will heal. Recognize that all pain brings knowledge. What lessons will you take from that which causes you suffering in this life? How you respond to your pain will determine whether you move toward love and joy—or toward the avoidance of pain. These are not the same paths in life. The person that remains open to love and joy remains open. They do not allow the words and actions of the past to scar their heart and disable them from union with others and the world around them. The heart that heals continues to hope. Remember, a heart that can break is a tender one. Beware of the heart that is frozen, numbed, to avoid pain it has learned to avoid love.

The association with Saturn in Libra in this card brings focus to our karmic contracts in this life. Graduating from the toxic binding agreements between you and others in this life will always come with a release of pain. The 3 of Swords can represent, at times, the failure of an attempted union along our journey, where the pattern of certain relationship dynamics (Libra) that no longer serve us (Saturn) finally deals our ego a heavy blow. And our ego must be dealt a heavy blow, my love, if we are to truly change our ways.

Nothing forces us to deal with our own personal insecurities more than rejection. It is not the rejection so much that destroys us, it is the beliefs we form around it that deals the most damage to our heart. An incompatible partner turns into "I am unlovable." A sour marriage turns into "I will never marry again." A harsh review of our art turns into "I knew I was kidding myself." These beliefs are a maladaptive attempt from the mind to protect the heart. Yet, all it is protecting the heart from is the chance to heal and to be loved in its most authentic expression. Whether we like it or not, pain is what matures the heart and soul.

Saturn in Libra disciplines our desire for union by forcing us to gain a higher understanding of our individual self. To exercise no restraint or discernment (Saturn) in your dealings with others (Libra) is to lack respect for your own heart. Yet, to guard yourself against the slightest showing of any weakness and vulnerability is to isolate yourself from all who would love to love you, my love. Remember, no matter the storms that your heart weathers in this life, your heart can only ever be deepened by pain. A heart that has chosen still to love in the face of so much suffering and rejection is powerful. We do not enter this world with the inherent capacity to love deeply. We learn to truly love in this life through developing compassion, forgiveness and understanding.

Does this mean you should let people hurt you as much as they like? No, but you also must understand that even the things that you love deeply in this life will still cause you pain. Who and what is worth that suffering? Who and what will you allow to deepen your heart? For the heart that has suffered, in the end, has the capacity to receive the most love, for it appreciates so little so much. And, so, welcome that pain, the gratitude later will have been worth it all. Love, love, love, my love . . . and learn.

IN A READING . . .

ASTROLOGICAL INFLUENCE—SATURN IN LIBRA: The subject's pains of the heart caused by the rejections and actions of others and themselves are brought into focus. Reflect upon the accumulative pain caused by certain actions or patterns of thinking that are now ready to be acknowledged and released.

UPRIGHT (DIRECT): Working through heartbreak and rejection. Processing deep-seated insecurities. Pain that heals and teaches a powerful lesson. Bringing maturity and discernment to the heart. Ending the cycle of an imbalanced relationship dynamic with yourself and others.

REVERSED (RETROGRADE): Old pains of the heart reemerging to be healed. Reevaluating your inner fears of rejection and abandonment. Having to learn the same lesson a final time. Finally addressing the core wounds of your heart. Building inner strength, boundaries and discipline. No longer tolerating what continues to hurt you.

THE 4 OF SWORDS

MINOR ARCANA

Astrological Correlation: Jupiter in Libra

In the suit of swords, the suit of action, we have instead found inaction. How could this be? Should we not be taking inspired action? Should we not be moving toward everything we desire? How could it be, in the swirling winds of this journey through the element of air, that we find the fourth sword in a place of rest, that we stumble upon a sleeping knight? Yet, the choice to not act is still a very important and inspired action. To be able to recognize our limited knowledge from our current perspective and to desire a kind of recalibration.

This is the 4 of Swords, the part of your journey where you develop the wisdom of peaceful deliberation, of creating space from the aforementioned swirling winds of life and focus your attention on reconnecting with your inner truth. Correlated with Jupiter in the sign of Libra, the 4 of Swords brings an expansion of consciousness through the experience of inner harmony.

The scene of the 4 of Swords is one of peace and tranquility. The figure is not arrogantly holding onto their sword, instead they acknowledge their imperfection through the surrender of prayer. You cannot always know what to do and how to do it—and to think you do is to be sure that you will receive humility before anything else you truly desire in this life. When the 4 of Swords presents itself to you along your journey, it is time to recognize the importance of rest and finding solace in that which expands your perspective (Jupiter). This is why the setting of a church is depicted in this card, a holy sanctuary where one can be away from the actions, words and influences of the chaotic world that surrounds. It is time to heed a higher wisdom.

The presence of Jupiter in Libra here emphasizes finding connection with an individual who can bestow spiritual illumination. A counselor, a trusted guide or another individual that brings a peace of mind could be necessary to accompany the contemplation, reflection and isolation that otherwise characterizes this part of your journey. It could very well be the instruction of your own inner teacher.

Inaction is not always the most exhilarating part of life, but it is a necessary step in bringing all karma (Jupiter) to a halt. Destructive patterns of behavior are destructive because they are patterns. They repeat and repeat, and are only interrupted by significant periods of time spent in reflection. We must, at times, be ready to rehabilitate ourselves from ways of being that disorient us from a clear mind. A clear mind is needed to take action clearly.

Time spent in the peaceful sanctuary of the 4 of Swords allows a natural process of rebalancing forces to work on our mentality. The halting of previous karma allows you a blank slate from which to work. When you rise again—and you will—your inspired actions will come from a higher awareness as opposed to the old ways of being, thinking and doing that drove you into respite in the first place.

Honor your temporary reprieve from the world and absorb knowledge in your silence. Listen within you for when you are ready to reengage with life again in a new way. There is only so much knowledge you can gain while shielding yourself from the external influences of life. Eventually, you must be ready to practice what you have preached and return to the active parts of your life with a newfound understanding. So, enjoy the solace of prayer for a little while here, my love, I'll be waiting for you outside. Goodness, perhaps what you need is a reprieve from the sound of my own voice.

IN A READING . . .

ASTROLOGICAL INFLUENCE—JUPITER IN LIBRA: The subject's purposeful inaction and harmony through retreating is brought into focus. Reflect upon where there is the opportunity in the subject's life to gain a higher perspective and wisdom by creating space from that which causes distress.

UPRIGHT (DIRECT): Rest and rejuvenation. A time of peace that brings clarity. Expanding beyond previously-held perspectives. Choosing not to act rashly. Allowing peace to find you right here instead of chasing it somewhere else. Temporary pause and surrender that heals worries about the future.

REVERSED (RETROGRADE): Investigating the source of your inner restlessness. Requiring an expert opinion. Resolving volatile moods. Being forced to rest and retreat. Needing a new foundation in order to think clearly. Committing to bringing back your inner peace. Focusing on your mental health. Temporary isolation that brings newfound understanding.

THE 5 OF SWORDS

MINOR ARCANA

Astrological Correlation: Venus in Aquarius

The sky almost looks like it would be clear if not for the gashes of gray clouds that linger above. And there, up ahead, the fifth sword clanks to the ground at the conclusion of some duel. Prides have been wounded. The fallen swords indicate disappointment and defeat. Actions, ideas and words have seemingly failed to achieve what they were meant to achieve. We have given up on something here, too disheartened by our "failed" actions in the face of our enemies. Most of the time, that which brings us the deepest sense of defeat is actually the enemy that is within us.

In the 5 of Swords, you will experience the first visceral resistance to you moving forward in life. It is a resistance that both comes from within and comes from without. It is doubt in all of its forms. A part of us pushes toward victory and another belittles us, questions us, reduces us back to where we arose from. Why? Why do we punish our own actions toward self-realization so severely? Does not the world resist you enough already? Often, the resistance we experience in our external environment only reaffirms where we have already accepted defeat within ourselves.

It is in the inner and external skirmishes of the 5 of Swords where we give up on the creative projects that mean so much to us. It is in the beating down of our own self-confidence that we allow the first "No" to our greatest dreams to be our last. Do anything but give up on yourself in this life, my love. Of course, we cannot always be fighting and resisting every tide of the universe, we must choose our battles. Yet, a battle for your right to experience the inspirations of your heart is always worth fighting. To let the doubts of yourself or others dictate your own journey of self-discovery is to sap all of the joy of personal victory from your soul.

Having accepted defeat in the battle for yourself, you will only come to win the battles of others. You will be detached from the victories you celebrate, for the greater inspiration and meaning of your life has been "doubted" out of you. Affirm, "I will never walk away from the path of my highest truth. I will never allow doubt and personal insecurity sabotage what truly matters to my heart and soul." The defeat you feel, the disappointment that minimizes your courage and self-worth, is an indicator that you are not satisfied with an outcome. That something matters to you, more than perhaps you even thought it did! Will you whittle away off the grand stage of your life? Will you really let that be your final punctuation?

A story that ends in defeat is not a complete story. It is unfinished. You are unfinished, my love. The 5 of Swords will bring up all that discouraged you, so that you cease to be discouraged moving forward in your path of self-knowledge. The victor that smiles as you walk away in this card is the voice within all of us that scoffs, "I knew you couldn't do it. I knew that was the extent of your power." And, so, we walk off, yet only five of the swords have been collected in this quest through the suit of ten cards, of ten swords of self-knowledge. To conclude here is to conclude without knowing the full story of who you are and what you are truly capable of. Turn around, my love, and face yourself. You are your enemy and you are your defender, if you so choose.

Halfway through the suit of swords, you come to the understanding that to wield the sword of your personal truth is at times a battle. You will need to prove yourself, yet the only "proving" that truly matters is to yourself. The mirrors in your life will only reflect back to you the quality of that inner conversation. The doubt you give yourself will only give others more reasons to doubt you. And doubt can be good. It is evidence of a soul that actually thinks before acting. To withstand a barrage of doubt is to truly know the strength of your inner truth.

Heed this, my love, in the duel for higher self-understanding: What is always true for you will always fight for you. It is a sword that you will always know how to pick back up. That which is not true for you is easily defeated by opposition and resistance. And so it should be, lest it bring more confusion to your path! Pay attention to what you cannot help but fight for and against, and separate your losses from the loss of your dream. Losses can only support your dream. The loss of a dream is a choice, not the result of life's circumstances.

The astrological correlation with Venus in Aquarius here brings to light the ultimate intention of the 5 of Swords: the inspiration (Aquarius) of newly found values (Venus). By coming to terms with the battles that we have won and lost, the 5 of Swords brings us to a higher consciousness (Aquarius) in our dealings with ourselves and those around us (Venus). We learn to make peace and detach ourselves from the personal insecurities that have been triggered in a particular situation, so that we can remember the true goal of our future.

The Aquarian aspect of the 5 of Swords emphasizes social unity, reconciliation and a setting aside of personal differences so that a collective vision can be attained. The presence of Venus in this scene of the conclusion of battle reminds us to hold a love for ourselves and those who oppose us. Despite our differences, we are all simply trying to discover our personal truth. We may not agree with everyone's choices, but what truly matters is that we are happy with the choices that we make. When you learn to value the bigger picture of life beyond the minor duels that come and go, Venus in Aquarius will bring you a love for all of mankind and the capacity to detach from your personal ego in order to realize your highest contribution to fellow humanity, which always runs parallel to the highest wishes you have for yourself.

So, let us move on from these petty scenes, my love, and remind ourselves of what we are really doing here, of the vast beauty and interconnectedness that we can find with one another in so many moments. Let us go onward and not turn away in defeat, for if you saw the full story, only excitement could glaze your face.

IN A READING . . .

ASTROLOGICAL INFLUENCE—VENUS IN AQUARIUS: The subject's ability to relate to others with a healthy detachment and take actions that bring unity and not further division is in focus. Reflect upon where conflicts within or externally are giving the opportunity to reconnect with a higher goal. Where are the thoughts and opinions of others sowing unnecessary doubt in the subject's mind?

UPRIGHT (DIRECT): Being tested by the thoughts, opinions and actions of others. Learning to be the bigger person. Calmly holding firm to your truth in the face of attack. Creating a healthy detachment from that which causes distress, doubt and antagonism.

REVERSED (RETROGRADE): Addressing inner conflict caused by doubts and fears. Momentarily withdrawing from distressing conflict. Resolving miscommunication in relationships. Reevaluating your opinions and perceptions of others. Reflecting upon and processing past conflicts. Resolving "black or white thinking" (i.e., only having enemies or perfect friends).

THE 6 OF SWORDS

MINOR ARCANA

Astrological Correlation: Mercury in Aquarius

And now, with the sixth sword among us, we find ourselves on a boat heading somewhere, somewhere we may not know, but with the hope that it will help bring a little more peace and joy. This is the 6 of Swords, the point in your journey where the thoughts of the mind align with the feeling of the heart and a great peace descends. We can finally move forward peacefully. There is still a sense of grief in the process and an uncertainty around if where we go next will truly bring us closer to our highest aspirations. Yet, we go anyway, because there is nothing left for us here where we have been. There is nothing left here that we already do not know.

It is in the 6 of Swords where we are taking action toward our greater good. The mother and child present in the card also symbolize the need to do that which will protect us from further harm and help move us toward a healthier emotional environment. The 6 of Swords of heavy thoughts, actions and words weigh down the boat, yet they do not deter its path, indicating that, at this point in your journey, what you have decided has not been taken lightly. There has been heavy deliberation and many reasons as to why the path you are now choosing is the best course of action moving forward. Sometimes, it is quite simply because, for whatever reason, you have no other choice. You have no other choice but to take the risk that something better awaits you at the end of your voyage.

The sixth sword of inspired actions is the act of transition. In the 6 of Swords, you are in transit. There is nothing behind you and you can only guess at what may be ahead. Yet, you must press on, you must trust that greater forces will help move you forward, even when you don't have the energy or the resolve. Your willpower, my love, is an inexhaustible gift. The man on the gondola is using only a wand, the principle of attention and focus, to move all the weight of the boat forward.

There are times where you will be able to focus on nothing else but the journey of moving forward. The future will be too uncertain, the past too burdensome and you will have to continuously direct your attention to the voyage at hand. And the voyage of the 6 of Swords can, at times, feel like a deathly limbo. The card itself conjures up images of the River Styx in Greek mythology, the river that created a border between the world of the living and the world of the dead. Can you find peace within the process of transition, my love? Where you are too far to reap the rewards of where you were and too far to reap the rewards of where you will be? Where you must source a deep trust, surrender and willpower from within yourself, to keep yourself carrying forward toward a higher wish and dream?

You cannot take back past actions, but you can use them as momentum toward your newfound understanding of yourself and your inner truth. And, at no other point in your journey will you experience more of the haunting thoughts of regret than in the voyage of the 6 of Swords. What would the souls that are carried on the River Styx from the world of the living to the realms of the dead think about along that journey, my love? Would they think about everything they wish they did or did not do? Perhaps, it is the hope that in their next life those wishes could be fulfilled.

And here you are living, my love, with a chance to fulfill what has not yet been fulfilled! On this boat now, contemplate if you would regret moving forward toward your wish more or never having taken the journey itself. With the 6 Swords loaded onto this boat, you can be sure that even if your journey brings you nothing else, it will bring you the invaluable gift of self-knowledge. To understand on a deeper level why you think and act in the ways that you do. To gain a greater understanding as to why you have had to experience everything that you have experienced up until this point.

To take the journey of the 6 of Swords is to seek out a greater context for your pain, to not let the fear of regret paralyze you from fulfilling the totality of your journey. Though the journey may be long and uncertain, look at the still waters that surround you, my love. What do you really have to fear? If you were really so lost and heading toward the wrong path, don't you think a little more chaos would surround you? Don't you think an insufferable storm would and could swipe you off your little boat at any moment? Yet, stillness surrounds, my love. Yet, the only reason you are moving toward a greater peace is because you are already experiencing that greater peace. Don't you think the universe has an endless arsenal of ways to move your little boat where it requires to be moved? Yet, you are on this boat now, wading, moving, albeit slowly. There is no immediate threat to your security.

And, so, you must trust, my love, that you are moving away from chaos, not toward it. Trust yourself, trust those six swords, those multiple reasons that stand up firm in the movement of your vessel. Though you may feel fragile and vulnerable, never has your will been stronger. A current still pushes you onward.

Astrologically, the 6 of Swords is connected to Mercury in Aquarius, which brings our attention to the thoughts, ideas and actions that are inspiring a deeper connectedness to the world at large. Though the 6 of Swords is often moving away from something, it is only with the intention that beyond the horizon lies many opportunities to fulfill your hopes and dreams.

IN A READING . . .

ASTROLOGICAL INFLUENCE—MERCURY IN AQUARIUS: The subject's focus and attention is on the fulfillment of a higher aspiration that will bring freedom, liberation and detachment from wounds of the past.

UPRIGHT (DIRECT): Detaching from hurtful, isolating or oppressive situations. Taking action from the inner peace of the heart. Being in a significant transition. Moving toward new freedoms and possibilities. Pursuing a like-minded community. Trusting that there are "others out there like you."

REVERSED (RETROGRADE): Contemplating the need for a significant life transition. Resolving doubts and fears about moving forward. A boat that for now is still anchored to the bay. Gaining more information before setting sail. A deep inner spiritual journey. Being afraid of your own freedom.

THE 7 OF SWORDS

MINOR ARCANA

Astrological Correlation: Moon in Aquarius

Be careful not to draw attention to us! Stealth and strategy are the games of this part of your journey. Outwit or be outwitted! There comes a point in your journey where you may be faced with a moral dilemma, when honesty and integrity conflict with getting what it is you think you want. Oh, how the lines blur in our road toward self-realization! Why do we feel the need to deceive? It is often to accomplish something that we otherwise would not be able to accomplish by being completely transparent.

The 7 of Swords represents these games of deception. Deception itself is not your enemy. Any strategy will always involve some form of deception, simply through the fact that the first step is put in place to allow the final step to occur. If we were more honest with ourselves, we would come to realize how much we actually deceive ourselves and those around us in order to take action toward what we truly desire.

Deception is not your enemy. What you must keep in mind, however, is if your strategy is indeed taking you closer to your true goal or further away. Sometimes, it is we who will get caught in the deceptive webs we weave and, instead of playing the field around us, we end up only playing ourselves. Self-deception runs rife when you consciously or subconsciously hide information from yourself, when you choose to ignore the presence of damning information or evidence that would expose the futility of your behavior. And, yet, powerful self-understanding is always gained when we come to terms with our own self-deception, when we dare to confront our own denial.

Notice, my love, the figure up ahead that is whisking away, holding stolen swords, representing the possession of knowledge that others do not have. It is a powerful and precarious place to be to know what others do not yet know. The 7 of Swords is an omen to use your knowledge wisely and to remain faithful to the overriding goal of your plans. Be wary of getting lost along your way toward your personal victories. Remember that though many things in life may be a means to an end, do not lose sight of the nobility of that end, of remaining true to who you really are. In fact, the only souls that are truly able to use deception are those who remain true to who they are, for only the deeply self-knowing can truly discern what is a hired truth and what remains eternally true for them.

What truths are you hiring, my love? Is it that you are indeed the most renowned dancer even though you have only just attended your first class? Or is it that you are actually someone who suddenly cares about meditation being a part of your daily life? The 7 of Swords is the act of faking it until we make it, of blurring fantasy with reality so that we can progress and succeed in ways that we otherwise wouldn't allow ourselves to. I must remind you, however, that illusions can only serve you if you recognize them to be illusions.

Be aware that any success or momentum you have achieved through the art of deception is borrowed. It is not yours to keep because, in a sense, you have stolen it. Understand that, at some point or another, unless you are able to overcome the glamour of the successes you have gained and remember your integral objective, what you have temporarily hired must eventually be taken back from you. Deception of yourself or others must always serve a higher inner truth. It must remain under the instruction of a personal aspiration that will do good for you and the world around you.

You must consent to the understanding that what you take as a result of being under a veil will be taken from you once that veil is lifted. What is not taken from you once your veil has been lifted was never gained as a result of that veil—you gained it through your authentic expression. And what a beautiful surprise that can be, my love. To recognize that the deceiving dances we enact toward our true desires, in the end, were perhaps not as necessary as we had previously imagined.

The 7 of Swords is connected to the astrological placement of the moon in Aquarius, where the instinctual and intuitive (Moon) part of one's nature is utilized for a more advanced objective (Aquarius). In essence, this speaks on the 7 of Swords as premeditated action. Actions and responses to life that are not the result of emotional instinct, but calculated to achieve a particular goal. Through the moon in Aquarius, it is impossible to not become truly consciously aware of the motives and thoughts driving our actions when we are presented with this part of our journey. It is a chance to assess the integrity of your conscience.

Are you aware of the personal strategies that are playing out in your reality? This is why the 7 of Swords has often been associated with the act of procrastination, where a strategy of self-deception and denial is put in place so that we avoid having to confront the deeper fear that is at the source of our behavior. Remembering the moon in Aquarius here, your subconscious mind wants to protect you, my love. It will weave elaborate stories to justify what is actually futile, irrational and nonstrategic behavior.

And how easily we fall into our own traps—and we must! For how else would we become aware of how we play against ourselves. Indeed, we all have an inner thief whose mental tricks we fall for every now and then. There is no removing this thief in your own mind, they still serve a purpose in allowing you to gain self-knowledge by wearing different guises and false identities. You must instead learn to beat your inner thief at their own game. This little thief will steal your faith in yourself just before the arrival of great success. They will whisper to you the need to have an upper hand in every situation you partake in, for showing up in your authentic expression is (according to your inner thief) just not enough. For "Who do you really think you are?" And how could someone like you be deserving of success? And how preposterous that anyone would like you if you took off your guise and showed who you really are? Yet, these are all the sabotaging words of the inner thief that carries five swords of "reasons why you're stupid" and leaves the swords of your higher truth behind.

Try as you might to lie to yourself, my love, your inner truth will always eventually reveal itself to you one way or another. Try to deceive the whole world and your inner thief will show up again to spite you. "What would happen if you dropped the act?" Maybe you would lose "everything," but still those two swords behind stand upright, as they always have and always will. For they are rightfully yours.

By dropping the act of false pretenses that have substituted for what is ultimately true for you, you will stop sabotaging your own success. You will finally confront what it is that you truly want and you will come to terms with how so much of how you were acting was an elaborate guise for that one true purpose. Yes, you may lose everything, my love, but you will gain one of the only things that makes life bearable—an honest and pure conscience.

IN A READING . . .

ASTROLOGICAL INFLUENCE—MOON IN AQUARIUS: The subject's capacity to strategically achieve their objectives is in focus. Reflect upon where the subject's inner fears of being "exposed," imposter syndrome and lack of self-trust could be sabotaging their authenticity.

UPRIGHT (DIRECT): Strategic action. Trying to cut corners. Being aware of hidden motives. Faking it until you make it. Goals that require planning well in advance.

REVERSED (RETROGRADE): Resolving imposter syndrome. Feeling "fake." Analyzing your own emotional patterns. Reevaluating your strategy and objectives. Accepting your "gray" morals. Exposing your self-sabotaging and procrastinating tendencies.

THE 8 OF SWORDS

MINOR ARCANA

Astrological Correlation: Jupiter in Gemini

And over there, the eighth sword on our journey toward your inner truth. It appears to be participating in a kind of cage that entraps that poor figure up ahead. Yet, what is really entrapping us here? For along the path of swords, the path of our own inspired thoughts, words and actions, it is only ever ourselves that could bring us into this position. And, so, we should be entrapped, for it serves a purpose in the unfolding of our self-knowledge and eventual self-realization. Just as cages can trap us, don't forget that they can also protect us from further harm. Indeed, they keep what is in from going out, but they also keep out what wants to trespass within.

In the 8 of Swords and its correlation with Jupiter in Gemini, it is actually knowledge and wisdom beyond all else that is trapping or protecting us in the "cage" of what we currently choose to believe. And, so, we should be skeptical. For does that philosophy truly fit for us? And do those ideas really represent us? It is this process of deliberation that often appears as mental paralysis and inaction.

It is a difficult position to be in, my love, because what you have always known has now got you stuck and you are still uncertain about adopting new beliefs or perspectives that could liberate you from your mental prison. Accept and affirm that what you have known has served you up until this point! Yet, to proceed further in your journey, you must be willing to commit to a new belief. To commit to a philosophy that cannot be unraveled through self-criticism, skepticism and self-judgment. A philosophy that, try as you might, cannot have its truth unraveled into lies, that still gives you a sense of hope, inspiration and motivation.

This is enough of a reason to take action in its direction. Trust that after the grueling mental interrogation represented by the 8 of Swords, you are more than well-equipped to make wise and discerning decisions in your life. There is no need to allow healthy mental consideration to rot into mental paralysis. Mental paralysis comes from an almost obsessive desire to prove yourself wrong, to quash your path of self-discovery. If you do not believe in yourself, my love, you will not find that belief unless you start believing in yourself. And how silly does that sound? But it's true when you understand the nature of belief. And the nature of belief is to be able to trust yourself in the absence of confirming evidence. You are never stuck; you are simply safe in what you've always known. Yet, that safety is not so fun now, is it?

It is not very fun to not be learning more about yourself, my love, to not be on a path of unfolding your ever-unfolding potential. Your "stuckness," your mental paralysis, is so because your old approaches are no longer working for you. It is you, not anyone else, that is no longer believing what you once believed. In the 8 of Swords is a showdown between you and your own ideas, words and actions. Where have your approaches in life become stale? That is, where have your actions only brought you more of the same, and the same, and then negligibly different, but then the same again. To be motivated, we must remain inspired by empowering beliefs.

In the 8 of Swords, you are ready to bring a new level of inspiration to your life. As much as the woman appears to be "entangled," from a Jupiterian perspective of expansion, she appears to be in a cocoon. A breakthrough is imminent. You are no longer able to work within the confines of old perspectives that now only sap your joy. Don't be fooled into thinking that it is simply the actions of others lending you this mental paralysis. We all have a part to play, my love, but you are the main character. You are in control of what you choose to believe, speak into existence and take inspired actions toward.

In the paralysis of the 8 of Swords, we can isolate ourselves, feeling too overwhelmed and judged and picked apart by others. Yet, it is you who is picking yourself apart the most. I promise you, there is nothing anyone else will ever be able to say or do that comes close to the mental cage of believing you are not destined to be happy. You are destined to be happy, fulfilled and self-actualized, my love, or else you would have never decided to enter this godforsaken realm.

Allow Jupiter in Gemini here to bring you the spiritual significance to all that which you have ever thought. Allow an expansion of your perspective by expanding your awareness of others that share your beliefs in the hopes and dreams that you have. Trust that "stuckness" can only ever arise from you choosing not to pursue the direction of greater self-knowledge. You will only ever limit yourself in this life by what you are not willing to learn. Learn, expand, understand. And take small steps in the direction of what you don't yet know.

You will not fail, my love. In the worst-case scenario, you'll know a little more about yourself and the world around you. And that's a little bit more than believing that "where you are is where you will always be." This is a sorry philosophy, that you should be sorry for. For there is too much in you to discover in this life, there is no limit to the extent of that which you can experience and know. Affirm "I am always being guided toward my highest path through my inspired actions and even more so when I am wrestling against that which I no longer choose to believe."

You are endlessly powerful, my love, so powerful that you are able to find resolution and the way out of the most complex mazes that the universe could ever construct for you in this life. The secret? It is that it begins with a shift in mentality, not a shift of action. A prison cell becomes more bearable when imagined and experienced as a hotel room. And a hotel room becomes unbearable when imagined and experienced as a prison cell.

Allow imaginative and optimistic Jupiter to expand and shift your mental perceptions (Gemini). And know that in the center of every storm, even mental, there is an eye of that storm. There is a stillness, a peace and a certainty that all is happening to serve your greater good. Your true, core beliefs will never entrap you, they will only further empower you.

Consider where you have allowed the mental projections and fears of others to define the cage that is your reality. Remembering the duality of Gemini here, be also ready to recognize where you have entrapped yourself in an echo chamber of what you want to believe, even though it is clearly not working for you. Your true beliefs will never need to shut out every other opinion in order to survive. In saying this, letting the beliefs of others completely constitute your reality is a recipe for dread. Let that be them. Let that not be you. And let us press on, for there is still so much to discover about yourself.

IN A READING . . .

ASTROLOGICAL INFLUENCE—JUPITER IN GEMINI: The subject's mental perceptions and limiting beliefs are called into question. Reflect upon where there is the opportunity to absorb new philosophies and ideas that will bring inspired action. Surrounding or clarifying cards may point to where in the subject's life they may be experiencing boredom, fear and feeling trapped.

UPRIGHT (DIRECT): Actions that yield the same results. Mental loops. Protecting yourself from the opinions and beliefs of others. Brainstorming a new perspective. Being aware of what is no longer working.

REVERSED (RETROGRADE): Eliminating toxic and limiting beliefs. Resolving fears and doubts that have led to mental paralysis. Reevaluating what you believe. Recognizing a dead-end situation. Seeking out a new, inspiring direction. Reaching your limit with something. Cleansing yourself of other people's thoughts, ideas and mental projections.

THE 9 OF SWORDS

MINOR ARCANA

Astrological Correlation: Mars in Gemini

How dare you awaken with such an unnecessary fright and disturb my sacred beauty sleep, my love? And what is that? You saw the ninth sword of our journey toward your eternal inner truth in a nightmare? Well, of course, that's where it is. For the ninth sword in the suit of swords is an illusion. It is not real. Well, not to the anxiety-inducing extent that you believe it to be. Look at you, all worked up for what? And now there's no hope that you'll get any more rest tonight. Neither will I it seems, for I cannot sleep near the possessed.

So, I might as well tell you about the 9 of Swords then. Anxiety, my love, anxiety. What you must first know is that our anxieties are fueled by attempting to have control over what we cannot currently control. And what makes some of the anxieties of the 9 of Swords so destructive is that what we believe we cannot control is our impending doom. The 9 of Swords viscerally illustrates what happens when we obsess over what we do not yet have or what we fear might happen to us—both mental complexes created by the survival instinct of our ego.

Astrologically in this card, with Mars always comes an element of aggression and in Gemini we are aggressively seeking an answer to something that would dispel the fear, worry and anxiety in our mind. The sharp mental pain of this card comes from the fact that just because we add more force doesn't mean we arrive at our answers more quickly. In fact, it only causes us to inevitably stray further and further away from the present moment and into the terrifying possibilities of our future—of which there are an endless supply.

In the language of Mars, in order to succeed we must be ready to conquer our enemies. And, so, in this card, we see the result of where we have conjured up our own mental phantasms, hidden enemies and demons that keep us restless and awake at night. We obsess over what another may be thinking, plotting or strategizing and we are desperate to ease the pain of a burning dilemma in our mind—usually a situation that is out of our current control.

What makes this tarot card so challenging is that the mental state it reflects is a painful road to nowhere. Mars in Gemini here easily translates to a war in our own mind and, though our ego-fueled mind will do its best to point the blame to everything and everyone outside of us, ultimately, we are the ones being our own enemy. Letting our mind run rampant with painful thoughts is self-destructive and it is what causes us to despise being "alone with our thoughts." When we fear being alone with our own thoughts, we should, because our thoughts have become our greatest enemies.

The 9 of Swords is about this psychological battle to restore the rightful dominion we have over our own mind, to temper the aggressive, survival instinct that is a mind out of control. It is a mind that has enslaved itself to a primal instinct of survival. You are not here to be enslaved by a primal instinct, my love, you are here to recognize your free will and capacity to be the conscious and self-loving host of your own mind. Once again, I do not sleep near the possessed. You are here to have the great power and drive of your survival instinct be under the instruction of the peace that always naturally flows through you.

Through the 9 of Swords, we learn to apply mental force not toward fulfilling what the ego is fighting for—"What will they say? Do they love me back? What if I fail? When will I be happy? What happens if I don't get the job?"—but instead toward what we can control. Trust that you are doing the best that you personally can right now. And your "best" can only be done when you are still operating from a place of being centered and content with your present reality. Work done anxiously will always give rise to more work to be anxious about. When will you choose to be the host of your own mind?

The Mars aspect of this card naturally brings up the importance of using our willpower to make our mind a tool for self-empowerment. When we focus on what we cannot control, we can only disempower ourselves and experience frustration. And we should be grateful for this, because it is through these painful states of being that we begin to take the necessary steps to restore our rightful place as the ruler of our own mind and, consequently, the ruler of our own life.

When you are centered in the driver's seat of your own mind and not falling for the aggressive fears produced by the survival instinct, you are able to better channel that aggression into a productive, sustaining and enjoyable progress in your reality. This is not about "slowing down and being less busy." This is not about spitting on the city and exiling yourself to a remote countryside. This is about actively mastering that which gives rise to the primal instinct, so that you can withstand every pressure of life and truly realize that you are always in control. It is the giving of your power away to the thoughts, inner demons and reactive actions that makes you feel otherwise.

How's that for a bedtime story, my love? It seems my sermon was enough to send you right back to sleep. It brings joy to my maternal instinct though my ego is stung. It is what it is. Let us sleep, then, and let us rise with the grace of dawn and let my thoughts and yours be illuminated by the one force that flows through us all.

IN A READING . . .

ASTROLOGICAL INFLUENCE—MARS IN GEMINI: The subject's anxieties and mental distortions are brought into focus. Where can nervous and erratic energy be channeled into productivity in the subject's life?

UPRIGHT (DIRECT): Opportunity to expose illusory fears. Feeling the pressure and urgency of something. Anxious thoughts and behavior. Catastrophizing the unknown. Opportunity to ease many worries at once. Obsessive and compulsive behavior that masks deeper fears.

REVERSED (RETROGRADE): Exploring the fears, anxieties and worries in your psyche. Regaining control over your own mind. Resolving psychological wounds from the past. "Waking up from a bad dream." A situation not as bad as you thought it would be. Ending a period of suffering in silence. Resolving where productivity turns into burnout.

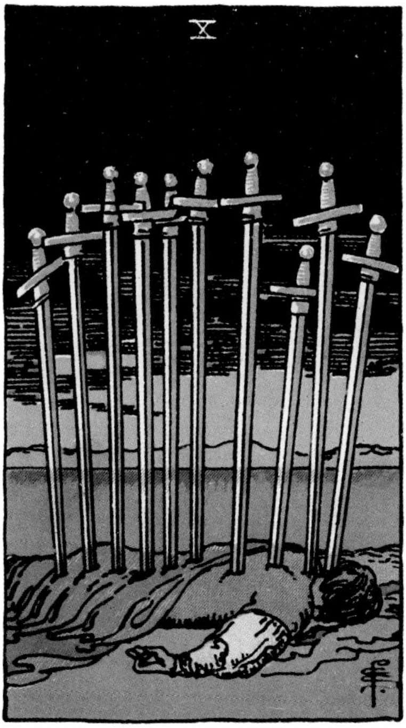

THE 10 OF SWORDS

MINOR ARCANA

Astrological Correlation: Sun in Gemini

Do not be horrified, my love. The soul has already moved on from the body. What we are seeing is no different than the shed skin of a snake. Did you expect to see something different at the end of our journey through the suit of air? I suppose I should have told you earlier that the discovery of a new truth marks the end of an old identity. Pay your respects to who you were, but in that form you are no longer.

The 10 of Swords, correlating with the sun in Gemini, enlightens us to the fact that the ideas we have about ourselves and who we are must significantly change throughout our life. Who we thought we were at age 7 will (hopefully) be different by the time we've reached 27. The catch is that for anything to undergo change, it must first be willing to "die."

The 10 of Swords is painful because it is the symbolic death of a previous version of ourselves that must occur if we are seeking to move into a new cycle of creation. By accepting where in our life the breath of spirit and inspiration no longer resides, we give ourselves the freedom to end a cycle and resurge with new life. Finally, we are able to drop an old identity that has served its purpose. We are able to breathe new life into our mind and welcome in a new cycle of creation.

Like death, this is a natural and essential process to our journey of self-discovery. And, truthfully, by the time you reach this point of your journey in the 10 of Swords, there is nothing to particularly end, for what has meant to end within has already died. It is only up to you now to catch up to the inspiration of your soul, who has already caught the winds of spirit toward a new purpose and a new expression of the one light.

Indeed, there are many correlations that the 10 of Swords has with the major Arcana card #13 Death. However, #13 Death speaks more to the deep psycho-spiritual process of inner transformation, whereas in the 10 of Swords, we have most likely already completed this process, and are at a place where we are ready to bring a decisive end to old ways of being.

The feeling of the 10 of Swords is like looking in the mirror and no longer recognizing your reflection. It is the feeling of doing, but not seeing the joy of your own spirit being reflected back to you. For your spirit has already moved on, a new identity has already begun to emerge. Are you willing to pursue the horizons of your ever-unfolding identity, my love? Are you willing to remain curious about yourself, even when you think you've had it all figured out? Do you want to know what is written on some of these swords that bring death to an old identity? Heed: "I know this is who I will always be."

With all of the love of the universe let me say: You know nothing, my love. You are an ever-evolving entity in which no labels or anything of the physical world will ever be able to perfectly categorize. To attach your self-definition entirely to your body and physical experience is to isolate yourself from the limitless potential of the limitless light that flows through you. Remember, my love, spirit changes matter. Matter will not change matter. You will see this in greater detail when we meet the fiendish one, #15 The Devil (page 218). It is your newfound awareness of self that will alter your identity to better match who you are becoming. A new physical experience may not change your old self-perceptions. If a florist does not feel worthy as a florist, he will not suddenly feel worthy by becoming a lawyer, for the primary source of this unworthiness was rooted in unworthiness, not the labels he attributed to it. And all forms of unworthiness arise from completely attaching ones (eternal) identity to (finite) matter.

Accept your ever-unfolding identity as an essence of spirit that informs the actions you take in this life. When you are operating from that essence, you will be guided toward the thoughts, words and actions that will help bring more of your unique light into physical expression. The changing of your physical reality is a byproduct of the powerful process depicted in the 10 of Swords—death and rebirth of identity.

And it is painful, my love. It is not easy to leave behind an old skin that is fueled by old beliefs and mental perceptions. Often, it is the mental processing and unraveling of false beliefs that is far more difficult than the physical changes we inevitably make in our lives. Set yourself free by committing to your ever-unfolding and multifaceted identity that is not sourced in your physical world. It is expressed in your physical world. Just as much as you are a body with a soul, you are a soul watching over your body. She who knows this does not suffer from the ten swords that will inevitably descend upon the flesh. For a new truth must arrive, for the beautiful expressions of your soul must continue to create anew!

Authenticity beckons you, my love. And there is no other way to discover a new level of our authenticity unless we are willing to be mentally back-stabbed by thoughts, ideas and beliefs that once used to serve as our truth. Oftentimes, these swords can also represent the words, opinions and actions of others that have served to construct a husk of who we never really were. They are not to blame; it is rare to stumble across those who recognize the eternal soul behind your body.

Here and now, the reference to the sun in Gemini beautifully illustrates the dawning of a new identity in our minds, one that will not be felled by the painful thoughts of your past, for you have learned from them and paid the price for that invaluable knowledge of self. Many fear the 10 of Swords for the degree of shock and instinctual defensiveness that this card evokes upon first glance, yet this is precisely its intention. Defensiveness almost always comes from the fragile ego that is trying to preserve an identity that has its roots in the physical world. The criticisms that cut you deeply do so because they attack the weakest parts of your identity and we should be thankful for them, for that sharp pain gives you the chance to heal those wounds that stifled the full expression of your personality.

It is in the 10 of Swords where we are finally able to let go of unfitting attachments and labels about ourselves and allow a deep process of self-transformation and evolution to occur. Indeed, when we finally come to accept this transformation of our identity, we feel nothing of the swords that once caused us so much pain and strife. For no longer is it our body that they pierce, but a skin that has been shed in the name of self-love.

Know that when this card appears, you are paying the highest mental pain for the highest level of self-understanding, clarity and truth. Nothing is wasted in death and you will see how what you have experienced has given you invaluable wisdom and the freedom to celebrate more of who you truly are without the baggage of old truths you no longer believe about yourself.

Look at you, my love, powerfully and boldly transforming yourself and your mind . . . and how much lighter and freer you will feel again. And how you will be reborn with the joy of a child, but with the increasing wisdom of a sage, again and again and again.

IN A READING . . .

ASTROLOGICAL INFLUENCE—SUN IN GEMINI: The subject may be becoming aware of another aspect of their identity that is conflicting with previous versions of themselves. Reflect upon where in the subject's life they may be experiencing a death of identity and the possibility to embark on a new journey of self-discovery. Surrounding or clarifying cards may speak to the area of life this is likely to be affected the most.

UPRIGHT (DIRECT): Death of identity. The final blow of an exhausting cycle. Solemn acceptance of circumstances. Full clarity and awareness. The truth that hurts then heals. Nowhere to go but to transform. Rebirth.

REVERSED (RETROGRADE): Finding the blessing in painful circumstances. Reflecting on who you no longer are. Resolving attachments to old ways of doing things. Receiving closure for unexpected circumstances. Letting go of deeply held resentments and painful beliefs. Clearing the way for an emerging new identity.

THE PAGE OF SWORDS

MINOR ARCANA: COURT CARD

Astrological Correlation: Air and Mercury

A youth practices against the unrelenting yet unresisting opponent of the wind in the distance. Here we are, in the vast plains of the Kingdom of Swords. Is it not entertaining to watch this Page of Swords, timid yet persevering in their actions? Trusting yet cautious?

Learn from this learning page, the joy of having a go. Their movements are light, tentative and uncommitting. There is a curiosity about "What could happen if I just . . .?" Oof! A little too much force and too little grace. They stumble to the ground, dusting themselves off and trying again. The Page of Swords has learned by doing. Every self-taught master has begun as a Page of Swords. Persistence and curiosity refine our abilities. The discipline of practice and the joy of practice. Sometimes they coexist, often they do not. Yet, still we learn, we mature, and what we once approached with a shakiness and uncertainty, eventually becomes second nature.

The Page of Swords is learning to wield the sword of ideas, words and actions. They are in the process of discovering their inner truth, by testing it out in their environment. Your inner Page of Swords, my love, is responsible for bringing a freshness of perspective to your life, to pique your curiosity and to allow you to trial life without the fear of punishing consequences. They bring the gift of light-heartedness and detachment, the ability to shift focus and attention to many things at once, for they must satisfy their inherent need for mental stimulation.

The combination of Mercury and the air element here creates a character that is primarily concerned with communication, information and the multifaceted possibilities of life. What is the first thing coming to your mind right now? What do you wish to say or do? Say it, do it, pursue it. Perhaps, greater self-knowledge awaits you on the other side.

Your approach may, at this stage, lack a level of refinement, yet that should not deter you from taking the first step. Remember the joy and discipline of practice. Your inner Page of Swords loves nothing more than the acquiring of new information and skills. What if you sent that message? Applied for that position? Read that book? Researched that topic? Just made a start somewhere?

Try not to hold any expectations here. And, here, now our lovable sword fighter has something to say, "The less you commit, the more quickly you will recover!" I believe they are just talking about their little skirmishes, yet a valid wisdom for much else in life too. Indeed, this little page is always looking to outmaneuver and outsmart their opponents. It is both their intelligence and their immaturity, for there will come a point where to advance any further in their self-knowledge, commitment will be necessary.

Maturity will eventually temper their flighty spirit, but for now they share with us the delight of a bird learning to fly. And they will fall, again and again, but look, already they are back up! Humble and playful they are, unaware of what a master they are already becoming. Let us take something from this too, my love, and throw ourselves at life every now and then like birds eager to fly for the first time.

IN A READING . . .

ASTROLOGICAL INFLUENCE—AIR AND MERCURY: The subject's curiosities, self-study and communications are in focus. Reflect upon where there is the opportunity to learn new information and express an exciting new idea.

UPRIGHT (DIRECT): New ideas. Playful communication. New field of interest. Being good on the first try. Following what mentally stimulates you.

REVERSED (RETROGRADE): Resuming or pausing learning something. Shift of priorities. Communication and opportunities from people in the past. Reevaluating your interests and preferences. Reviving your love of learning. Observing and studying someone you admire. Holding back saying something for fear of how it will be received.

THE KNIGHT OF SWORDS

MINOR ARCANA: COURT CARD

Astrological Correlation: Mars and Gemini

Your journey hastens, my love. There's little time to think, for so much is already moving. The Knight of Swords has a mission and there is nothing that you can say or do to deter his direct path toward his objective. Consequences will be dealt with later, for right now calls for swift and decisive action.

This knight combines the powers of Mars and Gemini to generate a powerful momentum forward. Whatever is meant to be done will be done quickly. There is no hesitation of mind here, and it is both this knight's talent and what often topples him off of his high-speed steed. The Knight of Swords operates on a momentum that can accomplish a lot quickly, but it cannot be sustained. Your inner Knight of Swords is responsible for the single-minded conquest of a particular task or goal. What matters is that it is done. What happens afterward is none of his business.

Mars in Gemini gives an insatiable restlessness to this knight and a primal desire toward all forms of conquest whether it be in the arena of love, business or the fulfillment of some personal truth. Hear him yell as he rides heroically into battle: "Don't wait for the mind to still before action. The mind is stilled by action!" There is a time and a place to wait patiently, and there is a time and a place where you must allow yourself to be taken in by the whirlwind passions of your heart.

Where the Page of Swords (page 205) danced back and forth in a testing and trialing manner, the Knight of Swords rushes in headfirst toward his most pertinent ambitions. The momentum that has been generated does not allow a change of direction to be likely at this time and recovering from a fall will not be easy. It is your inner Knight of Swords that seeks out the high risk for the high reward.

If not a single doubt could inflect itself upon your mind, what would you do next? Where would you go? The Knight of Swords, imbued by the powers of Mars in Gemini, thinks, speaks and acts with a great assertiveness and command over the entirety of his being. This is the fighter you would want to have for your cause. Not once would he question that which commands him, he only desires that those commands be fulfilled. The Knight of Swords is the protector of your word and will die for that which will ultimately bring you freedom.

Mars in Gemini does not take back what has been said and done. Every time you affirm in the direction of your personal truth, you have deployed a Knight of Swords out into the field of your reality. He will not relent until he comes into contact with that which will and must confirm the truth you have spoken. And, so, command him wisely, for your Knight of Swords will obey all commands without hesitation. Truly, this knight is the embodiment of the power of word. "Your will is my command!" he will yell before you are able to finish your sentence. He travels as fast as sound itself, for he is sound. He is the power of your affirmation. Affirm, my love, "I follow my words with assertive and decisive action! What I affirm will be confirmed! Nothing can intercept the power and speed of my word."

And, so, the relentlessness of the Knight of Swords will lead him to complete his mission or die trying. At times, he will be defeated by his own recklessness and lack of contemplation. And it will hurt, yet it will also stop the momentum toward any further damage. A fallen, burnt-out, unsuccessful or remorseful Knight of Swords is a safe Knight of Swords. The inability to go further in a particular course of action forces reflection, self-realization and course correction so that his passion can be steered onto the right path once again.

IN A READING . . .

ASTROLOGICAL INFLUENCE—MARS AND GEMINI: The subject's ability to act swiftly and decisively is in focus. Reflect upon where there is a sense of moving toward a specific objective in their life.

UPRIGHT (DIRECT): Following your word. Getting things done quickly. Fast movement forward. A clear and specific goal will be achieved. Running with your truth. Needing no further convincing.

REVERSED (RETROGRADE): Reevaluating your approach to a specific goal. Reassessing your objective. Running around too much. Temporary pause to catch your breath. Recovering from falling after moving too quickly. Repairing and optimizing things to run more smoothly.

THE QUEEN OF SWORDS

MINOR ARCANA: COURT CARD

Astrological Correlation: Moon and Libra

The Queen of the House of Swords approaches us, seeking to offer her wisdom to your journey. Notice how she assesses you with the eyes of a hawk and an owl. Not only does she possess the intelligence and highly developed mental faculties common to all her kin, she also carries with her the gift of intuition.

A profound wisdom emerges, my love, when you combine reason and intuition. It is a wisdom that allows your inner Queen of Swords to perceive reality accurately. To perceive reality accurately is to be able to perceive it coldly, not tinted by the colors of fleeting emotions or passions, or by the delusions of false promises and expectations. When we perceive a situation clearly, there is an internal balance that may even strike those around us as cold, unfeeling or heartless. True justice can only be delivered with a cold blade.

The Queen of Swords will be misunderstood in her life only because she understands the consciousness required in giving a balanced assessment of any given situation. Her sword is lifted toward divinity in complete submission to a sense of balance and justice that is above her own personal wishes and desires.

Unlike the King of Swords (page 214), her sword is positioned in a way that signifies the inherent power of her word and not its capacity to execute and accomplish. Her sword is lifted, but she gives no indication that it is required that she use it. In fact, it is her hand that extends further, displaying the grace that she holds, preferring to find resolution through the revelation of truth rather than through a display of brute force.

The Queen of Swords holds the weight of a cumbersome responsibility. She feels the weight of justice. She knows how even one action inspired from a clear and balanced assessment of reality can save a soul from a thousand actions taken from a false foundation of reality. There is a deep empathy in this, my love. Do you not see the pain in the eyes of this "unfeeling" queen? The weight of decisions made that have had no clear outcome of victory. Decisions that have not left anyone involved unscathed? Decisions where pain could only be balanced with another kind of pain?

The Queen of Swords carries with her a wisdom that can only come from pain—the pain that comes from choosing to see the truth and choosing not to see the truth. She translates all of this suffering into lived experience and profound wisdom. She knows better than anyone else that to bring back into balance what has become unbalanced, often what is required is a taking away of something. So attuned is she to her own responsibility in relation to every dynamic she finds herself in that the sight of something unfair or unbalanced cannot go unnoticed by this queen.

Your inner Queen of Swords knows when she is experiencing injustice. She does not need tangible evidence of this in her reality, her sense of justice is based on the inherent balance of all things. In fact, physical evidence is, oftentimes, the last kind of evidence that needs to appear in order for this part of you to confirm what you have been feeling all along.

The Queen of Swords is assigned the zodiac sign Libra, the scales of justice themselves. The Venusian sign of Libra again emphasizes the very human aspect of this queen, who has derived wisdom and insight from an understanding of forces between people, wisdom gained through understanding her relationships and the balancing of opposing wants and needs.

In line with the values associated with the planet Venus, the Queen of Swords perceives truth as something artful, graceful and beautiful, where resolution is simply a product of warring forces that have found harmony with one another. Her counterpart, the King of Swords (Saturn-ruled Aquarius), carries a far more disciplinary aspect in affirming the truth of a current situation that is disregarding of the personal values of those involved.

This heart of the Queen of Swords is her greatest gift and the bane in the delivery of her judgment. The more she allows her personal emotions to infiltrate the steely blade of truth and reason, the more she departs from her rightful throne as an avatar of justice and into the hissing winds of personal attack. The fury of a Queen of Swords singes not through its heat, but through its sheer ice.

If she lets her wrath go unchecked, her innate sense of balance may give in toward the need for personal retribution. Indeed, a vengeful Queen of Swords can be calculating and cruel. She represents your inner desire to "settle the score" and will tirelessly work to protect your reputation. And, so, respect her by respecting yourself, my love. In return, she will bless your relationships and endeavors with fairness and honesty of heart.

IN A READING . . .

ASTROLOGICAL INFLUENCE—MOON AND LIBRA: The subject's innate sense of balance, justice and righteousness is in focus. Reflect upon where there is the opportunity to trust the accuracy of your perspective.

UPRIGHT (DIRECT): Being a reliable source and witness. Powerful foresight. Being fair and just. Cutting through lies. Seeing everything for what it is. Maintaining your integrity and poise. A graceful victory. Getting to the heart of the matter. Being respected for your unbiased perspective. Calling out misbehavior.

REVERSED (RETROGRADE): Reevaluating your perception of a situation. Feeling "gaslit" or like your perspective was not honored. Investigating something further. Grace in defeat. Not feeling like you have the whole truth. Waiting for someone to show their true intentions or prove themselves.

THE KING OF SWORDS

MINOR ARCANA: COURT CARD

Astrological Correlation: Saturn and Aquarius

We have reached the King of the House of Swords. He does not offer the friendliest welcome, but do not take it personally, as his primary field of mastery is the mental plane of reality. Intellect, truth and achieving through direct communication is his specialty.

The King of Swords represents the aspect of you that is responsible for delegating, deciding and affirming the truth of who you are in this world. His approach is not bound by the subjective realms of emotion or the impulsivity of passion or desire. Fact, logic and a matter-of-factness is in control here, which allows you to make decisions on an objective view of your reality.

If anyone will teach you the art of detachment, it is the King of Swords. His only attachment is to that which represents his truth and integrity. Truth can be as cold as a sword, my love, and the King of Swords is prepared to act in accordance with that truth no matter the cost. His mind is unbendable and, though this lends to his stubbornness and inability to be moved by the subjectivity of others, this is also his strength.

The King of Swords is responsible for the inner truths you hold that should be unbendable. To hold your own truth with the same stoicism as the King of Swords will grant you one of the greatest gifts in developing your truth in this lifetime: the ability to trust yourself. To be able to trust how you think and what you do is an essential part of actualizing yourself in this life.

The King of Swords will fall on the sword of your truth. He is committed to what you personally believe. He will die for your perspective of yourself and the world around you. Not because he necessarily loves you or is moved by your plight, but because it is his duty to uphold what is true and just. Part of this responsibility entails the affirming of yourself against the thoughts, ideas and actions of others that may threaten the integrity of who you are. The King of Swords will coolly cut away that in your external environment which does not respect the truth of who you are.

When you seek it, the King of Swords will always offer you wise council and clarity in how to go about taking action in the direction of what is ultimately "right" and reasonable for you. Where you lack logic, a strong mental reasoning and boundaries between your truth and the truth of those around you, the King of Swords appears to bring order and clarity back into your life. He is precise and a master at execution. His final word is the final word, for it will always be signed with the permanency of wisdom and a well-deliberated truth. When he speaks, there is a resounding finality, a piercing answer to every nebulous problem. There is no confusion, hesitation or uncertainty. How could there be? When the King of Swords decides to finally speak, it is the final product of a vigorous mental simulation of every possibility. If the King of Swords is not speaking, he is thinking, simulating and processing. Though he would hate for you to say this about him, is it not warming to feel the presence of such a wise counselor and strategist at the beck and call of your destiny?

Is it not infinitely empowering that you have enlisted a servant of truth and perfect execution to assist in the cutting away of every illusion, distortion and deception that will ever threaten the unfolding path of your soul? The King of Swords holds the antidote to every confusion, every dark haze of the mind, every delusion—all of this falls to the cold and clean truth of his blade. These psychological distortions cannot contaminate his personal wisdom, for his wisdom was born from the provability of science and rational thought, not through our, at times, fallible feeling nature. Delusions of the mind can only grasp those that are easily swept away by the subjective tides of emotion and passion.

The King of Swords is the part of your nature that has sacrificed his own capacity for pleasure, euphoria and passion so that he may see your reality truthfully. For only when we are seeing things truthfully can we hope to gain any level of control over our reality. The counsel of the King of Swords comes from what he has seen before, not what he has felt before. He places a greater trust in the wisdom he has gained from the world, not the wisdom inherent to the soul.

A double-edged sword, this mind of probability and calculations that he holds in high-esteem, for what is also true is that not everything in this world is as it seems. Contained to only seeing, the King of Swords will miss what goes unseen and unsaid. The rigidity of his blade will, at times, deny him the foresight found only in intuition and the wisdom of the heart. His logic and detachment from the emotional realm can also deny him the capacity for intimate connections with others. Intimacy is formed through embracing the warm advances of other hearts, not by piercing them with the intellect.

Astrologically, the King of Swords is granted the Kingdom of Aquarius, the "fixed" air sign, which aptly speaks to his extreme intelligence and equally as extreme mental rigidity. Once the King of Swords has decided that he knows, there is no changing that knowing unless a more valid and provable argument can be presented to him. His Aquarian nature will reveal to you that he holds truth in very high regard, for his consciousness is geared toward deciding what is for the good of all rather than what is good for you or them.

By embracing your inner King of Swords, your actions and sense of the world will be imbued with the sociopolitical and scientific awareness contained within the sign of Aquarius. Genius, quick wit and the capacity to challenge the prevailing truths of yourself and the world around you will become available to you. The strong, consolidated truth of the King of Swords will always invite many who will seek to listen to him and seek his crystal-clear counsel, naturally allowing him to assume positions of leadership where his intellect and mastery of communication is on display.

Have I introduced this powerful avatar of the mind to you well enough, my love? Are you ready to work with him and seek his council through the many questions you will have along your journey? He is quite the character, generally serious but, at times, mysteriously humorous. He means well. Allow the King of Swords to fight for you with the power of a strong, reasoning mind. If you allow him, he will protect the sword of your truth with his life for it is your inner truth that gives him his life and purpose. He will speak upon your behalf as a clear mirror of your objective consciousness, but you must also take it upon yourself to know when he should speak or remain silent.

If you allow the King of Swords too much reign over your inner kingdom, you may find everything around you to grow cold and distant. Criticism, judgment and a general harshness on yourself and everything around you will replace the subjective pleasures and pains of the heart, and a cold numbness will bar anyone access to the tenderness of your soul. If you allow this king's rigidity to completely overtake you, a clinical order and predictability will replace the spontaneous, magical moments of life, and storms of mental clutter and overanalysis will take away the authenticity of the way you move through the world.

Take this wisdom, my love, in your dealings with this player. Be aware of what truth you are standing on, for, as I have said, the King of Swords will take that truth and build a kingdom out of it. As a loyal servant, he will do exactly as you say without a single error in your detail. Remember, the King of Swords always takes things literally. You will only have yourself to blame when you look around and realize that the truth you used to carve out your personal kingdom was never your truth at all. Yet, this is how your King of Swords builds his wisdom. Try not to criticize your endeavors too harshly.

Following a wrong truth that unravels itself into the realization of a deeper truth is nothing other than a profound blessing, and part of trusting yourself is recognizing that only by pursuing your "wrongness" will you ever hope to find what is ultimately "right" for you.

IN A READING . . .

ASTROLOGICAL INFLUENCE—SATURN AND AQUARIUS: The subject's mature intellect, their ability to stand in their authority and their highest truth is in focus. Reflect upon where there is the opportunity to step into a new level of authority using their ideas, words and strong convictions.

UPRIGHT (DIRECT): Taking action with cold, hard reason. Being respected for your truth, wisdom and counsel. Being more decisive and straightforward. Having a high position and noble duty. Leading important and difficult conversations. Having the answers that many are seeking.

REVERSED (RETROGRADE): Reevaluating the truth you have been standing on. Learning to value your intelligence and contribution to discussion. Having all the answers but withholding them. Needing to build more confidence in your writing and speaking. Learning to become more emotionally detached, yet firm and unbending in your position.

#15 ◆ THE DEVIL

MAJOR ARCANA

Astrological Correlation: Capricorn

Suddenly, the light dims and we find ourselves in some impenetrably dark chamber. There is the clink of chains, and the light of a burning torch illuminates a fiendish figure. A fiendish master of the naked man and woman beneath. You have reached the point in your journey where it is time to confront #15 The Devil.

Do not be afraid, it only feeds its insatiable appetite for power and control. And, what really is the devil? In order to even begin to understand this card, you must first be ready to swallow the difficult pill that, like every other major arcana archetype, #15 The Devil is a part of your nature. This is not some evil force that exists outside of you. Nothing can exist outside of the one that flows through us all, my love. Even the devil was once a part of the One. Even the devil is one of the expressions of the godly force that operates in all things.

Some have connected the devil to being the archetype of your shadow. That is, the darker subconscious persona within you that is the amalgamation of all of your most unbecoming traits, desires and characteristics. The shadow contains the vicious aspects of our subconscious human nature that are completely driven by base survival instincts. When left unintegrated or repressed by our conscious personality, our shadow personality can be extremely destructive to ourselves and the people around us. If we are able, however, to acknowledge this darker persona and give it instructions under the divine will and good of all, our shadow can become a deep and powerful reserve of vitality, material mastery, sexuality and creativity.

In this way, whether you like it or not, the devil does indeed exist within us all and plays a role in the sustaining power of the material world. Look around you at the natural world: Everything operates on its base instincts. Yet, due to our free will and conscious personality, we have the opportunity to improve the nature of all things, including our own. Isn't that powerful, my love?

And, so, in our journey toward self-realization, #15 The Devil is an essential archetype that represents the world of appearances (that is, the material world and the craft of manifestation itself). This is why the earth sign Capricorn is associated with this card. Capricorn deals with our path toward the attainment of wisdom and mastery over the material world. Capricorn is ruled by the planet Saturn, which also lends #15 The Devil an important connection with the karmic cycles of life. That is, the spiritual consequences for the actions we choose in this life and the patterns of behavior that trap us into re-creating old cycles of manifestation that no longer serve us. Capricorn is a sign characterized by its discipline, self-control and integrity, but these qualities are only developed as a result of mastery over its vices.

The same energy that #15 The Devil represents can both materialize worlds and destroy them. How will you use the power of manifestation in this life? Notice the reversed pentagram that actually covers the devil's third eye (that is, spiritual foresight). This is the same pentagram that represents perfect application of the forces of the universe in order to bring about manifestation. This is the entire premise of the path of pentacles, the suit of earth in the tarot. However, this pentagram is reversed, indicating that what gives rise to the malicious expressions of #15 The Devil is when the world of appearances (that is, the physical realm) is actually taken as the complete truth of reality.

To see things only for their appearance is to remain ignorant to their true nature. To perceive nothing but the physical manifestation of things is to inevitably fall to the delusion that you are powerless in this life. And feelings of powerlessness will always transform in either two ways: the desire to overpower others or the desire to awaken your true power by seeing beyond the world of appearances. To put it simply, to see beyond the world of appearances is to see beyond the five senses, to no longer be enslaved by the animalistic forces of gluttony and lust, represented by the animal tails of grapes and fire that are pictured in this card, respectively. Heed this to dispel many worldly delusions all at once: Matter does not create matter. Spirit creates matter.

The problem with #15 The Devil is that spirit has been taken entirely out of the equation of manifestation. The divine force that grants us love, compassion, good will, peace and joy is no longer being woven into the material world. You can imagine now that this subversion in the cycle of manifestation is what gives rise to man's most sinister expressions and creations.

So, when the devil presents itself along your journey, my love, there is a focus being placed on seeing beyond the world of appearances and metaphorically "breaking out of the matrix." Pay close attention to where you are sourcing knowledge from. Return to the spiritual knowledge and personal beliefs that align you with love and compassion for yourself and every being on this planet. A world of matter without spirit is a deeply distorted and divided one. Notice where you are isolating yourself and holding deep-harboring emotions that demonize and cause division in the things around you.

The seven deadly sins are directly linked to this card. Where are expressions of lust, gluttony, greed, sloth, wrath, envy and pride dominating your life? And, why, my love? Give yourself the grace to penetrate what your vices are seeking to protect you from. They are usually protecting you from facing what you must face in order to establish true power in your life. They are usually offering you a short-lived shortcut to the fulfillment that you truly seek.

This is why #15 The Devil has often been associated with the idea of temptation, for it is deeply tempting to succumb to the rush of power that the aforementioned vices bring. Yet, the devil never gives without taking. And what it takes is far more valuable than the power you are temporarily hiring. For a rush of momentary power and control, you have shackled yourself to a world of matter without spirit. You have abandoned the source of your own power and, thus, the external world of appearances will continue to have power and influence over you.

This is the complete opposite (remembering the reversed pentacle) of the divine law of manifestation, of the idea that it is you who always has a power over your external experiences in this life. Temptations will always cheat you; they offer a power external to you that will never match the force of creation that flows through you. And, still, we should not judge ourselves for falling for temptations. This is part of the journey for all of us in this material realm. We live and we learn. As we go off onto our own paths, we inevitably come to discern better what leads us astray and what leads us back home to the heart.

Passing through the trials of the #15 The Devil is an essential process toward wielding the power you will gain in this life with responsibility. Recognize that #15 The Devil is the creator and breaker of chains, for to become aware of its influence upon your life is to liberate yourself from all that which has previously kept you in bondage. And that which keeps us in bondage keeps us powerless in manifesting what we truly desire.

You are not here to be powerless, my love. You are not here to be enslaved by the world of appearances. You are here to penetrate the mysteries of all that is "seen" so that you may discover for yourself the truth of who you are and the truth of what lies in your heart. You are here to bring spirit into matter, so that all can benefit from the grace only you could have brought into this world. Do not let anything or anyone tell you to disown the wisdom of your heart. Do not let anything or anyone shackle you to beliefs that do not stem from the deepest vibrations of your soul.

Heed that with every word you read, with everything that will enter your sensory perception in this life: That which can tell you what to do has control over you. Hear what people say to you, but listen to your own wisdom. If you will come to a conclusion about anything in your life, make sure that it happens in the serene truth of your heart, for the heart is your gateway to spirit and can never be divorced from it. The heart can recognize the good in all things and wants to do good. The animalistic passions of the ego, when left unchecked, bring all that is good to waste through vice, the abuse of power, domination and manipulation. Recognize your capacity to abuse yourself and to abuse the people around you. Only through awareness will you have the power to not let these parts of you dominate your life.

Number 15 The Devil presents itself when you are on the cusp of breaking free from that which has, up until this point, controlled you. Affirm, "I see beyond the world of appearances! I am more than matter in a world of matter. I am spirit incarnate and, therefore, the true and only creator of my reality. I return all power that is rightfully mine back to me in service to the highest good of myself and the world around me."

When you awaken to the true source of your power in this life, you simply cannot remain shackled to anything or anyone. You open yourself to allowing what were once siphoning attachments to transform into loving relationships. You come to realize that nothing can have power over you unless you choose to give your power to it. You are not helpless; you are a creator. You are not limited; you are bringing a limitless source of power into a limited world.

Enough of this dark chamber, don't you think? This fiendish demon would have us believe that this small room is the extent of our entire world and the end of our journey. Look now, he is already bargaining with us. No, my love. There is no price that can match sacrificing your personal freedom. Too wise are we now for the tricks of this great salesman.

IN A READING . . .

ASTROLOGICAL INFLUENCE—CAPRICORN: The subject's shadow persona and attachments to the material world are brought into focus. Reflect upon whether there is an aspect of the subject's life that is operating from base survival instincts and what fears they are now ready to confront.

UPRIGHT (DIRECT): Becoming aware of toxic attachments. Integrating your shadowy qualities. Pushing through deep fears. Being presented with temptations. Sexual awakenings. Creative power.

REVERSED (RETROGRADE): Uncovering malicious intentions and foul play. Breaking free from the "twilight zone," abuse and manipulation. Gaining control over your own inner demons. Integrating your true power. Successful manifestations. Reconnecting with your spirit.

THE ACE OF PENTACLES

MINOR ARCANA

Astrological Correlation: Earth

Finally, the Ace of Pentacles descends, the crystallization of everything that you have learned and experienced up until this point. How far you have come, my love. Through the trials of will in the suit of wands, the fantasies and illusions of the cups, the tribulations of the swords and now, finally, the harvest of the pentacles.

The Ace of Pentacles opens up the suit of earth, the suit of all matters pertaining to your physical experience in reality. This is the suit of physical embodiment and the craft of manifestation. Take this pentacle now and affirm, "I am receiving a great opportunity!" And how deserving you are of all that it is you wish to bring into fruition.

Begin now with this pentacle, with this seed of manifestation. Though it is only just beginning to take form in the physical world, do not forget that it is also a masterful product of your mind. It is you who creates your reality and it is you who creates its opportunities and possibilities. Look into this pentacle and see what you have earned, see what is only just about to take form as evidence of the remarkable creator that you are. What you have earned is the ability to build worlds from this single seed. And what you will learn through this journey of the pentacles is the path of turning opportunity into opportunities, of building prosperity, wealth and abundance by learning to recognize the seeds of potential in your reality at any given moment.

The Ace of Pentacles represents your inherent power to create value from any given circumstance. To succeed in this part of your journey, you must affirm that the universe is generous with opportunity. You only need to look at the abundance and perpetual regeneration of nature to understand that this world gives more than it takes. Opportunities are constantly scattered like seeds across our lives, it is truly up to us to recognize them and decide which of them we will nurture.

Contrary to how many people live, there is almost never a time where one's priority should be waiting on some kind of opportunity. The universe does not make you wait for opportunity. In the cycles of nature, there is always something in season. When opportunity in the world does not present itself clearly to you, look a little closer at life and you may come to realize that it is because an opportunity of highest value has already been given. You are not here to be "awaiting the blessings of the universe." Your existence as a crafter of worlds is a blessing. You must plant a seed in the fields you plow if you truly want something to wait for, my love. Not a single soul that is reading the words that you are reading right now did not come with the divine ability to manifest. Affirm, "I am always receiving opportunities of the highest value!"

Don't let your ego snag you here. The opportunities of highest value to you are not always the ones that promise the most luxurious life or financial abundance. Your highest-value opportunities are those that give you the most room to grow, that respect your worth as a creator and allow you to utilize your energy in ways that both complete and sustain you.

When the Ace of Pentacles presents itself along your journey, know that you are being granted and are granting yourself a significant seed of manifestation. The entirety of the universe is reflected in this one pentacle. The energy of everything that has ever been brought into physical embodiment exists now at your fingerprints. Is that pentacle beginning to feel a little heavier in your palm? Are you beginning to recognize the true value of everything that is currently in your life and will be in your life moving forward?

Beauty is in the eye of the beholder because of our personal perceptions of value. Beautiful things will always have the highest value. Oh, the interconnectedness of everything, my love. The opportunity in everything! Would you like to know a secret before you embark on this part of your journey? A gift from me to you to celebrate the gift that keeps on giving that is the Ace of Pentacles! The one who knows the true secret to abundance is the one who is able to see beauty in all things. So, let us create beautiful things in this world. A path of great manifestations, prosperity and wealth of soul awaits you. And to create wealth from a wealth of soul is truly to live in paradise on Earth.

So, will you step with me now through this wonderful little orchard gateway up ahead? Will you bring everything that you are into this life? Will you create your personal paradise on earth? The mountains in the distance suggest that it will not always be easy, yet great heights will be reached in the process, from which you will be able to look down on everything that you have created. In the Ace of Pentacles, is the infinite value that exists within you. You will find nothing of greater value in this world than your ability to create value.

In the Ace of Pentacles are contained all three of the zodiac signs under the earth element: Taurus, Virgo and Capricorn. Taurus, ruled by Venus, represents all the pleasures that the material world has to offer and our ability to experience self-love, strong values and plentiful resources in this life. Virgo, ruled by Mercury, deals with our health and the development of routines and skills that improve our ability to create with higher levels of efficiency and detail. Capricorn, ruled by Saturn, governs the legacy that we will leave behind in this world and the great lessons that will lead to even greater achievements in this life. Harnessing the self-esteem of Taurus, the consistency of Virgo and the ambition of Capricorn, let us go forth and become masters of this temporal realm!

IN A READING . . .

ASTROLOGICAL INFLUENCE—EARTH: The subject is being granted a new cycle of manifestation. Reflect upon where they are ready to invest themselves in bringing forth something new to their physical reality. Surrounding or clarifying cards may speak to what this new cycle will resolve.

UPRIGHT (DIRECT): New investments. New opportunities. Implementing knowledge to build something new. The promise of future stability and success. The start of something solid.

REVERSED (RETROGRADE): Reevaluating your intentions for investing in something new. Doubting your ability to manifest. Being distracted by potential material gain. A new opportunity is ripening but not quite ready yet. Waiting for what is "meant" for you.

THE 2 OF PENTACLES

MINOR ARCANA

Astrological Correlation: Jupiter in Capricorn

And, would you look at that, in the juggler up ahead we find the second pentacle. The pentacle of managing and mastering time. As the juggler artfully, albeit with a degree of uncertainty, balances his two sources of energy, it is in the 2 of Pentacles where we navigate our priorities. What is currently of greater priority in your life? What is of greater value?

This is not always a simple equation of choosing one or the other, for there could be two or more things that are bringing essential sources of value and energy to your life. The juggler can juggle because he allows the position of his pentacles to shift. He operates with the knowing that what goes up will come down and what goes down will come up. The value we place on things in our life changes with time. And it must, for to remain stagnant in what we value and choose to invest in is to risk losing everything altogether.

The infinity symbol in this card indicates a mastery over the flow of time. In the temporal world, our time and energy are finite. To invest more here means to invest less there. When the 2 of Pentacles presents itself, this is your opportunity to readjust the flow of your life and your investments. To inquire more deeply as to if your commitments are assisting you in overcoming and mastering the constrictions of time or enslaving you to a rhythm that you did not choose.

The 2 of Pentacles is correlated with the planet Jupiter in the kingdom of Capricorn. The presence of Jupiter here reveals that this is one of the points in your journey where there is a potential to understand the cosmic order of the universe, to gain a higher understanding and, in the sign of Capricorn, a higher understanding about the laws of time itself. Did you think this playful juggler would have so much depth, my love? The Jupiterian aspect of this card brings luck, abundance and expansion to those who are able to circulate the energy of their investments. Jupiter does not generally enjoy the constricting rules and regulations of Capricorn!

As the great beneficiary, the ideas of limitation and conservation of Capricorn discipline Jupiter's idealistic visions into practical reality. This forms the crux of the dilemma of this stage in our journey: How can you maintain a holistic awareness (Jupiter) of your path of self-realization while also tending to the responsibilities that give you the structure and freedom to do so (Capricorn)? Are your commitments serving the totality of your path or are they spinning you in a karmic loop of lack? The juggler who is able to effectively circulate energy can do so because he has an understanding of how his pentacles fit in the context of his divine plan. The individual that cannot connect his commitments to a higher understanding, purpose or goal will inevitably become enslaved by them.

In its most difficult expressions, the 2 of Pentacles indicates being trapped in time, where our freedoms (Jupiter) are entirely dominated by worldly obligations (Capricorn) that may not mean much to us in the grand scheme of things. Affirm, "I allow my energy to flow toward that which will expand me and empower me! And I allow my energy to return to me from that which no longer serves my personal sovereignty!"

You are here to experience your infinity in time, my love. Where the circulation of your energy becomes a pleasure, not a responsibility. You are not here to infinitely experience the constriction of time. To be always "not quite there yet," constantly having "too much on your plate" or endlessly juggling irreconcilable investments of your time and energy.

In the 2 of Pentacles, we can easily be caught in the black-and-white thinking of an existence ruled by time. We will tell ourselves that we are trying to "find a balance between work and life" instead of finding our life's work. We will balance between "being in a relationship and being alone" instead of enjoying our individuality while in relation to others. Where have you unknowingly limited the totality of who you are? In the 2 of Pentacles, Jupiter spiritualizes your understanding of the physical realm (Capricorn). You will become aware of the patterns of your reality that are and are not leading you to higher self-understanding, abundance and opportunity in your life. Freedom from the constrictions of time is the ultimate goal of this point in your journey.

Consider where in your life you have given the excuse of "not having time" instead of the more accurate "not being priority." Bring a Jupiterian idealism and sense of optimism to where you have automatically restricted yourself in life. What would change if the highest priority of your life became the fulfillment of your wildest dreams? This is not about denying your worldly responsibilities, but it is about ensuring that they are serving your highest wishes. So, let us make time serve our highest wishes and not let time make servants out of us. On a side note, did you ever learn to juggle? I do admire this ridiculous skill even without all the philosophy attached to it. The bizarre things humanity comes up with . . .

Anyhow, juggle time or be juggled, my love! Once you've gotten the hang of it, we'll be ready to venture deeper into this world of manifestation.

IN A READING . . .

ASTROLOGICAL INFLUENCE—JUPITER IN CAPRICORN: The subject's ability to balance their priorities and find a greater flow in their physical reality is in focus. Reflect upon where the subject is investing their energy in their reality and if it is giving them favorable results.

UPRIGHT (DIRECT): Balancing your priorities. Temporarily doing everything at once. Building resources. Finding a flow to life that works for you. Shift of financial circumstances.

REVERSED (RETROGRADE): Reevaluating appropriate use of time, energy and money. Focusing on budgeting and money goals. Wanting to bring more value for time spent. Reflecting on where work opportunities are taking you. Wanting to have more charge over your own time.

THE 3 OF PENTACLES

MINOR ARCANA

Astrological Correlation: Mars in Capricorn

There, the third pentacle! Engraved in the architecture of this grand cathedral. The pentacle of skill. What incredible things we can create in this world. What wonders we can bring into manifestation! A conversation here happens between the one who commissions and the commissioned. The young apprentice is granted the opportunity to showcase their skill and talent to those that have the capacity to increase their reputation.

The 3 of Pentacles is connected to the planet Mars in Capricorn, lending this stage of one's journey a strong will and drive to succeed. Mars in Capricorn is drawn to prove itself to those that have great authority. Yet, what Mars must inevitably learn in the kingdom of Capricorn is that great achievements require a great control over one's natural willpower.

The 3 of Pentacles is about yielding to the discipline required to progress toward our ambitions. The talented and skillful youth here will learn to channel their natural ability in a way that will also fulfill the blueprint of the project that has been set out for them. It is in the 3 of Pentacles where you are able to turn your inherent passions and gifts into valuable skills that will provide a great service to you and the world around you. All the threes in the suits of the tarot represent the first contact between self and the greater world that surrounds. In the journey of the pentacles, the "greater world" represents collaborating and working with those who have the capacity to turn what you value into what many others will value.

Mars in Capricorn here brings the promise of being admired and respected for your unique ability. Often, we do not even realize the unique power of our own talents and gifts until we encounter someone who perceives it as valuable! You possess remarkable and valuable qualities, my love. It is your birthright to experience the joy of work through developing your personal craft in this life. You do not have to be a mural painter for cathedrals to have a personal craft. Those who work with joy in sculpting their backyard gardens are mastering their personal craft. Those who work with souls who have experienced intense traumas are mastering their craft. Those who love nothing more than closing a deal are mastering their craft.

Allow the 3 of Pentacles to introduce you to what you can do that no one else can in this life. The journey of discovering, refining and mastering this aspect of yourself is the coming into of your life's work. It all begins here, in this seemingly mundane conversation in a cathedral. Where personal value turns into worldly value. Where you first become acquainted with your true worth as a masterful creator of worlds that only you can create. How else can I articulate to you how infinitely talented you are at being you? There are so many who would want to lift you up for all the world to see.

When the 3 of Pentacles presents itself to you in your journey, realize that an aspect of your life is ready to experience a higher level of success, that an opportunity for promotion awaits you. Your skills, talents and personal values are coming to a point where they will be able to manifest more opportunities for you. Is it not a wondrous blessing? When a single plant gives birth to three fruits? Take pride in your abilities and pay attention to the level of respect you are receiving in your reality. Do you feel that your personal attributes are being valued in your life by those around you? Are you valuing yourself? Or are you allowing opportunities to pass you by as a result of a lack of assertiveness in your abilities?

When Mars allows its personal will to be too constricted in disciplinarian and duty-bound Capricorn, we can, at times, find that what we personally want has been lost against the stronger voices of those around or above us. Be wary of allowing your personal drive to be subsumed by the goals and ambitions of others. When Mars in Capricorn allows its inner fire to be dulled, it will slave tirelessly for the dreams of everyone around it except its own.

Do not waste your talents on those who cannot see your value. You will always be forced to overextend for those who cannot see your inherent worth. And those who will overextend you value your servitude more than your skill. You are not here to be replaceable and disposable. Servitude can be easily replaced, a skilled craftsperson cannot. Who will you choose to be in this life?

Mars in Capricorn affirms in the 3 of Pentacles great success will always await those with a great passion. And a great passion can only be sustained when you are doing something for no one but yourself. There is no honor in remaining in work, my love, that kills your drive. No monetary compensation is worth destroying your will. Your will is your key to personal freedom.

If you are ever at a point where you are routinely working with no will, you will find that it is because your will has already begun casting other plans for you. Summon the strength to find and pursue where your will has gone and you will begin to see your value once again. Recognize your skills, my love! I cannot wait to see what wonders you will build with them.

IN A READING . . .

ASTROLOGICAL INFLUENCE—MARS IN CAPRICORN: The subject's ability to develop their skills is in focus. Reflect upon where there is the opportunity to receive greater recognition and success for the subject's inherent talents and gifts. Where will their discipline reward them?

UPRIGHT (DIRECT): Excellence. Building your craft. Talents that can bring remuneration. Collaboration. Important projects and meetings. The beginning of successful work. Being supported in your goals. Future opportunities for growth and promotion.

REVERSED (RETROGRADE): Working on your talents in private. Returning to a skill that you have stopped using. Discovering a talent. Secret projects and meetings. Wondering if your efforts are being appreciated. Seeking out extra support for your goals and ambitions. Taking a break from work. Starting your own business endeavor.

THE 4 OF PENTACLES

MINOR ARCANA

Astrological Correlation: Sun in Capricorn

I almost didn't see the fourth pentacle tucked so closely to that king's chest. It is the pentacle of conservation. And, look, a well-developed and impressive city stands tall behind this stoic ruler. It seems as though he and his people have withstood great challenges where they are. Yet, for this protection, they have sacrificed the desire for anything more than what they already have.

In the 4 of Pentacles, you will learn to admire the strength that discipline, self-control and restraint will grant you. After all, it is the sun in Capricorn that is astrologically correlated with this card. The sun is responsible for our vitality and spirit and, in the kingdom of Capricorn, the spirit is rejuvenated through conserving its power.

Understanding the limits of your own resources can make you sturdier. The frugal soul has often been disapproved of, yet it is their conservation of power that more wasteful individuals inevitably envy. To be able to show restraint is a sign of maturity and authority. If you want the power in a room, be the last to speak. If you want to withstand the financial uncertainties of life, save a little when financial certainty is at its peak.

All the fours in the tarot have to do with consolidation and, in combination with the earth element, the 4 of Pentacles is the quintessential card of stable foundations. To progress any further in the path of pentacles, the path of mastering the temporal realm, you must be able to create a solid foundation for yourself. However, what many do not realize is that the solid foundation in the 4 of Pentacles is not in and of itself monetary. Financial security is only a symptom of the foundation built in the 4 of Pentacles. The essence of foundation refers to one's ability to conserve resources and energy on all planes of reality. It does not matter how secure your job is, if your unrestrained emotions end up spending all your resources. It does not matter how stable your relationship is, if you have no drive toward your individual happiness.

Indeed, the foundation that is depicted in this part of your journey is the result of developing maturity and a level of restraint in one's willpower (wands), emotions (cups) and actions (swords). It is this recipe which naturally gives rise to the financial security and stability essential to the suit of pentacles. Many fail to realize that the physical embodiment of security is a product and not the primary objective. For when financial stability becomes one's single-minded focus in and of itself, it is far more likely to become a crutch that represses the fulfillment of all other areas of life.

Greed, hoarding and stinginess are not examples of mature restraint; they are examples of a lack of restraint in all of the other arenas of life aforementioned. What is the source of your foundation? What if I told you that as long as the source of your foundation is something purely physical, you will never experience the comfort of true security? Let us go deeper.

Observe, the pentacle that still balances atop the king's head. This stoic and frugal ruler we have been observing can be seen as your inner miser, the part of you that is responsible for holding what you value most dearly close to you.

Your strongest values will always be found in what is never more than an arm's length from you. When you can become aware of what you hold most dear to you, you will be able to develop your own personal sense of what foundation means for you. Your inner miser will always make sure that you stubbornly never let go of that which is a fundamental part of your inner foundation. Yes, that's right, you have the permission to be insufferably stubborn when it comes to your personal foundation. For without it, anything you build will always feel as though it is on shaky ground.

Of course, there are times where we cannot be so set in our ways, where our own conservatism and familiarity with what we've known has turned us into a relic of the past. And how do you know if your own rigidity has worked against you? You'll be awfully isolated, my love. You'll be the ruler of a kingdom of one. Accumulating much of something that no one will be able to enjoy but yourself. The misery of the miser. Now, that's not much fun, is it now? Such are the lessons of the 4 of Pentacles! The physical manifestation of foundation upon which many wondrous things will be built. It is the foundation that will allow you to persist through the harsh winters of life and emerge with greater wisdom and greater wealth.

Affirm with me, as we progress further within the world of manifestation, "I allow my discipline and restraint to illuminate to me the most valuable aspects of my reality!"

IN A READING . . .

ASTROLOGICAL INFLUENCE—SUN IN CAPRICORN: The subject's ability to exercise self-control and restraint is in focus. Reflect upon where self-control can help build a stronger foundation. On the other hand, where is the subject's rigidity making it difficult to share more of their generous spirit?

UPRIGHT (DIRECT): Being grounded. Realistic. Protecting your energy. Developing gratitude. Building financial stability. Sticking to the tried and true. Maturity and self-discipline. Saving.

REVERSED (RETROGRADE): Reevaluating your financial situation. Reflecting on the worth of your material possessions. Reassessing your values. Work that isolates you. Allowing yourself to indulge a bit more. Resolving trust issues. Reevaluating your comfort zone.

THE 5 OF PENTACLES

MINOR ARCANA

Astrological Correlation: Mercury in Taurus

What horrid conditions, what a depressing sight! Can you make out the fifth pentacle? There, depicted on that stained-glass window. A barrage of snow and rain beats down upon those wounded wanderers up ahead. Alas, this is the 5 of Pentacles. The point in your journey where the contrasts between having and not having—of the rich and the poor, of the abundant and the impoverished—all become painfully visible.

You cannot ignore the cold here—it bites with every rush of wind. Opportunities seem as far and as remote as the morning sun is from a dark, stormy night. A dread plagues us and all of the foundations we built in ourselves somehow elude us now. We no longer know where we are going, who we are or what we are worth.

What the 5 of Pentacles truly depicts is what reality feels like when one has forgotten their own godly powers of manifestation. The soul that is perpetually helpless to circumstance cannot recognize value or opportunity in their reality. And can you blame the sick for being afraid that they will become sicker? Can you blame the soul that has never known abundance to easily expect riches? Can you fault the soul who rejects love because love first rejected them?

Crisis, suffering, rejection and abandonment are the lessons that force us to remember our true value once again, our infinite value as designers and sculptors of our reality. The worn yet resilient figures in this card, through no fault of their own, are far departed from their own self-value. And, without self-value, they cannot hope to create a new world for themselves. They can only brace themselves for more suffering. Through their eyes, everything around them can only affirm how undeserving they are of blessings and goodwill. And how could it not? "Look at reality!" these figures will cry. "Look at the state of my body! The state of my wallet! Look at how everything and everyone has turned their back, closed their doors, left me out in the cold! Look, look, my compiling misfortunes!"

You are not wrong when you feel this way, my love. This is your reality. It is not your perception that is troubling, it is the fact that you are chasing value instead of creating it. You are looking for something or someone outside to welcome you inside. The abandonment you may be experiencing in your world is nothing compared to the way you have abandoned yourself by denying your ability to manifest the changes that you truly seek to make in your world.

Beyond all the losses and forms of poverty that the 5 of Pentacles can be associated with, the greatest loss here is one's loss of connection to the manifesting powers of the universe. This has nothing to do with losing anything on the physical plane of reality, this is first and foremost a loss of knowledge.

That is why the 5 of Pentacles is astrologically correlated with Mercury in the sign of Taurus. Mercury governs our ability to acquire information and commit it to memory and also our capacity to discern and differentiate phenomena. Mercury in Taurus here emphasizes the overriding purpose of this grueling part of your journey: the discernment (Mercury) of what is truly valuable (Taurus) to us through loss. How will you appreciate your fireplace if the weather never turns cold? How will you come to know what you truly love if you never lose it?

Such are the lessons of the 5 of Pentacles. And, if you lose everything in this world, my love, hang on to this one piece of knowledge and the world will remain entirely in the palm of your hands: "I am opportunity." Know that you are the embodiment of opportunity and know that you are deserving of opportunity at every stage in your journey. Do not let anyone tell you otherwise. Do not let the rejection, neglect or mistreatment from people in your life make you think that you are not worth the world.

The duplicity of Mercury in the sign of Taurus here should remind you that where there is lack, there will always be room for plenty. That where you have lost, by cosmic law, you will be sure to gain. The 5 of Pentacles is always a gateway through which you will come to recognize the true power of manifestation within you. Yet, first we must be plagued by worry. And, what is worry but a lack of faith in the endlessly regenerating opportunities of the universe?

How can you truly worry, my love, about losing anything in a world where energy can neither be created nor destroyed? Worry, fear and a lack mentality can only thrive in a mind that is far departed from the divine knowledge of manifestation. The manifesting soul knows that rejection and closed doors only affirm and bring them closer to their most direct path to fulfillment. Nothing is experienced as a failure or loss. Nothing is even experienced as a "missed" opportunity, for the manifesting soul creates opportunity.

Without recognizing yourself as a conscious creator of value in this life, your unconscious reactions to lack and loss in this life will only drive you deeper into all forms of poverty. Pay attention to the subconscious beliefs that are fueling your relationship to receiving abundance and opportunity. Be wary of getting stuck in the momentum of misfortune that is fueled by the soul that cannot help but run on survival instinct. That is, constantly fearing for your life and worrying that there quite simply will never be enough time, energy, resources and support for you in this life. No, my love. You are worthy of all of this and more. Learn to expect it. Learn to expect ease, grace and things working out for you in this life. Learn to pass through the 5 of Pentacles in your life, not to get stuck in it. Expect it to be a passing phase, not your constant reality.

When you are deeply isolated from the knowledge of true manifestation and other beliefs that keep you pointed toward improving your self-value, you will find that pessimism, cycles of misfortune and a general helplessness is much more likely to overcome you. You are more likely here to buy into the lies of the world of appearances (refer to #15 The Devil, page 218) and forget about the nature of your limitless power as a divine expression of the one that flows through all, including the rich and the poor, the arrogant and the humble.

Though this physical world may be far from achieving equality and a good quality of life and treatment for all, you can be sure that all creators are born with the same power to bring forth that which they truly desire. How could you ever allow yourself to believe otherwise? How could you accept that you don't have the power to attain everything you will ever desire?

You will attain what you believe you are worthy of attaining. This is not about vast riches and exorbitant lifestyles, this is about knowing, in the depth of your core, that you are of value. You are worthy of a life that allows you to live above the suffering of the survival instinct. Notice that the harsh conditions of the 5 of Pentacles make it very difficult to put your focus on anything other than your immediate pain and suffering. Allow Mercury in Taurus here to redirect your attention to that which gives a sense of grounded meaning and value to your life.

Do your best to base your thoughts, words, actions and general field of attention on images of plenty, abundance and the goodwill of mankind. Feelings of unworthiness were never yours to begin with, my love. You must understand that. Clear them by choosing the direction of your enough-ness and you will slowly but surely remember your true value. Your true ability as a builder of worlds with your words.

IN A READING . . .

ASTROLOGICAL INFLUENCE—MERCURY IN TAURUS: The subject's lack of mentality and current state of self-value is highlighted.

UPRIGHT (DIRECT): Braving temporary harsh conditions. Healing lack of mentality. Working through worry and fear of what is to come. Trusting that you will be and have enough. Knowing better awaits you. Waiting for the right opportunity.

REVERSED (RETROGRADE): Getting to the root of your self-esteem issues. Letting go of fears and worries that are not yours to hold. Reflecting upon what gives you value. A situation that brings up old feelings of abandonment. Reestablishing your self-worth. Learning to manifest again.

#16 ◆ THE TOWER

MAJOR ARCANA

Astrological Correlation: Mars

A bolt of divine lightning strikes down a tower in the distance. It is a scene of chaos, of a grand crumbling, marking the end of a self-inflicted suffering. Welcome to #16 The Tower, my love. Where all the bricks you have laid to isolate and protect yourself from your own highest potential must eventually show their weak foundations. It is the bolt of divine awareness that will and must destroy the false mental and physical guards we build for ourselves.

There is no avoiding it: #16 The Tower is, indeed, crisis. Yet, always at its core, it is a crisis of spirit. Because there is something that we now know that we cannot unknow. There is something we are now fully aware of that we can no longer afford to ignore. #16 The Tower is always, on some level, painful and challenging. As it should be, for at no other point in your journey will your attention and focus be snapped into exactly the right place than after the crisis of spirit represented by this major arcana. When the bolt of divine awareness strikes down our false foundations, we are instantly forced into doing exactly what we should be doing.

On the surface, and to the proudest souls, this will always appear as unfairness and punishment from the universe. That they are receiving of some bad luck and that the universe has turned its back on them. No, my love, it is we who turn our backs to the universe, for it is we who are given the free will to not know what it is that we do.

#16 The Tower is one of the expressions of mercy from the universe, never punishment. It marks the end of a structure of mind or physical circumstance that was, at its core, punishing to maintain. It marks the destruction of a structure that only further disconnected you from your most fulfilling desires.

The fiery and energized planet Mars is aptly associated with this major arcana, emphasizing the pure energy that accumulates and is, finally, climactically released at this point in one's journey. Mars is the destroyer and severer of that which restrains his path of freedom and self-realization, and in #16 The Tower, this is exactly what is unfolding. Simply put, the crumbling tower always brings freedom, freedom from the burden of upholding that which we no longer have the personal will to uphold. This card is a course correction from the universe and marks a complete redirection of our willpower. It is time for your energy and drive to be put toward that which will truly fulfill you moving forward. Mars is the conqueror of new worlds and does not do well locked away in a tower built of fear and familiarity. Eventually, Mars must seek out new levels of power.

Know, too, that not every tower takes the form of a life-changing crisis. The striking of a powerful new inspiration can easily bring about the process described in this card. Yet, no matter the scale of that which you are experiencing, you can be sure that your willpower, focus and power of creation is being returned to you, not stolen from you. Let what is no longer working no longer work. It is time to build a new foundation from a newfound will.

In many cases, #16 The Tower can represent that of an existential crisis, where what once granted us passion and drive no longer does so, where we must accept that it is not that our willpower and motivation has vanished, it is that it has already begun to seek out new horizons. And, now you have no choice but to go in the direction of those new horizons, for your current vantage point and the limiting perspectives it had is collapsing as we speak.

Let it burn, my love. You must understand that Mars, our willpower and desire nature, must undergo a process of maturity in this life. We do not begin life knowing what we truly want from life. We go toward what others want, what others want for us, what we think we want, what we want now but maybe not later, what makes us feel good, and what makes us money . . . and so on. #16 The Tower represents the process through which our desires are forced to mature. Impatient, stubborn and insufferably egoic Mars does not naturally know when to stop or change direction. It is both a great gift and a recipe for divine course correction.

Never despair, as the embodiment of your eternal and primal will to survive, Mars recovers more quickly than you may realize. The tower moments in your life will teach you one of the most powerful secrets to embracing new cycles of creation in your life. Affirm, as what must fall, falls: "Foundations only crumble when I no longer need them."

The planet Mars, the source of our primal will, is also, by extension, the source of our anger. In this way, #16 The Tower can, at times, present itself as the experience of a powerful uprising in your life. It is to affirm "Enough is enough" and to erect newfound boundaries and principles in your life that better serve your path toward self-actualization. Anger, when channeled correctly, is a potent tool that can help you break through the oppressive structures of your life and reaffirm who and what it is you truly stand for. You are not here to live in the oppression of others. You are not here to maintain structures that give power and freedom to others at the expense of your own. These are not secure foundations for you to experience your individuality and authenticity in this life.

The tower that finally crumbles does so only to bring you into greater levels of authenticity with who you are and who you are now becoming. Let it burn, burn, burn, my love, and step through the fire into the most empowered and sovereign version of yourself.

IN A READING . . .

ASTROLOGICAL INFLUENCE—MARS: The subject's ability to respond to divine course correction is in focus. Reflect upon where there is the need to let go of false foundations in the subject's life. Surrounding or clarifying cards will speak to what area of life will be most impacted.

UPRIGHT (DIRECT): Crisis that brings a blessing in disguise. Passion, energy, pure potential. Powerful realizations. Freedom from oppressive situations.

REVERSED (RETROGRADE): Finding deeper authenticity in yourself. Reconnecting with your anger, drive and sexuality. Postponing big changes until you are ready. Accumulating power. Preparing for a big shift. Resolving an existential or identity crisis.

#17 ◆ THE STAR

MAJOR ARCANA

Astrological Correlation: Aquarius

Are you not filled with hope as you gaze upon the Star overhead? How can you feel lost? How can you allow yourself to forget your interconnectedness to every being in this universe? To feel lost is to feel like a star that thinks itself to not be a part of a constellation. You are part of a grand constellation, my love, on every level of your reality.

You, in your essence, in your truest expression, are a fragment of the universal light. You are universal. You are felt universally. Allow the Star to connect you to the infinity of your being. You are timeless, my love. Your vibration, your frequency . . . it has and will continue to exist throughout space and time, echoing into the very fabric of everything.

Do you understand the magnitude of this? The magnitude of your consciousness? Connecting with the Star will connect you with the eternal aspect of your being. The cosmic self. What remains of you when you sink into the nothingness of meditation. What remains when you shed every memory, thought and temporary emotional turbulence. All of this sinks here into the eternal truth of who you have been, are and will be. This guiding star overhead is the same star that guided the three wise men to their destiny. This same star keeps you pointed to the eternal truth of who you are.

What is the essence of hope, my love? Is it not the sense that you are not completely lost? Hope is not to be mistaken with expecting something specific from the future. Expectation always disappoints. True hope never disappoints, for it is eternal and undefined in nature. True hope is an awareness of your highest destiny and your highest destiny is never a defined point or destination, it is the guiding star that remains out of reach only to be able to continue to guide you through the darkest periods of your journey.

It is this awareness of a true hope or destiny that allows you to connect to the people, places and things that are in complete alignment with the ever-expanding constellation of your life and soul on this physical plane. Is that not wondrous, my love? Is that not miraculous? What a miracle to be guided by an etheric and enlightened version of yourself that is not bound by time or space. What a miracle that, at every point in your finite journey here, there exists a connection to the infinity of you, where there exists nothing but the endless peace of your destiny as eternity. To glimpse even a fragment of this, to feel it for a moment, is to dissolve many of the fears, doubts and limitations you have placed on yourself as a result of the baggage we accrue in this physical journey. It is to experience a lightness and a peace that is unable to be articulated as anything but miraculous.

To truly understand this card, my love, to understand this part of your journey, is to unlock your rightful ability to experience eternity in a moment. That eternity is you. It cannot be anyone or anything else. What exists outside of your consciousness? What has not been thought up by you, experienced through you, become aware of by you?

Notice the figure in front of us pouring all of her experiences of her personal subconscious mind back into the cosmos. You may not see it upon first glance, but it is the Empress (page 24). The Empress' completely naked soul. You have seen her experience the infinite abundance and beauty that can be found on the physical plane, now you see her experience infinity in the etheric realm—both accessed through the miraculous portal of her heart. Will you join her? Will you surrender the pitcher you hold? The weight of everything that has impressed itself upon your subconscious and bogged you down from your highest destiny? The weight of pain, anger, melancholy, resentment, vengeance. The burden of wishing ill upon another, of carrying hatred and other contaminations of the soul. The burden of toxic emotional attachments to that which you cannot control, the pain of rejection, heartbreak, grief and loss.

Oh, how much we carry, my love! Oh, how much we hold. Pour the pitcher now, release that which guides you away from the peace of who and what you truly are, the infinity that is contained in that. Pour the pitcher and experience the tranquility of who you really are, the peace that you began with and will end with, the blessing of a conscience that is clear. Clear of everything that did not come from itself.

Discover here, at these cleansing waters, that what you hold was borrowed from the collective. The pain you hold, the agony, the confusion and the fear, it was never yours, only yours to experience and learn from. Here now, you have learned you are setting yourself free, back into your naked essence. Return these emotional turbulences back into the infinite water now. The weight lifted and gone, yet the wisdom remains.

Congratulations, for you have experienced awakening. It was not your first and it will not be your last, for that is the nature of a being that is infinite. Return here, my love, when it is time to give back what is no longer yours to hold. When you seek reconnection with the cosmic bliss within your being. When you seek meditation and rest from the turbulences and distortions that frequently mar the still waters of our soul. When you are emptied, all that can remain is what is infinite within you. When you are emptied, you open yourself up to be filled again with newfound awareness.

The Star will always bring you clarity, purpose and direction if you are ready to extract the infinite wisdom from your finite experiences of your journey. Aquarius is the sign associated with this tarot card and it is the zodiac responsible for the experience of human consciousness itself. You, as a human, are indeed a bearer and being of water, my love. A consciousness that continuously experiences and is purified, reaching higher states of self-understanding and evolution. It is Aquarius that carries with it the interconnectedness and genius of humanity. The connection of not simply body to body, but of soul to soul. The awakening to aspirations and visions that go beyond the predefined limits of our consciousness.

All of this is contained within Aquarius, the miracle of a humanity evolving into higher expressions of liberation on this physical plane. Freedom, equality, universality, community and evolution. All of this you open yourself up to experiencing when you allow yourself to pour the pitcher of your own personal experiences back into the "world pool." This is you sharing the uniqueness of your soul with the universality of the collective. This is you representing a collective truth so that you may appear as a guiding star on another's individual journey toward self-realization. There are no words for this, a miracle, miracle, miracle . . .

IN A READING . . .

ASTROLOGICAL INFLUENCE—AQUARIUS: The subject's highest aspirations, life path and destiny are in focus. Reflect upon where there is an opportunity to experience interconnectedness and unity with others who share the same ideals.

UPRIGHT (DIRECT): Fated meetings and situations. Being guided by a greater destiny. Connecting with soulmates. Revelations about your life purpose. Wishes being fulfilled. Following cosmic guidance. Recognition for your uniqueness. Community.

REVERSED (RETROGRADE): Reevaluating your aspirations. Reconnecting with your soul mission. Remembering who you truly are. Reflecting upon what brings you peace and a connection to the cosmos. Keeping a dream alive in yourself. Being an underdog. Channeling your uniqueness. Searching for your community.

#18 ◆ THE MOON

MAJOR ARCANA

Astrological Correlation: Pisces

And now a dog and a wolf howl up at the moon and, more specifically, an eclipse. It is the union of the two celestial bodies that share their light to our world and illuminate our paths. Under both the light of the sun and moon, all will be revealed. That which is unseen will become seen. That which we have felt within, but have not yet understood, will be realized.

#18 The Moon, in its essence, represents the process whereby what lurks in our subconscious mind, symbolized by the moon, becomes known to the conscious mind, symbolized by the sun. The pool of water in front of us stirs and ripples with deep emotions. We cannot progress further along our journey unless we are willing to process what must be processed, for there is a sense that something may be amiss.

Whether real or imagined, our subconscious mind is speaking to us, warning us, perhaps. For the subconscious mind illuminates your path forward by showing you what you already have known. All that you intuitively understand and know is so because of deeply imprinted memories in your subconscious mind.

The moon, better than anyone else, will illuminate to you the road home to yourself. Like a doting mother, she is extremely protective over your emotional foundation and personal happiness. Her frown depicted in this card indicates that as you suffer, so does she. She is extremely attuned and receptive to your environment and if the conditions around you allow you to blossom and thrive. The moon and your subconscious mind just want you to come home to yourself, my love. Where you will be safe, where you will be secure.

When #18 The Moon shines herself upon your journey, it is time to allow deeper, blocked or repressed emotions to come up and be illuminated. The concerns you have, above all else, stem from your emotional needs and your emotional memories. Gentility, patience and introspection are necessary to wade through the waters of your own psyche and to clear that which is alarming your subconscious mind or evoking fear in you. Confusion, deep uncertainty and mental haze often stem from a disconnect to our emotions and intuition. To feel emotionally secure and safe in ourselves, we must be willing to make decisions and choices that reflect who we truly are within. We must, to some degree, feel that the life we are living is aligned with our intuitive knowings about ourselves and our deeper emotional needs.

The union of the sun and moon reflects the union of the spirit (sun) with the body (moon). As above, so below, my love. #18 The Moon brings forth this integration. It brings forth the deep, subtle wisdom and psychic knowing of the body into the conscious mind. Naturally, dreams are an important aspect of this major arcana card. Dreams are also ruled by the zodiac sign Pisces, which is attributed here. Dreams reveal the subtle language of your subconscious mind and will always speak to your innermost thoughts and feelings.

The sign of Pisces is responsible for our receptivity to emotional vibration and our ability to attribute meaning to what we feel. It is Pisces that rules the subtle, unseen forces that draw us to people, places and things without us fully knowing why. And there is that sense here, in #18 The Moon, of responding to a calling from within even when we don't exactly know why.

All will be revealed in due time, my love, as long as you remain connected to what stirs within. If I could give you some wisdom for the emotional turbulence and vague uncertainty that often frequents this part of one's journey, I would tell you this: The answers you are seeking from the future will not be found in the future, they will be found by reflecting upon the past.

Remember, your subconscious mind operates on patterns formed from the past. It knows what it knows because it has experienced it before. This can be a double-edged sword when dealing with our future. At times, your subconscious mind will simply know if a direction will be right for you or not. But there are also the times where your subconscious mind is still playing out a maladaptive pattern of behavior that once served to keep you safe and secure.

There is a reason why people say that trauma is stored in the body. It is because trauma is also stored in the subconscious mind. The body and the subconscious mind are inextricably intertwined in ways we have yet to realize, for they both function automatically. #18 The Moon invites you to interact with the subtle waters of your subconscious and to address anything that may be worrying or bothering you.

This is an extremely important process, because whatever is lodged in your subconscious mind, you are constantly re-creating in your physical reality without your conscious awareness. This is beneficial to the soul that holds emotionally supportive subconscious beliefs and destructive to he who has only known pain, suffering and neglect. It is known that the subconscious mind forms very early on in childhood. It is during our childhood where we first become aware of our individual emotional needs. Yet, all too often, these needs are denied, shamed, neglected and distorted. And, so, we eventually develop maladaptive ways to find the emotional security that we always craved.

If you asked your inner child, my love, what they would need to feel loved, safe and secure right now, what would they say? Provide it for them right now. The past is always healed in the present. Give yourself the emotional attunement to your inner needs that you perhaps did not receive. You will be surprised to realize how much of your fears and uncertainty today come from the uncertainty you felt back then about having an emotional need be met. You can certainly provide it for yourself now and stop the maladaptive patterns that keep your emotional needs unmet.

In #18 The Moon are the tears of every time you had to believe that what you really wanted was wrong. You were never wrong, my love, you were a child who was deeply aware of your own needs. You are seen, you are held, you are supported. By reconnecting with this part of you, you will stop creating a life based upon what you were not allowed to have and start creating a life that truly represents the core needs that you developed as a child and have never changed. Tears will be shed, my love, and they must be. Cry for yourself, cry to the moon and then turn to the morning light arising.

IN A READING . . .

ASTROLOGICAL INFLUENCE—PISCES: The subject's emotional world, memories and past patterns are in focus. Reflect upon what their intuition is alerting them to in their present environment.

UPRIGHT (DIRECT): Needing introspection. Coming "home to yourself." Illuminating deeply held subconscious beliefs and memories. Trusting your intuition. Psychic experiences. Practicing caution.

REVERSED (RETROGRADE): Reevaluating your core needs. Healing the past. Breaking down your emotional walls. Resolving family issues. Reconnecting with your childhood. Roots and ancestry.

THE 6 OF PENTACLES

MINOR ARCANA

Astrological Correlation: Moon in Taurus

It is in the sixth pentacle, along our path toward worldly manifestations, that we encounter the importance of giving to receive. Do you know what it feels like to give from your heart, my love? To share the wealth of your soul? To give in a way where the pleasure is all yours?

A merchant here provides charity to the less fortunate. There is no expectation here around what he will receive in return. To be able to give without expectation for reciprocation is one of the greatest gifts you can bestow upon yourself and others in this life. The heart that can give before knowing if it will receive has everything it needs. To be able to openly give is to operate with the subconscious knowing that you are always receiving. And you are always receiving, if you pay close attention. Give, my love. Give with joy.

How else do I articulate the miracle of giving and receiving? Energy is here to be circulated. This is not about money, it's about energy. Allow others to share in the surplus of your energy. Receiving will always inspire giving and giving will always inspire receiving. This is the symbiotic relationship that allows every single being on this earth the opportunity to experience the goodwill inherent to the universe. And you will always have something to donate to the world around you. How many times have you been utterly replenished by receiving a kind smile along your journey? How appreciative are you when someone does a little bit extra just to make your life easier?

It is in these moments where you will experience the absolute miracle of this stage of your journey—the remunerating principle of the universe. There is no logical way to explain it, my love. When you give with joy, the universe infallibly gives back. When you give with the knowing that nothing can be truly lost in a universe that balances itself through a remunerating principle (that is, perfect compensation for every action [refer to #11 Justice, page 109]), you will bring greater joy, ease and harmony to your life and your relationships.

Astrologically, the 6 of Pentacles is associated with the moon in Taurus. This reveals to us that the harmonious circulation of resources illustrated in this card is the result of a subconscious mind that operates under the impression that there will always be enough to go around and that abundance, resources and surplus are things that should be expected. The moon in Taurus, in its exalted expression, is emotionally secure in the knowing that resources will always be provided. You will be provided for, my love. Whether it be through the divine orchestrations of the universe itself or through the goodwill of the mutually reciprocal relationships in your life, you will and must receive, for your energy is invaluable. You give so much by simply sharing your energy with the world around you. Do not compare what you give to what you receive. It is not up to you to match what another gives or expect something from another that they cannot provide. All harmonious exchanges in the world take place because one can give something that the other needs and vice versa.

The 6 of Pentacles speaks of transactions of equal value. Even if two parties are offering completely different things, in the dynamic of exchange, they become of equal value. For some, this allows mutually reciprocal relationships to blossom and prosper. For others, an inherent failure in compatibility will inevitably break the contract. If you are receiving gold in exchange for your wool, you are participating in an exchange where gold is now of equal value to wool. As long as both parties are overjoyed by this exchange, both will prosper. In another dynamic, one might say, "My gold is worth more than your wool! This is an unbalanced contract! Give me more than your wool!" "But I only know how to give wool," the other will say. This is a failure of compatibility.

Heed this and never forget it: Give only that which you know you can give openly, my love. That which you can give openly naturally arises from within you. It does not ask for anything in return, just as a tree grows and bears fruit without the faintest grumble of resentment. The tree bears fruit. Though its form may change through the seasons, it will always bear fruit. You are not much different, my love. Become aware of what you have and always will give.

The moon in Taurus is deeply aware of the limits of its resources and what it feels comfortable to provide. And what you will feel comfortable to provide is always that which gives you great personal satisfaction when you provide it. To give without personal satisfaction is, quite frankly, a violation of yourself and others. How does it feel to receive a gift wrapped in the nettle of resentment? Though the thought can be appreciated, the gift will always be painful to enjoy.

If you seek to fill your life and relationships with resentment, my love—it is very easy—simply give without personal satisfaction. Too many of us feel pressured to give what we cannot give in order to feel loved and appreciated. This will always lead you to bitterness and resentment. Give what you can openly give, my love, and you will open yourself up to receiving what others openly give too.

You will become invested in exchanges and trades of all kinds with the world around you. You will begin to consistently receive from others simply because you are sharing the surplus of what you will always have a surplus of. And what is it that you have a surplus of? Once again, it is that which naturally arises from within you.

The moon in Taurus is aware of the value attached to that which it intuitively knows it can provide. The woman who practically lives in her garden will always have a surplus of information regarding gardening. It is a pleasure to share this information with others because she finds it a pleasure to be in her garden. A baker, who seems to always have enough money at the end of the month, always bakes more than what will be sold so that he can give to those in need. He does not do this out of obligation, it is done with the inherent knowing that there always has and always will be enough to go around. If baking is what truly brings him joy, what does he have to lose by having more people literally ingest the love and joy of his soul?

All the sixes in the tarot represent a form of beauty. And, in the 6 of Pentacles, you will experience in your heart and soul the beauty of giving and receiving. Witness the love and beauty in your exchanges with others as you share what you already have so much of. Witness the compatibility of the relationships and contracts in your life strengthen and prosper as you become more aware of the joy you naturally bring others. You will never be asked by the universe to provide more than what you already are, my love. It is only humans that, strangely, do that.

Be wary of giving what you know you cannot provide. To do so is to subconsciously compensate for something that you believe to be inherently lacking in your personal value. This is the shadow of the moon in Taurus, where subconscious suggestions (moon) that we are "not enough" contaminate our exchanges with others and the world around us. It is what causes us to ask for more than we need and to give more than we can, throwing our dynamics out of balance.

And, so, my love, what you will ultimately learn through the 6 of Pentacles is that—are you ready for this secret?—the emotional security you seek that accompanies "having enough" in life will never be found in what you physically acquire, it will always be found in your ability to master giving and receiving.

IN A READING . . .

ASTROLOGICAL INFLUENCE—MOON IN TAURUS: A focus is placed on the subject's subconscious patterns of behavior that re-create their personal sense of self-love and self-value. Reflect upon their subjective perception (formed by the past) of their value in relation to others.

DIRECT (UPRIGHT): Harmonious and rewarding exchanges. Ease of giving and receiving. Mutual reciprocation. Remuneration from the universe. Giving and receiving of goodwill.

RETROGRADE (REVERSED): Reevaluating exchanges and balance in relationships. Compensating for something. Owing or being owed. Inequality. Differing values. Incompatibility. Needing to get back onto the same page.

THE 7 OF PENTACLES

MINOR ARCANA

Astrological Correlation: Saturn in Taurus

And, there, the seventh pentacle is uncovered atop a stack of leaves! Beside it, a figure considers their hard work. How far you have come along this journey of manifestation, my love! Have you taken time to consider this?

One must acknowledge that the path of the pentacles, as the suit of the earth element, is the slowest plane of reality. Hard work, perseverance and patience is, many times, required in order to build anything sustainable and fruitful in this life. Yet, the slowness of progress allows for many moments to marvel at just what wonders you are creating. Contemplate a little while here, my love. Acknowledge the effort and strain you have put into cultivating that which will bring you prosperity. At this point in your journey, there is a looming sense of having come so far, yet still with so far to go.

As one of the sevens in the tarot, it is a bridge between worlds and a test of one's spiritual resolve. It is here, in this mundane plateau of progress, that you must consider if what you are building is something that you would actually like to keep building upon. In the contemplative gaze of the figure toward his stack of leaves are all the questions like "Is this really worth it?", "Is this what I will be doing for the rest of my life?" and "Will it pay off in the end?"

The work in the 7 of Pentacles is not easy. It requires the investment of time, energy and resources. It cannot be sustained unless you are able to connect deeply with the long-term significance of what you are doing. Accordingly, Saturn in Taurus is correlated with this tarot card. Without a clear direction, purpose and goal (Saturn), it is very difficult to remain connected to our manifestations (Taurus).

The 7 of Pentacles is a card of facing the reality of a situation, the reality of the time, energy and resources that you must be willing to commit in order to bring something into fruition. It is actually at this exact point, in your most disillusioned state from whatever it is that you are building, that you will truly know how much it matters to you. It is easy to invest in things when they are going well and are progressing rapidly, for a little effort here goes a long way. Yet, seasons change.

At another point, you may find yourself investing double the effort for half the reward. Where will the source of your motivation come from then if it cannot come from the validation of rapid progress? Where is it, my love? It is in the long-term objective. It is in the ultimate reason as to why you are building this in the first place. It is in the reason that will remain long after you are gone.

Saturn in Taurus will teach you here, often in the harshness of slow progress and hard labor, about the strength of your long-term values. Saturn will strengthen your values here and give you an unshakable resilience to achieve what it is that truly matters to you. If you are not willing to persist through a dry season, there is no shame. Saturn has clarified for you that what you thought mattered greatly to you in actuality no longer serves you. If you are willing to invest in that which presently grants you little reward, then you are tapping upon something of your legacy, my love.

Welcome the disillusionment from what you are working toward and let it humble and ground you. When the glamour and adrenaline is gone from the pursuit of your desires, how do you perceive the progress that you have made? Can you marvel at the craftsmanship of your reality so far? Can you truly sit in peaceful contemplation and affirm "There is a long road ahead, but, still, right here, I am proud and fulfilled." If you are proud and fulfilled now, you will only become prouder and more fulfilled later, my love. If you are sapped of all of your vitality and cannot seem to restore it even in rest, do not fall into the Saturnian karmic trap that somehow fulfillment and ease will find you later. Even the hardest labor has its moments of deep, gratitude-inspiring satisfaction when it is aligned with your legacy. When you are not building toward that which will personally fulfill you, even the most simple task is tended to with dragging feet.

Honor yourself in this stage of your journey. You will look back at the times where you have invested yourself the hardest with a deep reverence for your resilience and discipline toward your long-term values and ambitions. Great struggle builds the strongest foundations. And if it helps, my love, heed this when you, too, will be contemplating upon your stacks of leaves: That which has come with difficulty leaves difficultly. That which has easily flown in flies away easily too.

IN A READING . . .

ASTROLOGICAL INFLUENCE—SATURN IN TAURUS: The subject's perseverance and dedication to that which they are investing in is in focus. Reflect upon where in life there may be a need to continue through slow progress or try a new approach. Surrounding or clarifying cards may give more information to the field of life that is reaching a temporary plateau.

DIRECT (UPRIGHT): Mastery through hard work. Being proud of your progress. Appreciating how far you have come. Building with integrity and maturity. Committing to the long-term reward. Meaningful work.

RETROGRADE (REVERSED): Reevaluating your work ethic. Finishing what you began. Finding an easier approach to a situation. Reconsidering your goals. Organizing and managing your finances.

THE 8 OF PENTACLES

MINOR ARCANA

Astrological Correlation: Sun in Virgo

The eighth pentacle is being worked upon as we speak, my love, by that skilled craftsman beneath the tree up ahead. Already, much of his work has been pinned up for display. And it seems that he has only improved with each of his creations.

This is the 8 of Pentacles, the process of refined and perfected craftsmanship. By this point in your journey, the personal craft that you began in the 3 of Pentacles (page 229) has now turned into a refined skill. What was once mere talent is now turning into mastery through repetition, consistency and diligence. Notice how the craftsman only has two pentacles that are awaiting completion (one of them already almost complete!), indicating that here we are at the final stretch of an endeavor that has required a high degree of investment in our reality. This is the artist perfecting the final details of her painting and the author writing the final chapter of his novel. This is the student preparing for their final exam before graduation and the mother who is in the final few lessons of a 12-week fitness boot camp.

Whatever the endeavor, whatever the chapter, recognize that, in the 8 of Pentacles, you are becoming a master. There is nothing else to do but to show what you are made of, to show the extent of your skills and abilities. Push through remaining obstacles with consistency, perseverance and repetition. The craftsman in front of us is not doing anything "new" at this point in the cycle of manifestation, he is simply getting better at doing what he has always done. He is refining his craft and perfecting it.

Astrologically, the 8 of Pentacles is correlated with the sun in Virgo. Here, our sense of vitality, identity and creative life force is being perfected, ordered and productively channeled. It is a time where we may be more perfectionistic than usual and harsher on our own abilities. By this point, you will simply hold very high standards for yourself in a certain aspect of your life. There is an anxiety to not "drop the ball" at the final moment and ensure no details are left unchecked. The sun in Virgo foretells that commitment, work and diligence during this time is also more likely to rejuvenate our spirits rather than burn us out.

Indeed, hidden in this card is actually the secret to vibrant physical health. Excellence is the goal of the sun in Virgo and the perfected expression of the spirit. What do you strive to be excellent at, my love? Who are you in your most refined and productive moments of your life? Where does it feel good to be orderly and productive? It is there where you will become excellent. Do not come to me with that foolish "but I am not good at anything." No one begins with excellence. Commit to that which brings you joy and you will become excellent at something. If you do not yet know what to commit to, commit first to yourself.

Indeed, the 8 of Pentacles is, at times, about working on yourself. Commit to yourself and become excellent at nothing but being yourself. It is from there that all of your hidden godly talents will emerge. Wherever you are, it is at this point that you are able to push a little further beyond your limit. Dedication and pride in your work will be greatly rewarded. Are you ready to commit to yourself, my love? Are you ready to become the best creator that you could possibly become?

The 8 of Pentacles will usually involve a significant narrow-minded vision so that important tasks can be completed. This is a card where you are being asked to become heavily invested in the physical realm. This may not be the time to yearn for another time, another place or another realm. A task at hand calls for your complete, undivided attention and focus. You are sculpting something that will be an expression of the highest form of your essence. Do you feel the weight of that, my love? Take the time you need to consider if what is claiming your undivided attention right now is aligning you with a path of personal excellence. Are you on a path that makes you feel proud of yourself? That is honoring your craft and is in service to your unique light?

When the sun in Virgo is dimmed by a lack of self-confidence (often under the guise of humility), the 8 of Pentacles can turn from refinement into drudgery. We focus all of our attention, resources and energy on insignificant details, menial tasks and stick to a routine that is not in flow with who we really are. We remain on a "humble" path in life even when our skills could take us very far. We work and work on our skills in secret, never feeling quite ready to actually take ourselves seriously or, worse, we give up on our projects entirely, paralyzed by procrastination and perfectionism.

Leave the inner critic for another point in your journey, my love. The hammer (wands) and nail (swords) that this craftsman holds indicate that only persistent focus and action will progress you further. This is a card focused on the doing, not on the "Why?" and the "Is it good enough?" and the "Who am I really?" Right now, you are at work and you are someone at work toward improving yourself and your personal craft in life.

Remembering the sun in Virgo, you are at work discovering the true essence of humility. That is, the discovery of a joyful devotion to your personal craft that will never change no matter where it takes you and what it brings you. It is to be your own competition, for the goal is to refine yourself in the eye of yourself, not for anyone else's (often fluctuating) personal perception of your value.

Anyways, I suppose I'll leave you to your work, my love. Oh, me? I'll do mine later. And that is why "excellence eludes me," you say? Hmm, remember when you were more ignorant at the beginning of your journey, my love? I liked you much better then.

IN A READING . . .

ASTROLOGICAL INFLUENCE—SUN IN VIRGO: The subject's ability to consistently invest themselves in order to bring something to fruition is in focus. Reflect upon where there is the opportunity to complete tasks efficiently and invest yourself in the joy of work, productivity and improvement.

DIRECT (UPRIGHT): Refining your skills. Completing tasks with excellence. Practice and discipline that is paying off. Making the final touches on something. Expressing joy through your work. Developing a healthy lifestyle.

RETROGRADE (REVERSED): Resolving harsh self-criticisms. Restoring faith in your abilities. Needing more time to perfect things. Reevaluating what the final product should look like. Reimplementing healthy routines and habits. Investing in self-improvement. Returning to things that excite and motivate you.

THE 9 OF PENTACLES

MINOR ARCANA

Astrological Correlation: Venus in Virgo

Oh, to frolic with you in this abundant garden, my love. And look, hidden among our bountiful harvest, the ninth pentacle along this journey of manifestation. Luxury, my love, luxury. The hard work is done and great rewards are reaped for what you have sown.

The 9 of Pentacles represents a state of being of high self-esteem, self-sufficiency and gratitude. It is truly the highest milestone for an individual along the long road of the pentacles. And it is not something exclusive to those with many physical riches. Physical luxury is only one of the manifestations of the state of being that is represented in this card. The figure in front of us is not luxurious because of what they have, it is because they exist in ease. To exist in ease is to have carved out a life for yourself that creates value from every single aspect of your being.

The figure in the 9 of Pentacles is in complete harmony and resonance with the environment around them. Their robe, covered in the sigils of Venus, indicates that they identify themselves as being someone deserving of ease, abundance, prosperity and love. It is because of this self-identification that reflected all around them is more than they even have the time to enjoy and consume. You are deserving of a life of ease, my love. You are deserving of being able to enjoy all of that which you are. Not only are you deserving, it is an essential process in order to experience self-sufficiency and personal sovereignty in this life.

The 9 of Pentacles illustrates to you how all the work through this path of pentacles of recognizing your true value within is what allows your true value to be shown to you without. It is easy for the figure in the 9 of Pentacles to recognize their highest value because, by this point in their journey, they are able to enjoy evidence in their reality of what they are able to create. Through persistence, dedication and a keen eye for what is valuable to them, they have been able to sculpt beauty into every aspect of their life. It is not that they somehow stumbled across beauty or got lucky or threw out their old life for a fancier one, they have worked with what they have always had and brought it to its highest expressions.

Truly, this is the essence of Venus in Virgo, the astrological correlation of this card. The ability to sculpt perfection into what is imperfect. The ability to raise the value of anything in your life by seeing its potential for beauty. You are a beautiful creator, my love. And already some will say, "Is that not never-enough-ness?! One should feel perfect exactly as they are!" No, my love. You are in the path of the pentacles, the path of bringing divine perfection into an imperfect, unmolded physical world. To say that you are perfect as you are is to say that a ball of clay is more perfected than the clay vase that brings you constant joy in your home. You are not perfect as you are, what is perfect is who you are. For who you are and always will be is a powerful creator able to turn what is valuable within into what is valuable without. It is a gift to be able to bring yourself and the world around you to its highest expression. The realm of Pentacles, the realm of physical embodiment, is not perfected. That is part of why you are even here, my love. I have said it once and I will only say it once again: Those who know the secret to abundance and prosperity can recognize the potential for beauty in all things.

With the presence of Venus in Virgo here, understand that to seek to improve the quality of your life is an expression of self-love. Love yourself enough, my love, to bring your life into its highest expression. The trap many fall into is that pursuing money in and of itself is what will bring a higher quality of life. Having more clay to work with will never make you a more talented sculptor, my love.

The fulfillment that you will feel in the 9 of Pentacles comes from appreciating what you have perfected in your life from what you first had to work with. This is what grants you a sense of self-empowerment. To obtain the riches of the 9 of Pentacles, through no sculpting of your own, is to inevitably feel empty inside. It is to feel trapped by a life of ease that is not easy to live. For the wealth of your soul is not what surrounds you, it is still within waiting for you to perceive it.

IN A READING . . .

ASTROLOGICAL INFLUENCE—VENUS IN VIRGO: The subject's ability to experience self-sufficiency and a high self-value is in focus. Reflect upon what in the subject's life creates feelings of worthiness.

DIRECT (UPRIGHT): Exuding high self-esteem. Luxury and wealth of soul. Things coming easily to you. Attractiveness. Enjoying life. Successful, yet humble.

RETROGRADE (REVERSED): Reevaluating your value. Reconnecting with your beauty and style. Reflecting on how to bring more ease and flow to your lifestyle. Resolving fears around being self-sufficient. Feeling like you deserve more. Being too humble.

THE 10 OF PENTACLES

MINOR ARCANA

Astrological Correlation: Mercury in Virgo

Finally, we arrive at the tenth pentacle, at the castle of a family of three generations. There is wealth here and there is legacy. There is the consecration and the concretization of all the work you have put into your reality. It is the final stage in a long journey of manifestation. It is both a place of completion and the foundation for a new cycle. A new cycle that is only now possible because of what has been previously crafted.

Welcome to the 10 of Pentacles, my love, the summation of . . . everything. To be at this place in your journey is to be experiencing the perfected conclusion of a cycle of manifestation in your life. This means that you have brought into physical fruition something that can never again be taken from you. For something at its final stage of manifestation is the most resistant to change. This is the essence of true foundation: that which can be relied upon to not change in its form regardless of what pressures and circumstances it undergoes.

There are no real words to completely describe the experience of the 10 of Pentacles, my love. It is life itself. It is spirit that has been successfully brought into its highest physical expression. It is immortal spirit that has achieved an immortal expression in the physical realm. This is extraordinarily powerful, because what you have crafted for yourself has perfected an aspect of reality even for those that will come after you.

The ten pentacles in this card are arranged in a diagram of the tree of life. A Kabbalistic symbol that, in the fewest words, describes the process of spirit turning into matter and matter turning back into spirit. To arrive at this point in your journey is to develop a conscious understanding of this process. It is to have wisdom about a cycle of manifestation that could not have been brought into fruition in any other way other than through you. And is that not a legacy, my love? To be the one who is remembered for that which only you have and could have mastered in this lifetime? This is never a process that is exclusive to those renowned by the world.

Every imperfect cycle of manifestation that has been brought into perfected harmony is an example of the 10 of Pentacles. This is the clearing of years and, oftentimes, generations of karma that has perpetually re-created suffering in your life and in the lives of others. The daughter who becomes the first person in her family line to attend university has broken a generational pattern of manifestation. The man who becomes an artist, in a family of a long line of dentists, has broken a generational pattern of manifestation. Have you thought, for a second, my love, about the titanic legacies that have led to your existence at this very moment? Do you recognize the foundations upon foundations that have made it possible for you to stand in this very moment? In one sense, you can say that the long line of dentists was the necessary foundation so that man could become the artist that he was meant to become.

We take for granted, my love, how these perfected foundations are constantly operating in our lives. When you can perceive this cycle of your life as the flower of everything that has come before you, you will never again doubt your power as a creator of worlds. For how many worlds were created and lived and experienced and lost so that you could blossom into this life? Yes, this history lives on in you whether you choose to recognize it or not. It is your choice to see it as a burden or as a blessing. It is your choice to contribute to the healing of imperfect worlds in this life by beginning with your own. It is also your choice to live out the years and years of karmic cycles that came before you, to remain ignorant of your powers and suffer in the exact same way as those before you. And how can you remain ignorant, my love? When in your very body you carry the wisdom of everything that has ever existed?

Indeed, the 10 of Pentacles is the definition of timeless wisdom. The legacy you will leave behind is a form of timeless wisdom, that is why it will never be forgotten. And your mark on this earth, my love, no matter how large you perceive to be the scale of your contribution, will reverberate through time and space forever. What you live through and what you choose to create with it will have lasting ramifications on everything that comes after you.

The 10 of Pentacles will, oftentimes, represent generational wealth because the cycle of manifestation that is perfected here lives on and on. It is able to create its own ecosystem. It has created its own ability to manifest itself, destroy itself and be reborn again. Quite literally, in the 10 of Pentacles, you are stepping into a new world for yourself and everyone around you. What is done is done. What is created will no longer undergo significant change. And nor should you want to change anything that has already happened, for it is forming the integral foundation (perfected to the minor detail) upon which you will accomplish everything that you seek to do in this life. If there was an end to this journey, my love, this would be the closest to it, for it captures the journey of living in its entirety.

To truly understand the 10 of Pentacles is to truly understand the one in all and the all in one. It is to come to terms with the grand evolution of the universe and how all of its expressions originate from a single energy that flows through us all. It is to know eternity now. I hope I have not overwhelmed you, my love, but the grand designs of this universe are wondrous and wild.

Astrologically, the 10 of Pentacles is associated with Mercury in Virgo, which tells us that what is ultimately important at this stage of one's journey is the knowledge that is obtained. Mercury in the sign of Virgo brings a self-conscious (Mercury) understanding of the systems (Virgo) that operate in our lives. From the system of our body to the system of our family, to the system of the world we are in and the system of our soul from which we have manifested from, what you will come to realize is that in their essence they all operate in the exact same way. Everything is connected, my love, and in ways that we are only just beginning to comprehend. Allow Mercury in Virgo here to highlight to you the hidden relationships that exist within your reality.

It is your capacity to make these connections that will grant you the knowledge essential to the manifestation of your personal wishes and dreams. There is no one magic formula. There is no one thing that will work for all. This is the work, my love, and you must choose to live in a way that works for who you really are. To achieve this is to become both the creator and the creation of everything that you are. And that is the closest you will ever get to the power that birthed the world and the world that is inside the power that lies within you.

IN A READING . . .

ASTROLOGICAL INFLUENCE—MERCURY IN VIRGO: A long cycle of manifestation is coming to its culmination for the subject. Reflect upon where the subject is successfully completing a significant chapter of life and where energy can now be repurposed. Surrounding or clarifying cards may point to the field of life where the subject is experiencing a significant milestone and the releasing of old karma.

DIRECT (UPRIGHT): Reaching a significant milestone in life. Accomplishments and achievements. Foundation for a new cycle. Long-term financial security. A successful and fully developed end result.

RETROGRADE (REVERSED): Reevaluating your milestones in life. Reflecting on your unique path beyond familial and material expectations. Releasing long-term or generational karmic burdens. Releasing ties with corrupt structures, institutions and material ideas. Reconnecting with deeper values and spiritual wisdom.

THE PAGE OF PENTACLES

MINOR ARCANA: COURT CARD

Astrological Correlation: Earth and Mercury

A humble page contemplates upon a pentacle in the verdant fields of this earthly kingdom. There is the sense of the world being their oyster. Possibility, possibility, possibility, my love. What will you bring forth into this realm with your little hands?

Though the Page of Pentacles may not be the most skilled, they are certainly the most ambitious, for they have not yet been beaten down and hardened by the losses of life. To the Page of Pentacles, there is no possibility for failure. There is a strong faith in a potential endeavor, the prospect of a destiny. They are eager to bring the world of their dreams to life. The Page of Pentacles is playing with the magic of manifestation. They do not know what they are truly here to master yet, but they are eager to learn.

Ironically, it is the wisdom-less page that carries one of the most powerful wisdoms: the importance of always remaining a student of life. No matter how much you learn about the world, my love, there will always be that which you don't know. It is in that unknowingness where you allow yourself to grow the most. The Page of Pentacles has the most to learn and that is exactly why they are the most likely to become a master. And now you look at me and say, "That clumsy, clueless fool? Who just now dropped the pentacle they were playing with, hoping no one noticed?!" Yes, my love, that clumsy, clueless fool. He doesn't look much different from another #0 The Fool (page 15), I know. And if they're anything alike, a great power lies beneath these clumsy veils.

Embrace your inner Page of Pentacles, my love, the one who will always know nothing and, thus, is inspired to know everything. It is your Page of Pentacles that raises the question inside of you: Why? Why do things work in the way that they do? What is my place in this grand plan? What truly is the extent of my ability to manifest what I desire? Yes, my love, some of the most foolish and insufferable questions you can ever ask yourself, for their answers will always evolve as you do.

Embody your inner Page of Pentacles, my love, and you will restore the power of humility in your life. This universe has a way of gracing the humble with the most potent blessings, for the humble do not know how to take advantage of what they have. In some ways, you are never more powerful and indestructible, my love, than when you are allowing your inner Page of Pentacles to help you invest in some new endeavor. Carried by the winds of naive excitement and adrenaline, initially, much progress will always come quickly. It will feel as if you are opening a portal to some profound new world or understanding. Yet, the more you learn, the more questions that will inevitably arise. Your ignorance will fail you and you will be blocked, at times, from moving forward in your manifestations because of it. Allow your Page of Pentacles to recover your ambition with a new question and a new approach. The learning of any new skill will always require consistency and diligence. In fact, there is no skill that will serve you more than the learning of consistency and diligence itself, my love.

The mercurial Page of Pentacles and the earth element here combine to bring the contemplation of a new value that has the capacity to improve your life. What if what you are insufferably interested in really does have value? What if that humble skill you never paid attention to has the capacity to change your life? Move forward in your endeavor with curiosity, humility and an openness to possibility here, my love.

I will only share with you a single piece of wisdom to accompany your journey that will save you the unnecessary suffering of many a Page of Pentacles. Remember that the most valuable part of any pursuit is the wisdom gained, not the resources it provides. Wisdom will grant you every resource you could possibly desire. Be wary of pursuing any endeavor purely for material gain. The soul that manifests money for the sake of money misses out on learning the wisdom behind money. The humble Page of Pentacles pursues the acquiring of skill, the naive individual pursues the glamour of coins.

When contemplating your next endeavor, my love, affirm "I offer up my skills to the universe and I will invest them toward the highest path that is shown to me!"

IN A READING . . .

ASTROLOGICAL INFLUENCE—EARTH AND MERCURY: The subject's ability to manifest opportunity and the excelling of a new skill is in focus. Reflect upon where in the subject's reality there is a seed of potential waiting to be curiously brought into fruition. They may require an open mind and a fresh perspective in order to best utilize this incoming energy!

DIRECT (UPRIGHT): Learning a new skill. Manifesting quickly. Opportunities that "drop into your lap." Building a solid foundation of knowledge on something. Having good common sense. Being able to create something out of nothing. Crafty. Financial gifts and bonuses. Good employment.

RETROGRADE (REVERSED): Reevaluating the types of opportunities you truly want. Reflecting on how to monetize your skills. Using skills you already have to your advantage. Being resourceful. Talks of a new employment opportunity or position. Receiving an opportunity that you previously missed out on or declined. Learning about finances, taxes, commerce and so on.

THE KNIGHT OF PENTACLES

MINOR ARCANA: COURT CARD

Astrological Correlation: Mars and Virgo

And, upon the slow but sturdy steed of the Knight of Pentacles, we persevere deeper into the kingdom of manifestation. Unlike the curious and clumsy Page of Pentacles (page 267) we came across earlier, this knight has a certain graveness about his goals and ambitions. He takes his mission seriously, for he knows the effort, resolve and commitment that will be required in order to bring what he desires into fruition.

In this tarot card, the knight's steed stands almost still, as if bracing for the long and arduous journey that is to come. This knight is aware of how much he will have to invest of himself in order to complete his goal. The Knight of Pentacles holds his honor, integrity and loyalty above all else. He must keep his promises, for to go back on his own word is to betray his own values. And a Knight of Pentacles with no firmly held values is doomed to wander aimlessly, allowing the slightest seduction from the material realm to derail him from his original mission. "Stay grounded in your mission and brace yourself for the obstacles that will try to stray you from your noble path" is what this stoic knight will tell you. It does not matter where his loyal steed will take him, what lands and treasures and temptations he will encounter along the way, his eyes remain on the prize.

And, what is the prize for your inner Knight of Pentacles, my love? It is the ability to make promises to yourself and to keep them, to be able to commit to bringing into fruition that which is important to you. One foot in front of the other, step by step. Consistency, diligence, patience, yet in combination with a fiery will. After all, though this Knight has a far more reserved and restrained temperament than the others in the tarot, he still carries the fiery planet Mars in his astrological correlation. The passion, inner drive and action-oriented nature of Mars takes on a different expression, however, when moving through the slow and considered pace of the earth element.

Here, Mars has its quick-burning energy spread out over time. It is forced to exert less effort quickly and more effort over a longer period. Instead of a great speed, in the Knight of Pentacles, we find that we will need great stamina. Learn from this knight, my love, the ability to focus and complete tasks that require a great deal of investment over a longer period of time. Your inner Knight of Pentacles inherently understands that all good things take time.

His correlation with the sign Virgo lends him his deeply devotional nature toward that which will bring good to himself and the world around him. Virgo also deals with themes of repetition, practice and consistency. The Knight of Pentacles understands that the key to long-term success is an accumulation of small progress every day. Though this knight may move very slowly, he will never fully stop until his goal has been completed.

Your inner Knight of Pentacles is the keeper of every promise you have ever made to yourself. As soon as you affirm what you must do, you have enlisted this loyal knight toward the realization of your promise to yourself. Though his progress may be slow and though even you may forget promises you have made to yourself, your committed Knight of Pentacles will never give up on those journeys. For if it is truly important for your highest path, no matter how long it takes, it must eventually be done. Remember what you truly value, for your values will always inform your habits. If you would like to know the quickest way to discard your own value, simply make a habit of breaking your own promises. Procrastination loves the soul that cannot keep their own word. Will you keep your word that you will do your best to keep your word, my love?

Mars in the earth element of Virgo here also grants the Knight of Pentacles a deep appreciation of the sensory world. Because of the slower pace of his journey, he is able to more easily "smell the roses" and truly take in the wisdom of life that can be found at every point in one's journey. Truly, the Knight of Pentacles understands the journey of life to be just as important as any destination he will ultimately reach.

And, so, let us smell the roses along the way, my love. Take things step by step and, before you know it, what seems like a mountainous challenge to you now will become one of the many mere hills in the distance, a pretty panorama of the past as you progress further toward the great things that await you.

IN A READING . . .

ASTROLOGICAL INFLUENCE—MARS AND VIRGO: The subject's ability to remain focused on a long-term endeavor is in focus. Reflect upon where in the subject's life could be a calling for commitment, perseverance and the embarking on of a journey that will bear many fruits.

DIRECT (UPRIGHT): Committing to a goal. Going to where opportunities will be. Remaining focused on your own path. Slow but steady progress with lasting results. Great achievements await you.

RETROGRADE (REVERSED): Reevaluating your commitments. Recovering your stamina toward a goal. Changing your plans. Getting clearer on your goals. Focusing on your health and body. Clearing obstacles and distractions toward your objective.

THE QUEEN OF PENTACLES

MINOR ARCANA: COURT CARD

Astrological Correlation: Moon and Capricorn

The Queen of Pentacles welcomes us into her kingdom with warmth and hospitality. It is as if the growth of nature itself is accelerated by her presence for anything that surrounds her is enriched. Queen of the earthly realm, she is a master at embodying the vibration of prosperity, abundance and self-love. When she breathes, all of life breathes with her, so attuned is she to the inherent beauty and resources of the earth she stands on. No matter the scarcity of her environment, the Queen of Pentacles is able to draw out its highest value because her vibration stimulates the growth of everything and everyone around her. Her vibration draws opportunities, resources and abundance to her.

And what is her secret, my love? How does she simply always manage to have, not only "enough," but more than she would ever ask for? It is because, on some level, whether she is conscious of it or not, her reality has been constructed upon this very affirmation: "Just as I provide my energy to the world, the universe and all beings within it will provide for me."

And who would not want to provide security and resources to sustain the Queen of Pentacles, my love? For she is the very vibration of abundance. The generosity she inspires in others is her gift to them. To be able to both give and receive openly is the hallmark of the self-loving soul and one of the great keys to abundance. And the Queen of Pentacles is the keeper of your sense of self-value. The pentacle she is tenderly tending to in her hands is the wholeness of who you are and the self-love that is always inside of you. She operates as the protector of your self-worth and self-esteem and everything that involves you feeling comfortable and valid in yourself.

As the queen of Earth, this also extends to your personal relationship to your physical body and sexuality. She understands the wisdom of the body more than anyone else because she is more connected to her physical vessel and its inherent spiritual wisdom than most. Your inner Queen of Pentacles, my love, is the voice of your body. What it rejects, what it holds, what it consumes, what it loves and what gives it pleasure and pain are all profound intuitions into the quality of your self-love and what your vessel personally requires in order to operate securely in this world.

A Queen of Pentacles who, for whatever reason, is not able to protect and honor her self-value will find that her resources are constantly depleted and that she simply cannot feel supported and secure in the world around her. Unable to trust her own vibration of abundance, she will constantly seek out things in order to compensate for the inner wholeness that she is currently unable to access. Yet, nothing in the physical realm can substitute for the power of her frequency. What could substitute, my love, for the rejuvenating and fertile force of nature that flows through her?

Affirm, my love, "I am tender, gentle and loving toward my own vessel, for I recognize it to be the instrument of abundance that attracts the highest quality of what I desire!" A healthy Queen of Pentacles is able to experience her sensuality and her indulgence in that which simply reflects the love she has for herself. Protecting her self-love and the values that help maintain it, the Queen of Pentacles allows the floodgates of fertility, creativity and abundance to flow through her and into the lives of everyone that is blessed enough to experience her. What she touches, indeed, turns to gold.

Connected with the moon and the zodiac sign Capricorn, the Queen of Pentacles is ultimately the master (Capricorn) over the body (moon). Her intuition is in her ability to see the value in all things, because she maintains her own self-value and self-love with high regard. The presence of Capricorn lends this queen a discipline over her own vessel and a high degree of concentration on building a safe and secure environment in which she and those she loves can experience plenty. Her connection to the nurturing moon lends her the part of her nature that is deeply concerned with providing the conditions for a strong emotional foundation in the material world.

And, so, let us relish for a little while in the abundant foundations of this Queen of Pentacles and her kingdom, my love. Her secret, ultimately, is the secret that is in you: Commit to loving yourself.

IN A READING . . .

ASTROLOGICAL INFLUENCE—MOON AND CAPRICORN: The subject's ability to embody the vibration of abundance and exude self-love is in focus. Reflect upon where there is an opportunity to feel worthy of receiving and being supported in the subject's life.

DIRECT (UPRIGHT): Exuding sensuality, prosperity and high self-esteem. Being firm in your values and allowing them to draw in the right opportunities. Having high standards that will be honored. Feeling grateful and abundant. Financial security that creates emotional security. Being highly respected for your unique and irreplaceable value.

RETROGRADE (REVERSED): Reconnecting with your body and sensual nature. Recovering your inherent inner value. Reevaluating what gives you a sense of security. Learning to love and accept yourself more fully. Protecting your energy and resources from being siphoned. Releasing doubts and fears around what you truly deserve.

THE KING OF PENTACLES

MINOR ARCANA: COURT CARD

Astrological Correlation: Saturn and Taurus

And, now, we approach the King of Pentacles in a rare state of repose, contemplating upon everything that he has built and achieved. He has matured and wizened with time like a ripened wine, cloaked in snaking vines, symbols of the long and wealthy legacy he will leave behind. So much wisdom has he obtained through not only absorbing the laws of this universe, but by learning to apply them, again and again, throughout time.

Truly, the King of Pentacles is a master of application. What he does works. Is that not one of the greatest milestones of our experience in this temporal world? To actually have influence and dominion over our reality? To no longer be subject to the arbitrary forces, causes and effects of this world and to instead create a world that we choose to live in?

This is the King of Pentacles, my love, the applier of wisdom to the physical world, the builder of physical worlds. Where others have time as their master, the King of Pentacles is the master of time. This King need not speak very much, for his empire speaks much for itself. Wisdom lies in everything he has built. If you seek to learn from him, learn from what he has done. Your inner King of Pentacles, my love, is the governor of your personal empire. He is the protector of your legacy, your ambitions and that in you which will allow you to overcome the constraints of time. His primary objective is to physically construct your life in a way where you have the resources necessary to achieve whatever you wish to achieve.

Through practical wisdom and application, the King of Pentacles is able to build a reliable physical foundation upon which all great kingdoms are built. And how does he do it? How does his success only grow with time? It is through deeply understanding the relationship between value and time. Your inner King of Pentacles is responsible for bringing you the highest amount of value to your investment of time. What you personally value will always inform how you spend your time. And, so, it should, for to spend your time doing what you do not value is to have time as your master. Affirm "I have the tools and resources required to become a master of my time. I take accountability and personal responsibility for where I invest my energy and for the consequences of what I choose to invest myself in."

Your inner King of Pentacles does not have time to waste. He invests himself for exactly the amount that is necessary, not a fraction more or less, for even that fraction must be held accountable for the value it brings. You have a right to own your time in this life. Your inner King of Pentacles will protect it dearly if you allow him to. Remember, it is not so much about the number of resources you have as it is about the amount of time you have to invest in in what you truly want to invest in.

An unhealthy King of Pentacles is driven by a materialistic hunger to acquire and acquire, neglecting the mastery of time which is required to sustain all of that which he comes to possess. When this king is only motivated by greed, social status and power, what he invests in will inevitably overpower him. Pursuing money for the sake of money will always lead to superficial results. If a King of Pentacles is to achieve the security he truly wishes to achieve, he must learn the mechanism behind his successes and losses. Many play the game of life, but a true King of Pentacles knows how to build the game.

Astrologically, the King of Pentacles is attributed the planet Saturn and the zodiac sign Taurus. His Saturnian influence lends him the sternness, self-control and collectedness required to maintain the power he tends to attain. The sign Taurus reflects the more sensual aspects of this earthy king, who indeed is not here to only work, but to enjoy what he has worked for to the fullest extent. Venusian Taurus makes the King of Pentacles want to attain the most of that which he personally values. It is the hunger and, sometimes, greed that pushes him onward toward greater heights and greater ambitions. It is an appetite that can only be understood by those who want to own the world. The King of Pentacles must be wary to not allow his entire worth to be founded upon how much he has.

Remind your inner King of Pentacles that the wisdom of the world is more priceless than any riches you will attain, for it is what you have learned that will allow you to better build whatever you seek to build. And, you will eventually have your riches one way or another, my love. The true question, however, is will you also have control over your time? Will you have others to share with everything that you have worked to attain? Will you still be in touch with the magic and romance of life and not allow the appearances of the material world to deceive you as to what is of true value?

A healthy King of Pentacles uses his power for the goodwill of the entire world, for the betterment of everyone who coexists in the game of life. He remains humble even when the entire world is grateful to him and he allows spiritual wisdom to guide his decisions, even when the temptation that accompanies power whispers otherwise. For the King of Pentacles ultimately knows that the strength he is given to accomplish what he will accomplish is not his alone. A higher force, the mechanism of the universe itself, is applied masterfully through him and the result is a better quality of life for all that he influences.

IN A READING . . .

ASTROLOGICAL INFLUENCE—SATURN AND TAURUS: The subject's ability to apply the wisdom of the material world is in focus. Reflect upon where there is the opportunity to gain greater mastery and control over an aspect of the subject's life by employing maturity, experience and practicality.

DIRECT (UPRIGHT): Gaining control over your finances and goals. Managing yourself and your time efficiently. Developing wisdom and maturity. Being respected for your worldly achievements and position. Achieving career and financial goals. Being your own foundation.

RETROGRADE (REVERSED): Reevaluating your connection to the material world and money. Reevaluating your ambitions, long-term goals, business models and life timelines. Recovering control over your financial situation. Reconnecting with your business sense. Reflecting on your reputation. Finding a new approach to creating financial security. Adapting your business, work and skill set to changing times.

#19 ◆ THE SUN

MAJOR ARCANA

Astrological Correlation: Sun

Do you feel the warmth of these morning rays of light, my love? The sun rises over your journey now. Are you not filled with a childish glee? #19 The Sun is one of the, if not the most, uplifting and joyous cards in the major arcana. Not because it represents anything particularly extraordinary to be joyous about, but because you are recognizing the joy within you. To the soul that has recognized joy within, the arena of life becomes a playground to experience their own self-expression. The soul that cannot find joy within lives impersonally, for the loss of joy within is always accompanied by the loss of personality.

#19 The Sun is, essentially, the experience of self-actualization itself, my love. It represents coming to the conscious realization of what truly brings you joy in life. It is to bring your personality to its highest physical expression. And a personality at its highest expression is exactly being who it really is. I know I make it sound simple, my love, and, in some ways, it truly is. Yet, it is the entire practice of psychology and spirituality to bring us back to this simplicity. To become exactly who you really are is not who you begin as.

That is why the journey, my love. The trials and tribulations. The tempering (refer to #14 Temperance, page 166) of our personality to bring about self-actualization. The exalted personality represented by #19 The Sun is the result of conscious integration of the many different aspects of your nature. It is the glorious amalgamation, the uniting and harmonizing of all of your nature so that you may come to know the one in all and the all in one, to experience yourself as both creator and creation, as an infinitely unique expression of the one original force.

Do you feel the magnitude of that, my love? Of being an irreplaceable child of the universe? Of being a flower of the world tree that will only ever bloom once through the vastness of time and space in this exact form? How could you see yourself, my love, as anything other than endlessly unique in this one life? How could you not come to recognize that the sun that all of life bows to is a manifestation of the energy that is within you?

Open are the arms of the child, open are the rays of the sun, every single soul on this planet is here to experience themselves openly. To radiate their unique light onto this earth. To remind us all of the infinite joy, beauty and creativity of the one force. The talents and gifts and beauty you admire in others, my love, are reflecting back to you your own light. Do not come to me with the "I am not original" or the "Nothing brings me joy" when you were birthed from the force of creativity itself.

Do not come to me seeking to become anyone else other than your divine expression that always shines through when you are at your most joyous. When you are filled with joy, my love, you are completely embodied in who you really are. You are delighting as both creator and creation. You are experiencing the beauty that is you and the beauty that you have created in this life. On the most cosmic level, you are the one marveling at its own self.

Yes, my love, that which has created everything on Earth did so for its own joy, did so to experience its own beauty. And, yet, you in this life feel guilty and afraid or even selfish for following the light of who you really are. The highest honor you can give to the creator of this universe, my love, is to become your personal expression of beauty. It is to allow the light within you to shine without.

A child is depicted in #19 The Sun because, as children, we know how to do this unconsciously. A child does not question itself. A child does not feel shame, fear or guilt about who they really are. Why? Because they are not even aware of themselves as a unique expression of the oneness. Their personal joy is the joy of the world. They do not try to be authentic, for they cannot help but to embody themselves.

And, so, should we all just simply regress to the consciousness of a child, you may ask? No, my love. Because you are not here to be a child. A child cannot have conscious control over its expression and, therefore, cannot consciously create its own reality. That is why, as children we are helpless to the forces of our reality and the wills of others until we develop the faculties necessary for the actualization of our individual will.

When #19 The Sun presents itself along your journey, it is time to become awakened to the miracle of who you really are in this life. It is time to perceive your own beauty and to celebrate a retuning to your innocence. And what do I mean by innocence? The exalted personality that #19 The Sun represents has nothing left to hide. Everything in themselves is illuminated by the light of spirit and, thus, everyone around them is illuminated in their presence. Notice, my love, when you are in your joy, you will always have this effect on others. For when you are in your joy, you are in your heart and, thus, cannot possess anything other than a love and beauty for the people and the world around you.

When you see #19 The Sun, follow your joy. Know that life is bringing about the conditions that will allow you to express the essence of who you are. This is not an easy process, and the joy and celebration that is correlated with this major arcana card often come after a period of weathering the storms created at the hands of our own unintegrated personality. The unintegrated personality cannot experience itself as a cohesive whole and as an expression of the oneness. Here, the division within does not allow us to experience the beauty of innocence and childlike joy.

Notice that the child rides on a gray horse. Gray is a symbol for the integration of opposites, as gray is always the product of mixing complementary colors (pigments that are opposite one another on the color wheel). In this way, your innocence and childlike joy can only be maintained upon the strong foundation of an integrated personality. And, oh, how gorgeous you are, my love, when you are in the joy of your spirit. Don't deprive this world of the life-giving force of your own light and self-actualized identity.

Astrologically, #19 The Sun is attributed . . . the sun. Yes, my love, because this major arcana card is what it is. Already, I have given you much too much for what is ultimately the very simple truth of being yourself. Yet, the journey to discover who we are is rarely that simple. Your entire journey of life is weaved to assist you in this process, for "being yourself" also evolves as you develop a deeper awareness of yourself. In saying this, however, there are some things in your ever-burning spirit (represented by the sun) that will never change.

The sun in astrology represents our identity, spiritual essence and self-expression. Though the expressions of your light may take on different forms in this life, your unique light itself is constant and eternal. It was there when you were a child and it is still burning deeply inside of you no matter how far you have attempted to stray from your personal joy. Maintain the simple joys in your life, my love, they will be constant reminders for the constancy of who you are in spirit. And when you find that the rays of your own personal joy and the world around you are no longer reaching you, when your light feels dim and depleted, you are on the cusp of discovering the most essential aspects of who you really are.

Look upon #19 The Sun and affirm "I bring all aspects of my personality under the instruction of my personal joy, and I am a divine and infinitely unique expression of the oneness." Be proud of who you are, my love. No one and nothing will ever exist that is quite like you. Make it your mission to witness the beauty of your own inner joy made manifest in this world. You will be doing everyone on this planet an invaluable favor. Never forget it.

IN A READING . . .

ASTROLOGICAL INFLUENCE—SUN: The subject's essential and self-actualized version of themselves is in focus. Reflect upon where there is the opportunity to tap into childlike joy. Surrounding or clarifying cards may speak to what aspect of the subject's life is receiving an influx of creative, joyous and enlightening energy.

DIRECT (UPRIGHT): Self-actualization. Radiance. Joy. Authenticity. Creativity. Integrated personality. Wholeness. The light of truth. Innocence.

RETROGRADE (REVERSED): Reconnecting with your joy. Recovering your creativity and self-expression. Recharging your inner light. Releasing fears and doubts around illuminating who you really are. Remembering your inner child, magic and innocence. Finding joy within.

#20 ◆ JUDGMENT

MAJOR ARCANA

Astrological Correlation: Pluto

Behold, my love, the time has come upon your journey for divine judgment. Everything you have ever experienced has prepared you for this moment of revelation and spiritual ascension. #20 Judgment is the nonnegotiable acceleration of destiny. An angel above blares its trumpet, calling all who are ready to be reborn into their true nature. The figures rising up out of their coffins are bare (symbolizing purity) and gray (symbolizing the integration found in #19 The Sun, page 279). All have their arms raised in an open and surrendered gesture, welcoming the call to ascend into a higher understanding.

How do I articulate, my love, the magnitude of what is signified by this card? What is certain is that when #20 Judgment descends upon your journey, you are being bestowed complete and perfect knowledge of a circumstance in your life. There is a final deliberation upon what exactly needs to be done so that you are able to be initiated into the next chapter of your life.

The spiritual call represented in #20 Judgment is nonnegotiable. Not because you do not have free will, my love, but because the revelations you obtain during this time dissolve all former beliefs about your reality. The call of #20 Judgment is a call to a higher responsibility in your life that is only now possible because of all the work you have previously done to integrate the spiritual lessons of your past experiences.

When judgment arrives, the revelations and spiritual truths that you receive about your current reality collapse all time and space. It is the experience of gaining sudden and profound awareness into exactly why the script of your life has played out as it has up until this point. There is a clicking into place for everything that you have experienced. There is closure and an emerging conviction about what you are now ready to step into. Divine judgment is never early, nor is it ever late, my love. It arrives when you have stopped running away from the wholeness of who you are and decide to face all challenges directly.

Originally, #20 Judgment was attributed to the element of fire. And, indeed, in this card is a kind of baptism by fire, where all the beliefs that are too heavy for the next phase of your reality must go to burn. Nothing not of your highest truth and destiny can withstand the rite of passage presented by judgment. For there is no more time, my love. The call is now. And to reject the newfound understanding that will be coming to you is to try and return to a coffin. It is like a snake attempting to wear an old skin that is no longer attached to its body. Bare and pure are the figures in this card and bare and pure you must be in order to move forward now.

You must be ready to let everything you have known be replaced with knowing nothing. Not because you were ever wrong, but because your old understandings of yourself and your world will no longer serve you in the next chapter of your journey. Trust that you have absorbed the wisdom of everything that you have experienced so far and allow your vessel to be reborn with new life. Are you ready to open yourself up to a new level of your destiny? Are you ready to experience a higher octave of your entire reality? Release your doubts and release your fears, my love, and affirm "I open myself up to receive divine instruction toward my mission on earth!"

The process represented in #20 Judgment is the same process that will lead you to discover a higher purpose and responsibility in your life. More correctly, it is the process by which your purpose discovers you. You do not need to find your purpose, my love. As long as you are committed to a path of self-knowledge and self-realization, the trials and tribulations that you will inevitably encounter will reveal purpose to you. Your higher responsibility to the world, your life purpose, is not something that you decide for yourself. It is given to you, it is the call that only you can hear from the heavens above and are, thus, obligated to respond to. And the universe can only hand you a higher responsibility when you have shown an understanding of the greater themes that have repeatedly shown up in your own path. When you truly come to understand the personal, the universal will be revealed to you.

In more recent times, #20 Judgment has been astrologically correlated with the planet of death, transformation and rebirth—Pluto. It is Pluto that deals with the major cycles of transformation in our lives. Pluto in astrology has been referred to as the god seed, the force of pure power that is perpetually pointed toward evolution. The energy represented by the planet Pluto is the energy that allows us to transform through the most seemingly impossible circumstances. It is Pluto that destroys the outdated cycles of our life and brings forth deeper knowledge about who we are and what we are truly capable of. Pluto also rules our deepest and most intense desires, the ones that do not allow us to rest until we have an answer for them. This answer, the answer to your deepest questions about yourself and life, your existential fears and a release from that which has had a powerful influence and hold over you, arrives finally in #20 Judgment.

So live, my love. Live now for now and live with the knowing that you will be reborn later. Do not chase the answer to questions you cannot answer without spiritual revelation. Divine knowledge arrives not a day early and not a day late.

When you are nearing the calling of #20 Judgment, you may feel hopeless and afraid. You may be reevaluating the deeply-held perceptions that once constituted your view of reality. You may even be wondering if you somehow have been "forgotten" by the universe or if you have missed the wisdom you were meant to heed. Never despair, my love, you can never "miss the memo" of your life. As long as you remain open to receiving divine instruction, perfect understanding will unfold in perfect timing. Live with the knowing that you will eventually come to know everything you need to know. No one is exempt from judgment. No one can avoid certain crossroads of destiny that have been specifically ordained for their evolution. When your path in life is meant to accelerate, know that it will infallibly accelerate. Nothing is outside of the powers of the divine oneness from which all of life has arisen.

When #20 Judgment calls, know that everything you have experienced has only just been the preparation for the blessings that are about to unfold for you. Lift your arms up openly and affirm "I align my personal will with that of the divine will." It is when you are in this place of surrender, in this grand emptying of your own personal egoic wishes and desires, that you are finally able to receive the calling that will grant you not only everything that your soul desires, but in a way that brings meaning, purpose and context to everything that you have ever experienced up until this point through time and space. How limitless your power is, my love, when the universe is able to work through you.

IN A READING . . .

ASTROLOGICAL INFLUENCE—PLUTO: The subject's ability to respond to a divine rite of passage is in focus. Reflect upon where in the subject's life there is the nonnegotiable call of destiny. Surrounding or clarifying cards may point to the specific area of life or internal process that this divine judgment is bringing to its culmination.

DIRECT (UPRIGHT): The call of fate and destiny. Divine understanding and revelation. Opening a new door to life. Divine intervention. Ascension. Overcoming significant fears and barriers. Clearing karmic tests. Awakening to mission and purpose.

RETROGRADE (REVERSED): Coming to terms with a powerful inner revelation. Reevaluating your overall sense of purpose and life path. Releasing fears around entering your next chapter. Awaiting more information before the "final verdict." Resolving final attachments before rebirth can occur. Bringing context, perspective and closure to the past.

#21 ◆ THE WORLD

MAJOR ARCANA

Astrological Correlation: Saturn

You've done it, my love, you have reached the card in which all the other cards in the tarot are contained. You've reached the point in your journey where all other points of your journey converge into holistic awareness, maturity, wisdom and manifestation.

Welcome to #21 The World, completion, the end of a cycle and the beginning of a new one founded upon the wisdom gained in the previous one. It is #21 The World that assures we evolve and do not repeat. It is this very point in your journey that allows you to move up the spiral of evolution and not fall back into the loop of a circle. The world is the end and the beginning, it is the full-circle experience of coming back home to yourself.

It is amazing to witness, my love, how this point in your journey can actually feel for a moment that you have actually regressed, for #21 The World will always reintroduce to you the major themes that have characterized the last cycle of your life. Remember, it is Saturn that has rulership of the final major arcana card and Saturn is the disciplining final boss that only grants power over the material world to those who have mastered their lessons. When we do not learn the spiritual lessons of what we experience, Saturn has a tendency to throw us back into the ring, re-creating the same scenario with a different cast of characters, until we finally are wise enough to choose a different ending, to choose the ending that prioritizes our path of evolution and the realization of our highest potential.

The figure in #21 The World is suspended in the air. They are no longer bound by the limitations of the physical realm. All that once weighed upon their soul, they have been liberated from. The four totems of Aquarius, Scorpio, Taurus and Leo are also illustrated here, emphasizing that it is the mastery over the four elements (the entire journey of the minor arcana) that grants one the reward of successful manifestation.

When #21 The World presents itself, you must recognize that a cycle of manifestation is coming to its completion. It is not about what you have manifested, it is about the shift of awareness that you now have as opposed to when you began whatever journey it is that you are on. It is this shift of awareness that will give life to a new cycle of manifestation with its own challenges and blessings and with its own array of human experiences that will allow for the further expansion of your being.

Ask yourself, my love, what have you truly learned across this last chapter of your life? What are you ready to complete? To come to the full understanding of? For when you are able to answer these questions, you are able to achieve mastery over that cycle and a mastery over certain aspects of your reality.

What is learned in #21 The World you can be sure is never forgotten. It is engrained in the fabric of your being and in the very foundation of your reality moving forward. You will never again have to suffer in the way that you had to suffer. You will never again have to experience the lessons you had to experience, because you chose not just to live, but to learn. You chose to bring a mastery over your physical reality by recognizing the creator within, by bringing wisdom and self-conscious awareness to the fool that you began as.

And the mastery that you are now finding is what will allow you to dance in this reality, just as the figure does in this card. You will dance in air, my love, because you are now free. Free from the clutches of time (symbolized by Saturn, lord of time). Time is what leads you to believe that you are "not where should be" and that you "are moving too slowly" or "moving too fast" or "running out of." Running out of what, my love? Running to what?

The world is a symbol of eternity in a single moment. The great game of it all is that what you are completing is also an illusion. For that sense of completion is something not bound by time, it is a state of being, the state of being completely whole in yourself. When you are really there, there is nowhere to go, there is nowhere to run from. You are here, and you are here, and you are here. Observing the wheel of time and experiencing it all. The feeling of completion is not something only reserved for the major graduating events of your life. Every moment in your present is a graduation from the lessons you have worked to learn in the past.

I hope I am not too confusing for you, my love, but how else do I articulate the circular motion of time? When you are in the state of being depicted in #21 The World, you are actually in the eye of the storm of time. You are beyond it and safe from its limitations. What shackles us to time is the world of appearances (refer to #15 The Devil, page 218), which, when we are wrapped up into it, is a world of limitation.

The figure in #21 The World understands the true nature of the world and is, thus, unlimited. They are able to dance with the curiosity, joy and presence of #0 The Fool (page 15), but now also with the wisdom, maturity and perspective of the world. There is no more resistance to what is and there is no more deception from the Saturnian world of appearances and its false limitations. Why? Because in #21 The World, my love, you understand that everything has its time and its place. You understand that everything operates in its perfect cycles. And, so, you will no longer fight against your reality here, but instead be able to observe it and attain its wisdom.

Naturally, as the final card in the spiritual journey of the major arcana, the meanings of #21 The World are various and complex. At this point, you have been on the road, my love. You have been on a long journey of wisdom. You have matured. Whatever has needed to be completed by this point has now effectively been completed. You're not going back at this point. For to go back would not work with the newfound understanding that you have gained. Yet, remembering that because we are dealing with karmic Saturn here, who deals with learning from repeated past actions, there is a sense of going back over old themes.

Now, however, you are approaching these situations with a completely new lens and maturity. Now you know where the pitfalls are. You are not entering blind as you were when you began this journey. And with the ushering in of this new cycle, you are able to pay back the accumulations of karmic debt to the lord of time.

Though there is so much freedom depicted in #21 The World, do not forget that there is also the pressure of Saturn. It can be unnerving to realize at this point in your journey that you actually cannot go back. For as you continue to progress further along the cycle of your evolution, Saturn is the ouroboros snake that eats away at your past. Allow yourself to feel the pressure of evolution, my love. Allow yourself to grow into the maturity that Saturn is now expecting from you.

You will feel the growing pains, but you must press onward. To reject the completion that is presented in #21 The World is to demonstrate an insufferable lack of maturity to the universe. It is to be in resistance to learning your lessons. It is to be fooled into the most paralyzing affirmation that you could ever say to yourself or anyone else in this life. "That's just the way things are." No, my love. This is the wisdom of a hamster on a wheel, not a creator capable of building worlds. Those who reject the opportunity for freedom that the world represents will inevitably face the weight of Saturn. For every action that you take that is not in the direction of your new cycle will feel especially taxing during this time.

Recognize the powerful checkpoint that you are in when the world presents itself to your journey, my love. It is time to come to a full acceptance of where you stand and to find peace with that. The Saturnian element of the world reminds you that all mastery over reality comes from practice, consistency and discipline. You are not here to wait for the next "exciting moment" of your life. You are here to be invested in the wisdom of your reality and to be applying your knowledge at every stage of your journey. To only wait for the windfalls of life is to lock yourself in the endless loop of time.

Be wary of enslaving yourself to the idea that life may somehow "become easier" in the future. #21 The World affirms that life is happening right now. It is the choice to bring more ease into your life now that will make your life easier then. All forms of time converge here in the world because we come to realize that our capacity to change the past and future lies in the present.

Lastly, at this point in your journey, you must understand that you are in control, my love. And you have earned it. You have invested, you have learned and you will now receive. Balance and harmony will be restored. As all who become watchers of the world know, everything operates in cycles, within cycles. Yet, unlike everything else on this planet, my love, you have a very special gift: the ability to break them.

IN A READING . . .

ASTROLOGICAL INFLUENCE—SATURN: The subject's mastery of a significant life cycle is in focus. Reflect upon where in the subject's life there is the experience of coming full circle, the fulfillment of old contracts and the opening up of new possibilities. Surrounding or clarifying cards may speak to what particular cycle is reaching completion.

DIRECT (UPRIGHT): Total awareness. Completion. Resolution. Melding of past, present and future. Mastery over significant life lessons. Cleansing of old karma and patterns of suffering. Turning over a new leaf. New possibilities. Profound wisdom gained. Life experience. Maturity.

RETROGRADE (REVERSED): Reflecting on the lessons of a repetitive cycle. Clearing the old to bring in the new. Working through the "final test." On the cusp of a significant shift of circumstances. Putting to use everything you have learned. Final endings.

ASTROLOGICAL TAROT SPREADS

As you begin to utilize your own tarot cards in your journey, my love, you may find it at first difficult to organize your thoughts in relation to the cards that you are pulling. It can be overwhelming to process the meaning of a single card, let alone a series of cards. This is why many tarot readers employ tarot spreads. A tarot spread is a specific arrangement of tarot cards that provides a clearer context, structure and intention for your tarot readings. Practice and experience will give you a better indication as to which tarot spreads give you the most effective readings. Some readers also prefer to pull tarot cards intuitively, abandoning the structure of tarot spreads completely. Find what resonates with your work, as all works stem from the one work in the end.

THE OPPOSITION

The opposition is an astrological variation of one of the most well-known and beginner-friendly tarot spreads: the three-card tarot spread. This particular arrangement involves laying out three tarot cards in a row. The goal of this tarot spread is to bring resolution, harmony and a way forward in a particular situation by uniting seemingly opposing forces.

An opposition in astrology is an aspect made by two celestial bodies that are 180 degrees (opposite) from one another. This particular aspect brings a culmination of events and a full awareness of any internal or external conflicts we have been experiencing. A full moon is an opposition between the sun and the moon. On the next full moon, pay attention to how you feel and what you are now ready to become fully aware of!

Using the opposition tarot spread, reflect upon two seemingly opposing forces in your life and draw two cards directly opposite to one another. Draw a third card right in the middle to indicate what can be done to harmonize these opposing forces. This tarot spread works in a myriad of circumstances, so get creative! I have listed some examples here.

EXAMPLE 1. PAST, FUTURE, PRESENT

Card #1 (Opposing) — Past: This card position indicates something of importance from your past that is seeking to be processed or integrated into your present. How can you learn from the past in your present reality?

Card #2 (Opposing) — Future: This card position indicates something that you desire (or fear) in the future that is seeking to be processed or integrated into your present. How can you begin to embody your future goals in your present reality? How can you dispel your fears?

Card #3 (Integrating) — Present: This card indicates how you can integrate both what has happened in the past and your desires for the future into the present moment. Successful integration will bring resolution to both the past and the future. What is the past and potential future bringing up for you in the present? What is in focus now in order for you to move toward your highest reality?

EXAMPLE 2. RELATIONSHIP DYNAMIC

Card #1 (Opposing) — Self: This card indicates your state of being in relation to the other person or the aspect of you that is of the greatest source of conflict and opposition in your relationship to the other. How is the other learning from the energy that you are embodying?

Card #2 (Opposing) — Other: This card indicates the state of being of the person in question and the aspect of them that is a source of conflict and opposition for your relationship. How are you learning from the energy that the other is embodying?

Card #3 (Integrating) — Union: This card indicates what is currently being alchemized for you both as a result of your current relationship. This is a "shared energy" that is contributing to both your individual growth and the growth of your relationship. The card placed here is what you are both processing, experiencing and highlighting in one another. This is also the energy that is required to bring resolution, harmony and a karmically balanced exchange of energy between one another.

EXAMPLE 3. CONFLICTING DESIRES

Card #1 (Opposing) — Desire A: This card indicates "desire A" that is seemingly in opposition to something else that you also desire in your life. The card placed here also indicates what you feel you are likely to encounter if you pursued this direction.

Card #2 (Opposing) — Desire B: This card indicates "desire B" that is seemingly in opposition to something else that you also desire in your life. The card placed here also indicates what you feel you are likely to encounter if you pursued this direction.

Card #3 (Integrating) — Integrated Desires: This card indicates the force that must be applied in order to bring harmony and integration to your opposing desires. The card placed here presents itself as a solution to the obstacles that may arise by exclusively pursuing desire A or B. How can you utilize the energy of this card to bring balance and temper the extremes of desire A or B?

THE 12 HOUSES

This is a 12-card tarot spread that harnesses the knowledge of the 12 zodiacal houses in astrology. These 12 houses represent different areas of life and holistically capture the state of every facet of your life. This is a powerful tarot spread if you are seeking an in-depth overview of your reality. Here, I have listed the essential meanings attributed to the 12 astrological houses that will be providing context to the 12 tarot cards that you will pull. It is advised that you arrange this tarot spread in the form of a wheel, similar to that of an astrological natal chart.

1st House (Card 1) — The 1st House in astrology correlates with Aries. This gives cards in this position the role of bringing you more in alignment with your authentic, individual self and your personal freedom. Cards in this position will indicate your individual path, your strongest individual desires and the personal perspective that everything else in your life is being viewed through. Consider, how can the energy presented by the tarot card placed here serve you in better honoring your individual needs and desires?

2nd House (Card 2) — The 2nd House correlates with Taurus. This gives cards in this position the role of highlighting your personal values, self-esteem and your relationship to material resources. Cards in this position will indicate what is currently of highest value to you and how you can find a greater sense of security in your life. Consider, how can the energy presented by the tarot card placed here serve you in improving your self-love and your ability to create a solid foundation in life?

3rd House (Card 3) — The 3rd House correlates with Gemini. This gives cards in this position the role of highlighting your speech, communications, connection to siblings and learning. Cards in this position will indicate what you are currently communicating or intellectually processing in your life. Consider, how can the energy presented by the tarot card placed here serve you in bettering your communication style? What are you ready to express?

4th House (Card 4) — The 4th House correlates with Cancer. This gives cards in this position the role of highlighting your internal world, connection to roots, family and the past, and your core emotional needs. Cards in this position will indicate what is currently driving your emotional desires and how you can build a stronger internal foundation. Consider, how can the energy presented by the tarot card placed here serve you in connecting more deeply to your innermost needs? What are you ready to be more vulnerable about? What from the past is coming up to be met with compassion and healed?

5th House (Card 5) – The 5th House correlates with Leo. This gives cards in this position the role of radiating your unique self-expression, creativity and developing a strong sense of identity. This is also the house that deals with children. Cards in this position will indicate what is currently influencing your sense of self and personal character. Consider, how can the energy presented by the tarot card placed here serve you in better expressing your inner light? How are you now ready to embody yourself more fully? What will bring you joy?

6th House (Card 6) – The 6th House correlates with Virgo. This gives cards in this position the role of highlighting your physical health, diet and nutrition, and daily routines. This house also includes your connection to pets. Cards in this position will indicate what is currently influencing your daily efficiency in life and overall well-being. Consider, how can the energy presented by the tarot card placed here serve you in better optimizing your physical reality?

7th House (Card 7) – The 7th House correlates with Libra. This gives cards in this position the role of highlighting your relationships, your connection to justice and how you desire to be perceived in this life. Cards in this position will indicate what is currently being reflected back to you in your external environment and what is influencing your connection to others. Consider, how can the energy presented by the tarot card placed here serve you in better connecting with others? What are others bringing out in you?

8th House (Card 8) – The 8th House correlates with Scorpio. This gives cards in this position the role of highlighting your deepest fears and desires and your relationship with sex, intimacy and taboo topics. Cards in this position will indicate what is currently influencing your underlying motivations and untapped power. Consider, how can the energy presented by the tarot card placed here serve you in understanding yourself on a deeper level? How are you ready to liberate yourself from old fears?

9th House (Card 9) – The 9th House correlates with Sagittarius. This gives cards in this position the role of highlighting your belief systems, long-distance travel, connection to religion and spirituality, faith and higher learning. Cards in this position will indicate what is currently influencing your core beliefs and your alignment with your highest truth. Consider, how can the energy presented by the tarot card placed here serve you in guiding you closer to your personal truth? How can you better pursue what inspires you?

10th House (Card 10) – The 10th House correlates with Capricorn. This gives cards in this position the role of highlighting your career, long-term goals and ambitions. Cards in this position will indicate what is currently influencing your professional life and your overall sense of mission and purpose. Consider, how can the energy presented by the tarot card placed here serve you in reaching a new level of authority, leadership and power in your life?

11th House (Card 11) — The 11th House correlates with Aquarius. This gives cards in this position the role of highlighting your network, connection to friends and community and overall sense of belonging. Cards in this position will indicate what is currently influencing your social circle and ability to feel interconnected with those around you. Consider, how can the energy presented by the tarot card placed here serve you in building a stronger level of community around you?

12th House (Card 12) — The 12th House correlates with Pisces. This gives cards in this position the role of highlighting your cosmic awareness, dreams, mental health and inner knowing. Cards in this position will indicate what is currently influencing you subconsciously and what you are being intuitively guided toward. Consider, how can the energy presented by the tarot card placed here serve you in connecting more deeply to your spiritual knowing? What are you ready to release control over so that you may align more deeply with your divine plan?

USING ASTROLOGICAL TRANSITS

("TAROT TRANSIT SPREADS")

Not every tarot reading must involve a "random" selection of cards. By translating current astrological transits into their corresponding tarot cards, you are able to gain a deeper insight into the collective themes that you and everyone around you will, to some degree, be experiencing. If you are seeking to gain more specific information as to how any particular astrological alignment is showing up in your personal life, simply draw the tarot cards corresponding to it and allow your mind to meditate on its significance. These tarot spreads do, however, require some knowledge of astrology to be most effective. I have listed some examples here:

EXAMPLE 1. FULL MOON RITUAL

Full moons are a great astrological transit to work with in this way, as it is the time where our conscious mind is most aware of our subconscious mind. This has the effect of bringing forth powerful realizations that move us closer to what we truly desire and who we really are. To construct this astrological transit using the tarot, let us break down the concept of a full moon into its fundamental pieces. A full moon is an opposing aspect between the sun and moon. Therefore, I will first draw #19 The Sun (correlated with the sun, page 279) and #2 The High Priestess (correlated with the moon, page 21) opposite one another. This particular full moon is occurring when the sun is in the sign Gemini and the moon is in Sagittarius. Therefore, I will also draw #6 The Lovers (correlated with Gemini, page 50) next to the sun and I will draw #14 Temperance (correlated with Sagittarius, page 166) next to the High Priestess.

Example Interpretation: #19 The Sun beside #6 The Lovers brings into focus significant choices and decisions (The Lovers) that will be made in the name of our own self-actualization (The Sun). To better make these decisions, we are being assisted with a full subconscious awareness (The High Priestess) of aspects of our personality that require integration (Temperance).

This is a still a very general interpretation, and you can dive deeper as you connect these wider themes to your personal experience. No matter whether you practice tarot or astrology or both, this exercise will add another layer of depth to your readings.

EXAMPLE 2. SATURN RETROGRADE IN PISCES

To construct this particular astrological transit using the tarot, let us break it down! I will first draw the tarot card that corresponds to the planet Saturn, which is #21 The World (page 287). I will then draw the card that corresponds to the sign Pisces, which is #18 The Moon (page 246). Saturn, in this instance is in retrograde, which means I will place #21 The World in reverse (upside down). Now, you will meditate on how the themes of #21 The World are working within the context of #18 The Moon in your life.

Example Interpretation: The reverse #21 The World brings to attention the final clearing and lesson learning of a long cycle of repeated patterns (Saturn, The World) in the context of childhood and deep-seated subconscious patterns of emotional security (Pisces, The Moon).

Bonus! This particular transit actually shows up in the tarot in the 8 of Cups (page 144). In this case, you could opt for just simply drawing the 8 of Cups (correlated with Saturn in Pisces) and turn it upside down to indicate its retrograde status. How are the themes of the reversed 8 of Cups playing out in your life under this astrological transit?

ADVANCED . . .

You can take this even a step further by applying your tarot transit to your personal astrological natal chart. Again, this will require some basic knowledge of astrology and your birth chart; however, it is not very difficult to grasp. Taking the example of the full moon in Sagittarius which hypothetically is occurring at 26 degrees of the sign Sagittarius, take a look at your natal chart and pinpoint what astrological house (page 293) 26 degrees Sagittarius falls in. If it is your 5th House, for example, you can attribute the themes of the 5th House as another layer of meaning to your reading. You could say here that your tarot transit reading is being laid out in the field of the 5th House. Good luck!

CONCLUSION

And, so, I hope this journey together has brought you somewhere closer to yourself, my love. It has been a great pleasure to accompany you and to have your company. What can I say? Keep the stars in your sights and your cards somewhere nice. I pray that what you have learned here will continue to serve the highest good of your spirit. And, though this may be the conclusion of one journey, you will know by now that endings is just another word for new beginnings.

Know that as long as breath moves through you, you are being reborn in every moment. You are only just beginning. Your life begins now, if you say it does, no matter how many times you've already lived. Anyways, I'm sure you've heard enough of my paradoxical ramblings for a little while. Good luck, my foolish little love. Go and live, will you? Quickly now, I must go tend to something in my eye.

ACKNOWLEDGMENTS

I would like to thank Page Street Publishing for the opportunity to bring this project to life. Special thank you to the ever-patient Marissa, Maude and to Meg and Katie for their beautiful work on the cover design.

Thank you to every soul that I met along the way from my first step as a Fool on this earth and my first word as a Fool on this project. Thank you to the moon, to my mother and to Marianna.

And thank you to all who seek to know the secret to themselves and the secrets of the universe. In doing so, you make this world a little brighter in your own unique way. What a gift.

ABOUT THE AUTHOR

Argus Kaldea is a professional tarot reader, a Western astrologer and an artist. He is also the host of The Oasis Podcast, where he offers spiritual guidance and esoteric wisdom. You can find him on Instagram @arguskaldea or on his popular TikTok platform @MoonPriest.

INDEX

M

N